How Edison's Lamp Helped Light the West

The Story of
Pacific Power & Light Company
and Its Pioneer Forebears

by John Dierdorff

Published and © 1971 by
PACIFIC POWER & LIGHT COMPANY

Public Service Building • Portland, Oregon 97204

Foreword

THOMAS EDISON and his inventions, notably the incandescent electric lamp, laid a foundation for today's vast electric utility business, but his unique background role in the beginnings of Pacific Power & Light Company gives this case history a little extra touch of human interest. At the same time, we should make clear that our general title "How Edison's Lamp Helped Light the West" is broadly inclusive in its intended sense. Indeed, many other electrical pioneers came to mind as we wrote our story.

We began our work on this volume after retirement from active Company responsibilities, and the project has been enlightening and enjoyable. Our principal regret is that we cannot look forward to chronicling the great years of accomplishment that lie ahead for this organization, accomplishments envisioned by leaders past and being brought toward fruition by leaders present. We believe that readers will find the closing chapters of the book taking on deeper significance if the developments of recent years are considered with an eye to the future as well as to the background of the past.

One admission we must make is that when a family member writes proudly about his lineage, the tendency is to emphasize worthy achievements and overlook imperfections. So it is, in a way, with this narrative about the early years, growth, adversities and successes of Pacific Power & Light Company, albeit the historical facts have been carefully researched.

From November 1, 1933, until June 30, 1966, the author was engrossed in the daily work of the Company, and took part in critical battles to preserve the life of the enterprise. He was fortunate to enjoy the friendship and counsel of many old hands in the organization, men whose careers had begun with or before the incorporation of the Company on June 16, 1910. A rich part of the educational process came from barnstorming the "old" Pacific system with Tully Bragg, Charlie Sanford, "Tam" McArthur and other beloved and colorful personalities. It should be noted that when "Tam" was at the wheel, a flow of salty PP&L folklore might well be interrupted by a sudden roadside stop so the raconteur could poke with his cane among the weeds to be sure a U.S.G.S. bench mark was still where he had helped to locate it.

The basic purpose of this history is to provide background information for recent generations of the Company family, but it is possible that others may find it useful as a supplementary reference in studies of electric power development in the Pacific Northwest.

The book is dedicated to all the stout-hearted men of whom Paul McKee often sang enthusiastically in the shank of the evening—and to their loyal, patient and remarkably understanding wives—all members of a dedicated organization that lives on with renewed spirit and energy!

JOHN DIERDORFF

TABLE OF CONTENTS

U.S.Flagship Trenton

*First installation of Edison's incandescent lamps in a Navy ship, the
U. S. Flagship* TRENTON, *in 1883 played a little known part in the sequence
of events leading to the organization of Pacific Power & Light Company.
S. Z. Mitchell, board chairman and a director of PP&L from 1910 to 1933,
was a cadet officer on the ship at the time and recognized the tremendous
market potential of the new invention. (U. S. Navy Photo)*

Chapter 1

Edison's Lamp Was the Nucleus

THE STORY OF Pacific Power & Light Company really begins 30 years prior to its incorporation on June 16, 1910, and a recital of certain events that occurred in those earlier years is a necessary part of the narrative.

One key character in the background story is Thomas Alva Edison, whose invention of the incandescent electric lamp in 1879 triggered a flood of human and economic forces to create the huge electric industry of today.

Edison's simple carbon filament lamp was the first electrical device that could be used anywhere—in homes, in offices, in factories, in stores or on a street corner.

The idea of a clean, safe lamp producing artificial sunshine at the turn of a switch was one to capture public fancy, and the huge market potential of the new device was quickly recognized.

One alert mind intrigued by Edison's invention was that of Naval Cadet Sidney Zollicoffer Mitchell, who enjoyed an opportunity to help install and operate an incandescent lighting system —the Navy's first—on the U.S.S. *"Trenton"*.

Born in Dadeville, Alabama, on March 17, 1862, Mitchell was the son of a doctor whose forebears had moved into the South from colonial Virginia. His mother died when he was three and he grew up in the home of a grandmother during the difficult days of reconstruction.

Young Mitchell gained appointment to the United States Naval Academy through competitive examination. Upon completion of the four-year course at Annapolis he was ordered to the *"Trenton"* in 1883 to begin the two years of sea duty then required before award of a commission.

Much of Mitchell's time at sea was spent on Navy ships in the Mediterranean. As the end of the period approached, he was detached to escort a group of 12 prisoners via passenger ship to the Brooklyn Navy Yard. He then went to Annapolis and received his commission.

These bipolar Edison generators, built at the Edison Machine Works, Schenectady, N. Y., were installed in the Byers flour mill in 1888 by Pendleton Electric Light & Power Company, of which S. Z. Mitchell was one of the incorporators. The units together could light 500 16-candlepower incandescent lamps. The meter rate was 20 cents per kilowatt-hour.

But a young naval officer's prospects were not promising in 1885. The navy of the period was ill-equipped. Appropriations for its support were at a low ebb.

On the other hand, the embryonic electric business held fascination for one who had just enough experience with an Edison lighting system to whet his appetite for more.

Resigning his commission, Mitchell went to New York and sought out Edison, whose need for talent was such that he had established the first training school for electrical engineers. Students worked days in Edison's original Pearl Street generating station, or in the machine shops on Goerck Street. At night they studied at the office of the Edison Electric Illuminating Company, 65 Fifth Avenue.

With his education and experience, Mitchell was welcomed to the Edison organization. At the machine shop he learned how to build a dynamo. Going through the city with wiring squads to connect new customers he learned about insulation, lamp sockets, power connections and distribution lines.

By September, 1885, Mitchell was ready for a new opportunity, and had earned enough of Edison's confidence to bring that opportunity within reach.

Henry Villard, known in the Pacific Northwest principally for his role as a builder of the Northern Pacific Railway, was a great friend of Edison and had earlier been granted the exclusive agency for Edison products in northwestern states. But in late September, 1885, Villard decided to give up this agency, to which he had been able to devote little time or effort.

Mitchell asked for the territory and, as his son and biographer has expressed it: "Mr. Edison must have been pleased with his work, for in that month Mitchell became exclusive agent for the Edison Electric Light Company and the Edison Company for Isolated Lighting in Washington, Oregon, Idaho, Alaska and British Columbia."

When he headed for Seattle in the early autumn of 1885, Mitchell took with him another Annapolis graduate, Frederick H. Sparling, whom he had enlisted in the venture.

Quoting again from the Mitchell biography: "At this time in the Northwest, people had heard about the use of electricity in the East but nobody knew much about it. However, this region was growing rapidly and each town was sure that it was destined to be the biggest city in the area. The young men believed that, if they could set up an electric company in one of the more up-and-coming localities, the rivalry among the cities would be such that another city would also insist on electric light.

"The problem was which city to work on first, and also where to get the money. Money has always been the greatest problem in the electrical industry where an unusually high investment is required to produce one dollar's worth of sales. This ratio has varied between $4 and $8 of investment for each $1 of gross sales. And, when to this is added the growth characteristic of the industry, an annual increase of sales of 6 to 8 per cent compounded each year, one can have some understanding of the additional money continuously required . . . ."

In the fall of 1885 Seattle and Tacoma were contesting to become the western terminal city of the Northern Pacific, then drilling a tunnel through the Cascade summit to give it a direct connection with the Puget Sound area. This rivalry was not overlooked by the young Edison salesmen.

Box factory workers posed for their picture at West Shore Mills on the Astoria waterfront on June 1, 1885, about the time J. C. Trullinger, mill owner, ordered two Keith dynamos and a string of arc lamps to give the community electric service. The first dynamo was installed in the shed marked with "X" and 30 arc lamps blazed into action on Christmas Eve, 1885. A bronze plaque now marks the mill site.

Starting in Seattle, they obtained contracts for the sale of 250 lamps and were able to finance a company to build a small steam generating station and distribution system along the waterfront.

Tacoma was next on their development program. A company was set up there with 600 lamps.

In three years Mitchell and his associates set up more than a dozen other lighting systems at such points as Spokane, Pendleton, Boise, Victoria and Colfax.

It was a roundabout way to sell Edison lamps, and it took long hours of work and exceptional talent for negotiation and organization. But, city by city, a market was opened for Edison products, sold through Mitchell's Northwest Electrical Supply and Construction Co.

In 1890 Edison General Electric Co. decided to unify its manufacturing and selling agencies and carry on all phases of the business in the company's own name. Mitchell's sales agency was purchased by the Edison company, which established Pacific Northwest district headquarters in Portland. There Mitchell had his office until 1902.

Chapter 2

Slabwood Made Astoria's First Power

IN THE SAME YEAR that S. Z. Mitchell arrived in Seattle, a salesman from San Francisco found his way to an Astoria, Oregon, waterfront sawmill to extol the virtues of Keith dynamos and arc lamps.

The mill proprietor he sought out was J. C. Trullinger, who had come to Oregon from Indiana in 1847. Following experiences in the California and Oregon gold fields, he built a water power sawmill on the creek now serving as the outlet of Oswego Lake and began sawing out boards for houses and stores in the small but growing Portland community nearby.

When untreated water pumped from the Willamette River started an epidemic of typhoid fever in Portland, Trullinger took a pessimistic view of the city's future, sold his sawmill and moved into the Tualatin valley to set up a waterpower grist mill on Dairy Creek, about three miles north of Cornelius.

Subsequently he went to Astoria and built a steam sawmill on a site now marked by a bronze plaque as the location of his West Shore Mills.

The lumber business was good at the time the adventurous Trullinger listened to the persuasive dynamo salesman. There seemed to be no reason why the mill shouldn't make more money.

"Look," the visitor told him, "you've got a steam engine and have so much waste slabwood that you're using it for lumberyard fill. All it takes for you to get into the electric business is to buy one of our dynamos and a set of arc lamps. When the mill shuts down for the night you throw a belt on the dynamo, toss some more slabwood under the boiler and the money you collect for the arc lamps is velvet."

The sales talk was effective. Trullinger ordered two 30-lamp machines at a cost of $7,500 each, including the arc lamps. The dynamos were built to order and the first one delivered was set up in the planer shed and connected to an extended line shaft.

A contract for ten street lamps was obtained from the city. The C. H. Cooper dry goods store put in four lamps and others of the initial 30 were taken by enterprising saloons and dance halls along the waterfront.

Feed wires were strung from house-top to house-top. Poles were erected only where vacant lots made too wide a gap. The rate charged was set at $16 a lamp per month.

Current was turned on for the first time about 7 o'clock on Christmas eve, 1885. *The Morning Astorian* of December 25, 1885, referred to the event as follows: " . . . *The Astorian* is glad that Portland is growing. It rejoices that the grand country to the north of us, Seattle, Tacoma and all that splendid region is coming out. It is pleased to note the progress of the country; it is our daily delight to share in that progress.

"As we write these words our newly elected mayor is starting the first electric light in Astoria in front of our office: its brilliant beams penetrate the darkness of the gathering night as the light of progress penetrates the primitive condition of the country . . ."

The second Keith dynamo was delivered a few months later and this, along with the first, was set up in a building erected for the purpose adjacent to the sawmill. Separate boilers and engines were installed, the engines being of 30 horsepower each.

Thad Trullinger, one of the mill owner's three sons, was interviewed by the author in 1934 and supplied many interesting bits of background information.

The engines had no effective governing device, he recalled. From the time the plant was started up at dusk until it was shut down for the night the engineer was kept jumping from one throttle to the other in an effort to maintain steady voltage.

The lamps had temperamental clockwork mechanisms to regulate the arc gap between the carbon rods, and it was one of the chores of the Trullinger boys to keep these working. Along with generator troubles and line troubles, they were kept on the go 12 to 16 hours a day.

Had it not been for the sawmill end of the business the power venture would have had a difficult time keeping alive. The Keith dynamos lasted only about a year and were replaced by two machines made by Thomson-Houston Co., which subsequently became a part of General Electric.

6

Equipment for this pioneer central Oregon power plant was hauled by teams and wagon over the old stagecoach route from Shaniko to Prineville in 1898. Built by Prineville Light & Water Company, the plant went into operation in 1900. It took four cords of slabwood per day to fire the boilers.

The old dynamos, representing an investment of $15,000, were sold for $150 to an electric company at Salem, Oregon, which needed spare parts to keep a similar installation in repair.

About 1890 a 75-horsepower Thomson-Houston dynamo was purchased to generate current for incandescent lamps, and Trullinger went out for residential as well as commercial business.

The first ten or twelve houses were wired free to get customers on the line. The house in which Thad Trullinger was living in 1934 was still being served by the original wiring.

It cost $1.50 to buy a 16-candlepower lamp. The service charge for business establishments was 75 cents a month per lamp for 10 o'clock lights, $1 a month for 12 o'clock lights and $1.50 a month for all-night lights. The residential rate was one-half the commercial rate, with the agreement that current would not be wasted.

A flat rate soon proved to be impracticable. Merchants would neglect to pay the night watchman to turn off their window lights at the appointed hour and householders fell into the habit of going to bed with the lights on. This led to the inauguration of metered service.

The rapid obsolescence of early-day equipment and constant demand for additional capital investment in service facilities made the electric division of West Shore Mills much less than self-supporting. In 1897, while discussing a city street lighting contract,

7

Trullinger declared he had $75,000 invested in the electric system. A project that had promised to convert mill waste into extra dividends had proved, up to that time, to be only an added burden.

At the turn of the century, in addition to the electric company, there were two other utilities operating in Astoria. A street railway company had been established in 1887 and a manufactured gas company had begun business in 1883, two years before Trullinger's arc lamps crackled into action.

The street railway was electrified in the '90s, with equipment bought from General Electric. When the streetcar operation later went bankrupt, the property was taken over by GE for debt on the equipment.

It was at this point that S. Z. Mitchell came into the situation. Then located in Portland as manager of GE's Pacific Northwest office, Mitchell traveled to Astoria with other representatives of the company to investigate their problem.

All but Mitchell were in favor of junking the equipment and taking the loss. Mitchell, however, had a better idea.

In the bankrupt Astoria property Mitchell saw an opportunity for constructive reorganization. With characteristic vigor he organized the Astoria Electric Company, which issued $50,000 in bonds. General Electric took $25,000 of the issue in exchange for the street railway property. Mitchell took $5,000 of bonds, as did an associate, J. A. Cranston. Three others interested in the problem also put up $5,000 each—S. S. Gordon, C. N. Huggins and C. H. Page. With the bonds went 3,000 shares of common stock on a pro rata basis. This was in 1901.

The new capital was used to extend the streetcar line and install a new power plant. The property took on new life.

Next Mitchell set out to effect a consolidation of the street railway, the electric company and the gas company. This was accomplished in 1902. Service was improved and earnings were sufficient to carry the bonds and pay some dividends.

One of the progressive steps sponsored by Mitchell was to institute 24-hour service from the lighting plant, a move that was viewed with considerable skepticism by some of the local investors. But it proved to be beneficial to the company's business as well as a customer convenience. Apprehensions of the doubters were quickly dissipated.

Chapter 3

Electric Bond & Share Parent of PP&L

THE SALVAGE OF General Electric's investment in the Astoria street railway did not go unnoticed by the firm's top management. Over a period of time, GE had accumulated a considerable portfolio of stocks and bonds offered in part payment for equipment sold to struggling electric companies short of cash. Other securities had been received in creditors' reorganizations.

Securities issued by companies operating in well-known cities presented no great problem. These usually could be liquidated within a reasonable time, at little or no sacrifice.

However, situations such as had confronted GE in Astoria were all too numerous There were hundreds of small, home-town electric companies scattered across the country, suffering from growth pains and in need of financial and management help.

Unsalable securities of such companies lying in GE's safe began to represent a large amount of unproductive, tied-up capital.

C. A. Coffin, then head of General Electric, was well aware of his company's problem. He had observed with interest the accomplishments of Sidney Mitchell in the Pacific Northwest, and asked Mitchell to come to New York for consultation.

The idea they discussed was to set up a company that would take over GE's miscellaneous assortment of utility securities and undertake to build up their value by helping the issuing companies obtain capital and improve their operations.

The responsibility of setting up such an organization was offered to Mitchell, and early in 1905 he took up his new duties in New York. The corporate vehicle organized for the purpose in February, 1905, was Electric Bond & Share Company. Its initial staff consisted of Mitchell, a bookkeeper and a stenographer.

The new firm began business by issuing to the public $1,000,000 of 6% preferred stock. General Electric received 19,995 shares of Bond & Share common stock and 20,000 shares of preferred stock in return for $1,300,576.90 in cash and bonds of certain companies and $1,476,000 par value of stocks.

9

(Left) S. Z. Mitchell, president of Electric Bond & Share Company and chairman of Pacific Power & Light from 1910 to 1933, as he appeared in 1934. (Right) Guy W. Talbot, president of PP&L throughout the 1910-33 period, was only 36 when named to the post. This portrait from the files of Oregon Historical Society dates back to the early years

Then began the task of providing succor to underfinanced companies represented in the investment portfolio and making available to them capable engineering and operating advice.

This was helpful, but a small, isolated electric system needed more. To realize the economies of volume production it needed larger generators, for example, units big enough to supply the needs of several communities. Similarly, the cost of competent management and engineering talent could just as well be divided among a number of local operations.

To accomplish such forward steps obviously required capital, particularly common stock risk, or equity, capital that would make feasible the borrowing of money through mortgage bonds.

How a holding company could help the progress of the electric industry was demonstrated when American Gas & Electric Company (now American Electric Power) was organized late in 1906 by Electric Bond & Share Company to take over the interests of an entirely separate holding company that had failed to recognize either the insatiable capital needs of its subsidiaries or the necessity of ploughing back a portion of earnings as seed money.

10

In 1909 American Power & Light Company was organized by Bond & Share, initially to help provide common stock money for the expansion of two utility properties in Wichita, Kansas, and make feasible their consolidation with small neighboring companies in a new corporation, Kansas Gas & Electric Company.

With the Kansas program on its way, it was natural for Mitchell's attention to focus on the Pacific Northwest as another area where American Power & Light might go to diversify its holdings. Mitchell knew the Northwest and many of the people in the electric business there.

Negotiations were begun to acquire properties that might be included with Astoria Electric in a new operating company. At the same time, a move started to acquire and consolidate the properties of the Portland Gas Company and the East Portland Gas Company. The latter program was consummated with the incorporation on January 10, 1910, of Portland Gas & Coke Company (now Northwest Natural Gas).

Editorial reference to this formative period was made in the March, 1915, issue of the Pacific Power & Light Company *Bulletin,* which noted that "March 1, 1915, marked the fifth birthday of the Pacific Power & Light Company, or at least marked the end of the fifth year since the Portland office was established."

The article recalled that American Power & Light had begun looking into utility property acquisitions in the region in 1909 and subsequently decided to open an office in Portland "with the idea that the organization there formed would later be the operating organization of the Pacific Power & Light Company which was to be incorporated later.

"Mr. (Guy W.) Talbot was the first new officer in the organization, having been elected vice-president of the American Power & Light Company, although he was at that time still acting as vice-president and general manager of the Oregon Electric Railway Company. He opened up an office in the Corbett Building, in Portland, on March 1, 1910, the office being in charge of Lewis A. McArthur, who, up to that time, had been connected with the Oregon Electric Railway Company, and he is, therefore, in point of time the oldest employee of the Portland office of Pacific Power & Light Company.

Office staff of embryonic PP&L in May, 1910, consisted of Lewis A. "Tam" McArthur, with the telephone on his desk at the right, and George L. Myers, a one-time news reporter who could write shorthand as well as use a typewriter. Myers became secretary to President Guy W. Talbot and McArthur was named assistant general manager. Later that summer the Portland office was moved from the Lewis building to the Spalding building at Third and Washington where it remained until 1918.

"Within a month the offices had been moved to the Lewis Building and in the middle of summer to the Spalding Building, where they are now located."

This anniversary note probably was written by George L. Myers, then assistant secretary and assistant treasurer and an associate editor of the Company *Bulletin*, who modestly refrained from mentioning how closely he followed "Tam" McArthur through the door to a desk and typewriter in the first office.

By June, 1910, in addition to Astoria Electric, properties in the American portfolio included the Yakima-Pasco Power Company and utility systems at Walla Walla, Pendleton and The Dalles, the latter group in the transitory ownership of Columbia Power & Light Company, through which purchase negotiations had been conducted.

On June 16, 1910, Pacific Power & Light Company was incorporated under the laws of the State of Maine, which also had been the state of incorporation of American Power & Light. In

*On May 25, 1910, three weeks before PP&L was incorporated, a
photographer took this picture of Yakima Avenue, North Yakima, as the
city was then known. Horse-drawn vehicles outnumbered automobiles.
Population was about 14,000. Yakima-Pasco Power Company was
one of the initial units brought under the PP&L name.*

that era, some practical consideration or matter of convenience
dictated the choice of Maine as the state of incorporation.
Whatever the reason, any legal or other advantage has long since
vanished and, except for all the red tape and expense involved in
a change of corporate residence, the Company today could be
incorporated in any of the states in which it operates.

The new Company began to assume its identity in very short
order. At a meeting of the Board of Directors on July 23, 1910,
$1,500,000 of 7% par value preferred stock and $5,997,000 par
value of common stock was subscribed for in behalf of American
Power & Light for the properties of Astoria Electric, Yakima-
Pasco Power Company and Columbia Power & Light, with the
property transfer effective as of July 1, 1910. The Walla Walla
Valley Railway Company, acquired at the same time, was not
merged into Pacific with the others but was held as a subsidiary.

Talbot was named a vice president of the Pacific Company
at this meeting but the major change from the temporary directors
and officers came at the Board meeting of August 20, 1910.
Talbot at that time was elected a director and named president of

13

the Company. S. Z. Mitchell was elected a director and chairman of the board. Edward Cookingham, a vice president of Ladd & Tilton Bank and later an officer of the United States National Bank, Portland, had been named a vice president on July 23, and on August 20 also was elected a director. Others named to the board were C. Hunt Lewis, Portland capitalist; Philip Buehner, lumberman, Portland; J. C. Ainsworth, president, United States National Bank, Portland; George F. Nevins, secretary and assistant treasurer of the Company; S. S. Gordon, Astoria banker; Miles C. Moore, president of the Baker-Boyer National Bank, Walla Walla; F. G. Sykes, subsequently president of American Power & Light; Josiah Richards, Spokane banker; H. C. Lucas, Yakima banker; F. L. Dame, of Electric Bond & Share, New York; A. S. Grenier, general manager of the Pacific Company; and Niel A. Weathers, of the New York law firm of Simpson, Thacher & Bartlett, who had worked in Portland on legal matters preliminary to organization of the Company.

Guy Webster Talbot, who served as president of PP&L until his retirement in 1933, was born in Centerville, Michigan, August 12, 1873. A biographical sketch published in 1911 said: "He comes of an old New England family, being a grandson of John W. Talbot, who with his brothers, the late Charles P. and Governor Thomas Talbot, of Lowell, Massachusetts, built and operated the first woolen mills in Massachusetts at Billerica.

"G. W. Talbot pursued his early education in the common schools of Des Moines, Iowa, while spending his youthful days in the home of his parents, Charles Robert and Sarah F. (Webster) Talbot. He afterward attended college at Emporia, Kansas, and crossed the threshold of business life as an employee in the local freight office of the Chicago, Burlington & Quincy Railway Company at Des Moines. Since that time he has been connected more or less closely with railway interests, and each forward step in his career has marked the recognition of his ability on the part of those whom he has represented . . . . .

"In 1906 Mr. Talbot became vice president and general manager of the Astoria & Columbia River Railroad Company and the Corvallis & Eastern Railroad Company, with offices at Portland, Oregon. In 1907 he was made vice president and general manager of the Oregon Electric Railway Company and in 1910

14

Office and interurban station at Walla Walla in 1910. PP&L's subsidiary Walla Walla Valley Railway had 12 miles of streetcar track and 14 miles of interurban line to Freewater and Milton. Before automobiles became common, the railway carried as many as 1,285,000 passengers annually.

became president of the Pacific Power & Light Company and the Portland Gas & Coke Company."

It is interesting to recall that it was railroad builder Henry Villard, who, when he gave up the northwest franchise for Edison electrical equipment in 1885, opened up a sales opportunity for S. Z. Mitchell. Then, 25 years later, it was Mitchell who reached into the railway business for a man to head the electric and gas utility companies he was organizing in the Pacific Northwest.

The Oregon Electric Railway provided other managerial talent for the new utility. George F. Nevins, who had been traffic manager and auditor for the railway, became secretary and assistant treasurer. C. S. Walters, Salem general agent for the railway, became general manager of the Walla Walla Valley Railway and later served as Walla Walla district manager. Walters subsequently went with Carolina Power & Light Company and became a vice president and division manager of that firm. W. H. Galvani, who served for many years as engineer in charge of Pacific's property and tax department, also was recruited from Oregon Electric.

D. F. McGee, an engineer with broad experience, was in charge of what was called the Columbia division, headquartered

15

at Walla Walla. He had been employed by Electric Bond & Share in 1908 to go west and first managed the Astoria Electric properties. In the fall of 1910 McGee was transferred from Walla Walla to Portland to become chief engineer, a responsibility he held until he went to New York in 1914 to join the engineering staff of Bond & Share.

A. S. Grenier, first general manager, came from Chicago. He went to New York in 1914 and became a vice president of Electric Bond & Share.

J. E. Davidson, new business manager, had been president and manager of the Consolidated Lighting Company at Montpelier, Vermont. He was named vice president and general manager of Pacific in 1912 and held this post until 1917, when he moved to Omaha and rose to the presidency of Nebraska Power Company.

As of July 1, 1910, the electric properties in the infant Pacific Power & Light system served 7,356 customers in 17 communities. Installed generating capacity totaled 11,875 kilowatts. The Company had 388 miles of pole lines. Revenues from the electric business were approximately $593,000 a year.

Oregon communities supplied with electricity were Astoria, Dufur, Freewater, Pendleton and The Dalles. In Washington, electric service was furnished in Benton City, Blalock, College Place, Kennewick, Mabton, Naches, Pasco, Prospect Heights, Sunnyside, Walla Walla, Wapato and North Yakima, as that city was then known.

Manufactured gas plants and mains were operated in Astoria and Pendleton, Oregon; Walla Walla and Yakima, Washington; and Lewiston, Idaho. There were 4,024 gas customers being served by these facilities, which yielded an annual revenue of $128,564.

Three water systems were acquired with the Yakima-Pasco Power Company properties. These were at Kennewick, Pasco and Yakima, serving 2,964 customers and producing revenues of $73,553.

The street railway at Astoria came into Pacific with the Astoria Electric Company properties. It owned five electric cars and 4.5 miles of track. Revenues in 1910 amounted to $37,300.

Ownership of the Walla Walla Valley Railway, a 14-mile interurban line between Walla Walla and the communities of

Linen dusters and tweed caps were in evidence when this official party inspected the Naches power plant September 10, 1913. From the left: No. 1 is Guy W. Talbot, PP&L president; No. 2 is George C. Sawyer, Yakima district manager; No. 3 is D. F. McGee, chief engineer; No. 6 is S. Z. Mitchell, president of Electric Bond & Share and chairman of PP&L; No. 7 is J. E. Davidson, PP&L general manager; No. 8 is F. G. Sykes, president of American Power & Light; No. 10 is W. W. Cotton, Company counsel; and No. 12 is J. H. Siegfried, superintendent of power.

Freewater and Milton, came in the package with the utility properties at the eastern end of the system. The railway company was held as a subsidiary of Pacific, retaining its corporate identity until the property eventually was sold to Northern Pacific. It had 12 miles of streetcar track in the Walla Walla community. On the more heavily traveled routes, there were cars every 20 minutes. The interurban line provided hourly service. Before the passenger business was decimated by the automobile, this little railway carried as many as 1,285,000 persons annually.

In all, the Pacific Company had annual revenues of $832,200 as of 1910. Electric, gas and water customers totaled 14,344.

"No breaking of the housewife's back—no wear and tear on your delicate lingerie," said this 1910 Pendleton newspaper ad for an electric washing machine. But it didn't suggest what might happen if mama's apron strings got caught in the belt drive! A competitive ad of the same period asserted: "No other washing machine in the world will do all this but the Thor-Electric. Wash the clothes. Wring the clothes. Work the ironing machine. Work the food chopper. Sharpen the knives. Churn the butter. Turn the grind stone. Freeze the ice cream and do scores of other household duties by attaching the Universal Rod (sold only with Thor)."

18

Chapter 4

More About Pacific's Predecessors

E ARLY HISTORY of the several electric systems that came into Pacific Power & Light in 1910 was much like the story already told about J. C. Trullinger and the 1885 dynamo installation in his Astoria sawmill.

Two years later, in Pendleton, W. S. Byers obtained a franchise for an electric light plant on February 17, 1887, and installed a generator at his flour mill. In June of the same year, in a separate venture, a generator was installed at the foundry of the Pendleton Manufacturing company.

On July 28, 1888, Pendleton Electric Light & Power Company was incorporated by W. S. Byers, R. G. Thompson and S. Z. Mitchell, with a capital stock of $25,000. It was a consolidation of the two early plants. Three new generators and a large water turbine were installed in the Byers mill. One generator was a Thomson-Houston dynamo of 50-arc-lamp capacity and two were Edison machines with a combined capacity of 500 16-candlepower incandescent lamps. The meter rate was 20 cents a kilowatt-hour. Flat rate lighting service at $5.00 a month allowed five 16-candlepower lamps to be connected, "not more than three to be in use at one time."

It is recorded that by the summer of 1890 the electric plant had cost $35,000 and the generators were being driven by steam power. Also noted were plans to double the plant's capacity to supply the demand.

In 1903 the Pendleton property was acquired by the newly organized Northwestern Gas and Electric Company, which also acquired the electric and gas properties in Walla Walla. In 1904 this company purchased from another group water rights and a hydroelectric plant just constructed on the Walla Walla River southeast of Freewater. A franchise to operate a gas plant in Pendleton was obtained in 1905.

The gas system at Lewiston was started in 1906 by Isaac W. Anderson, founder of Northwestern Gas and Electric, and this

One of the first rural power lines in the region brought electricity to the Hamblett farm near Hood River in 1906. It was wired by Alva Day, pictured at the site 30 years later. Day for many years was PP&L's rural service specialist in the Hood River district. One of his sales tools was a panel truck fitted out with various electrical equipment items for house to house demonstrations.

property, with the Pendleton and Walla Walla properties of that company, was transferred to a new company, Northwestern Corporation, in 1909.

A gas company was organized in Walla Walla in 1881 but no information is available concerning its early operations. Walla Walla Gas and Electric Company was incorporated September 12, 1889, to engage in the gas and electric business and this firm took over the property and franchise of the Walla Walla Gas Company in the same year.

A definite date for the start of electric service in Walla Walla does not appear in available records, but it is known that a 100-horsepower Ball tandem-compound steam engine was installed in 1890 for driving one or more dynamos. In 1892, a Pelton water wheel was installed on Mill Creek five miles east of Walla Walla to drive a 100-kilowatt, 133-cycle single-phase generator of an old Thomson-Houston type. This generator delivered power at 2,000 volts directly over a single circuit line to Walla Walla. There it was fed into a similar generator, operating as a synchronous motor, connected to a line shaft to which were belted the several dynamos furnishing current for the arc and incandescent lighting of the town. The steam plant was used for an auxiliary.

Service apparently was not of the best and in 1900 agitation resulted in the formation of at least two opposition companies, which obtained franchises but did not actually get into business. Capacity of the system then was estimated at 350 horsepower. Soon thereafter the steam plant was enlarged to take care of growth in load.

Following the acquisition of the Walla Walla and Pendleton properties by Northwestern Gas and Electric in 1903, and with completion of the Walla Walla River hydroelectric plant, both communities were connected with the new power source. In 1906, however, floods carried away the headworks and much of the flow line. Pendleton was without service for a number of days because the old steam plant was out of service. The Walla Walla steam plant was able to give only limited service. In repairing the damage caused by the flood, the new flow line was moved away from the bed of the stream and contoured along the canyon wall.

First electric service at The Dalles was provided by a small steam plant consisting of two 15-kilowatt generators run by a Corliss steam engine. This was operated under a franchise granted June 30, 1888, to J. E. Handley and Hugh Glenn. Handley died and his half-interest was sold in 1891 to G. V. Bolton for the sum of $10,000. It is reported that service in the 1891-1892 period was not very dependable and it was not uncommon for the lights to be out for a week at a time.

In 1893 The Dalles Electric Light, Telephone and Power Company was incorporated by members of the group then having money in the venture, with the French Bros., pioneer bankers, heading the new corporation. A new steam plant was installed in October, 1893, consisting of a 225-horsepower engine, two Edison dynamos, each with a capacity to operate 820 16-candlepower lamps, and a Thomson-Houston 50-arc-lamp dynamo. In the late spring of 1894, the great Columbia River flood inundated the steam plant and the city was without lights for three weeks.

Facilities of the steam plant were not sufficient to serve an industrial load of any size, and when the Wasco Warehouse Milling Company was organized in 1901 an attempt was made to secure

21

Delegation of Portland visitors posed in blankets for this picture taken at the Pendleton Woolen Mills in 1910. In shirt sleeves at the extreme left is Clarence M. Bishop, long active in the nationally known Pendleton business. His son, C. M. Bishop, Jr., was elected to the PP&L Board of Directors in 1970. In the center background, just to the left of the door panel, is Guy W. Talbot, PP&L's first president.

power from a hydro project at Hood River. When this failed to materialize, a site on White River south of The Dalles in the Tygh Valley area was purchased. Articles of incorporation of the flour milling company were amended to include the electric business as one of its purposes. The property of The Dalles Electric Light, Telephone and Power Company was purchased for $52,000 and construction was started on the Tygh Valley plant in the spring of 1901. The hydro plant began operating early in January, 1902. The original installation consisted of two 500-kilowatt generators driven by Knight turbines. These turbines later were replaced by Pelton wheels. The steam plant in The Dalles was sold for $4,000 in 1904 and service thereafter was dependent upon the hydro plant.

First electric service in Yakima came about five years after the establishment by Northern Pacific of the town of "North Yakima," as distinguished from the older "Yakima City," which later adopted the name "Union Gap." When the NP built its railway through the Yakima valley, property owners of the original town could not agree on a plan for the promotion of the townsite.

The rail firm then plotted the townsite of North Yakima about four miles distant and undertook to move buildings and residences on flatcars from the old city to the new. This was in the spring of 1885. The name "North Yakima" remained in use until 1918, when it was shortened to the present form.

Initial efforts to institute electric service in Yakima began in 1889 but did not mature. On January 13, 1890, a franchise was granted to Edward Whitson for the operation of a power plant and water system, and work was begun on the project. On January 31, 1890, Whitson, James B. Reavis and Fred Parker incorporated two companies—Yakima Electric Light Company and Yakima Water Company. The electric and water properties on which Whitson had started construction were transferred to the new corporations.

By May 1, 1890, 50 men were at work on the water works and another force was at work on a ditch and flume to carry water from the Naches River three miles to a power house and another mile and a quarter into the city. Pumps and two dynamos for arc and incandescent lamps were installed at the powerhouse, the whole costing approximately $150,000. The city agreed to pay $144.00 a year for each of seven arc lamps of 2,000 candlepower for a period of ten years. Electric lights were turned on for the first time on September 4, 1890. Temporary power from a planing mill was used until the water wheels arrived.

On June 2, 1891, Yakima Water, Light and Power Company was incorporated by the same owners to consolidate the water and electric properties in one corporation. A new electric franchise was obtained and when the city installed two additional arc lamps the charge per lamp was reduced from $12.00 to $7.50 per lamp per month.

The census of 1900 showed that Yakima had grown to a city of 3,154, and in 1903 the company announced the addition of two new dynamos and the establishment of daytime service.

In December, 1903, the properties of Yakima Water, Light and Power were transferred to Northwest Light and Water Company, organized earlier in the year by Robert E. Strahorn, A. G. Smith and R. J. Danson. On June 24, 1904, an agreement for a new franchise was reached with the city whereby the company agreed to make a general reduction of 25 per cent on light rates

Sledges had to be swung in skillful sequence to spare the knuckles of the man holding the drill on this 1900 construction job. Excavation was for the forebay of the Big Fork hydro plant on Swan River, near the east shore of Flathead Lake. The plant was for many years an important power supply source for the Kalispell district.

in force and to establish a minimum rate of 75 cents. With the installation of meters, lights were to be charged for by the amount of electricity used.

The new electric rates started at 20 cents per kilowatt-hour for the first 25 kwh used. The next 15 kwh cost 19 cents each, the next 20 kwh cost 18 cents and the schedule tapered on down in steps of one cent to a low of 13 cents per kwh for use in excess of 1,000 kwh a month. A discount of 25 per cent was given if the customer paid before the 10th of the following month.

Late in 1904 a new power plant was started 11½ miles up the Naches River. Completion of this plant was hindered by weather conditions, including a flood, and by delays in the transportation of equipment. It was September 14, 1907, before the first 1,500-horsepower unit had been installed. This was comprised of a generator, a water wheel and a steam engine. Work on the canal was all done with horse-drawn scrapers and manual labor.

Several false starts were made in the establishment of a gas system in Yakima, but in June, 1905, a gas franchise was granted to Isaac W. Anderson, previously referred to in connection with

24

An obedient horse that would stand still while a man was working atop the ladder was an important part of this outfit, built to make it easier to service street lamps long before the day of the mechanical "cherry-picker."

25

gas utility developments at Pendleton, Walla Walla and Lewiston. Construction of a gas plant was started in July of the same year, with the Minneapolis Acetylene Construction Company in charge of the work. Completion by December 1 was guaranteed.

Yakima Gas Company was incorporated November 15, 1905, by W. A. Aldrich and Ira P. Englehart, with a capital stock of $100,000. Anderson was associated in the ownership of this company and conveyed to it his interests in the gas system.

In Pasco, Washington, the first effective steps to establish electric service began on May 1, 1906, with the granting of a franchise to F. E. Elmendorf, whose associates in the organization of Pasco Light and Water Company were George H. Doerr, W. S. Gilbert and W. O. Parker, all of Spokane. The electric plant was to be completed and in operation by March 1, 1907.

The original light plant consisted of a 100-horsepower producer gas engine belted to a 75-kva generator. It began generating power about February 1, 1907. A new steam plant was started early the following year and put into service July 14, 1908. This consisted of a 175-horsepower Atlas engine, an Atlas boiler and a 120-kilowatt, 2,200-volt Westinghouse generator. Less than a month later, a fire of unknown origin totally destroyed the new power-house and the town was without lights and water. Pumps to give water service were installed within 24 hours, but the town was without electricity for several months.

The Pasco company was sold to Robert Strahorn on August 28, 1908, and he started work on the restoration of electric service. A submarine cable was laid in the Columbia River to connect with the plant in Kennewick, which Strahorn had also acquired.

The Kennewick system had been started by Clifton A. Cochrane, who obtained a light and water franchise December 27, 1905, and who, with Calvin E. Wood and Albert L. Smith, organized Columbia-Basin Water, Light and Power Company on May 22, 1906. The first electric plant consisted of a 75-horsepower Atlas steam engine belted to a 50-kilowatt generator. Service was first given about February 1, 1907, but shortages of coal caused lighting to be discontinued as much as a week at a time in the early days of the venture.

Strahorn and his associates in Northwest Light and Water Company at Yakima organized Yakima Valley Power Company

Storage batteries in the box hanging on the frame of this Yakima district electric line truck weighed nearly as much as the truck itself. Half a century later, researchers were still seeking to develop a light-weight storage battery that would make electric vehicles competitive with gasoline or diesel power.

on September 21, 1908, shortly after his acquisition of the Pasco and Kennewick properties, which were put into the new corporation. Construction was begun on a 500-kilowatt steam plant in Kennewick and on a transmission line from Kennewick to Yakima and Naches. Electric distribution systems were built in Sunnyside and Mabton in 1909, and in the latter part of that year two 150-horsepower boilers were added to the Kennewick steam plant.

The Yakima, Pasco and Kennewick systems were consolidated as Yakima-Pasco Power Company in April, 1910, and all the physical properties of the latter were transferred to Pacific Power & Light Company following its organization two months later.

Chapter 5

Additions Continued After 1910

C LOSE ON THE HEELS of the 1910 acquisitions came a series of other additions to the Pacific system in 1911 and 1912. Among these were the plants providing service in the Dayton, Waitsburg and Pomeroy communities northeast of Walla Walla.

A small hydro plant on the Touchet River provided Dayton its first electricity in 1889. Flow of the river varied greatly, and when Pacific acquired the property in 1911 water power could not be depended upon to meet the needs of the 400 customers. Fuel for steam generation was so expensive the system's owners could not afford to take on new loads. Capacity of the plant was only 150 kilowatts.

In Waitsburg there was a combined steam and hydro plant having 150 kilowatts of capacity, dating back to 1896. It is reported that one of the early plant operators slept on a cot in the powerhouse with a carbon-filament lamp hanging over his head. When lights began to be turned off at bedtime in Waitsburg homes, the water wheel would pick up speed and cause the lamp over the cot to burn more brightly. The operator would rouse himself and reach over to give a turn on the penstock valve to reduce the water flow. Come morning, the light would dim as system load picked up and give the operator notice that the control valve needed adjustment to bring the generator up to speed.

In Pomeroy it was the Tucannon Power Company that began providing electric service in 1903, initially from a 150-kilowatt hydro plant on the Tucannon River at Marengo, about six miles west of town. An early difficulty with the hydro installation was that it could not be operated in winter because of ice in the power canal. It became necessary in 1906 to install a 100-kilowatt steam generator in Pomeroy to provide some degree of service protection to the 300 customers. Electric rates in the community started at 17 cents per kilowatt-hour.

In the mid-Columbia area, Pacific on February 28, 1911, acquired Husum Power Company, which in 1909 had begun

PP&L office and staff at Dayton, Washington, in 1915. Window displays promoted electric cooking, Edison Mazda lamps, electric irons and heating devices. From left, those pictured are Fred Sparks and Myrl Walsh, linemen; Fred Florine, chief clerk; Dorothy Griffith, clerk; "Dynamite," the district mascot; and H. A. Mott, district manager.

serving the town of White Salmon, Washington, from a 75-kilowatt hydro installation at a natural fall in the White Salmon River about five miles north of the community. It served about 190 customers.

Two months later the Company acquired Klickitat Light & Power Company, serving Goldendale, Washington. Its power source was a 150-kilowatt generator located in a 600-foot canyon at the confluence of Blockhouse Creek and Little Klickitat River about nine miles west of Goldendale. Three attempts were required to get the generator into place at the bottom of the canyon. Twice the generator fell and had to be returned to San Francisco for repairs. As a rule, only night service was furnished in Goldendale and the town was dark on an average about five nights a month due to a failure of either the generator or the line into town. During part of the summers of 1909 and 1910, service was supplied from 8 A.M. until noon, primarily to take care of a 15-horsepower motor at the ice plant. At the time Pacific acquired the property, there were 197 customers on its lines.

Electric and water properties at Prosser, Washington, were acquired in April, 1911. The Prosser Power Company had a 200-kilowatt hydro generator at a fall in the Yakima River, and a

29

200-horsepower steam engine for standby use. The electric system had 309 customers, and operated under a franchise granted in 1905. Part of its power supply was obtained from the Yakima-Pasco transmission line under arrangements that had been made with the Yakima Valley Power Company.

Also in April, 1911, Pacific acquired Hood River Light & Power Company, which began supplying service in 1901 from a 50-kilowatt hydro generator located on the N. C. Evans property on Hood River. The early company encountered rivalry from one organized in 1904 with the object of acquiring the pioneer enterprise. Failing in this, it built its own power plant at the old Powerdale site. The two properties later were combined, following which N. C. Evans organized another venture, the Hydro Electric Company. This firm built a 300-kilowatt plant on Hood River at Tucker Bridge and in 1912 entered into strenuous competition with Hood River Gas & Electric Company, then operating the other system. The state railroad commission ultimately had to step in to stabilize rates before one or the other company went bankrupt. In 1915 the two properties were put together and operated as a unit by Pacific Power.

The Reservation Electric Company, serving the town of Toppenish, Washington, was acquired by Pacific on October 23, 1911. This company had started operations in 1908, supplying customers from a steam generating station consisting of a 120-horsepower Lycoming steam engine connected to a Westinghouse 60-kilowatt generator. The population of Toppenish had increased from 500 to 2,000 over a three-year period and service demands soon exceeded capacity of the electric plant. Construction was started on a larger plant in 1910 and a 100-kilowatt generator was delivered to the plant site, but on account of financial difficulties the rest of the plant was never installed. Arrangements were then made to get power from the new Yakima-Pasco transmission line.

Pacific's 1911 construction program brought service to ten communities that had not previously had electricity. Among these were Bingen, Centerville, Grandview, Granger, Kiona, Outlook, Richland and Beverly, Washington, and Umapine, Oregon. The following year lines were extended into Mosier, Adams and Rowena, Oregon, and into ten Washington communities, including Moxee, Selah, White Bluffs and Zillah.

In 1913 the Company brought service to the Parkdale and Mt. Hood communities in the Hood River Valley and to Cowiche in the Yakima district.

Extensions in 1915 and 1916 gave service to Warrenton, Hammond and Flavel, Oregon, and Underwood, Wallula, Gleed, Prescott and Sawyer, Washington.

The Seaside Light & Power Company and the Gearhart Park Company were acquired in 1916. Electric service in Seaside dated from 1906 and the Gearhart distribution system, which obtained its power from the Seaside company, was organized in 1913. The Seaside system, when acquired by Pacific, had three steam driven generators with a rated capacity of 425 kilowatts. During the vacation season it served as many as 578 customers. Soon after the acquisition of these properties, the Gearhart distribution lines were rebuilt and the two communities were connected with the Astoria system by a transmission line. The small and inefficient steam plant was then retired from service.

Some years later, in 1928, Pacific added Cannon Beach to its Clatsop county service area by the purchase of a small diesel-powered plant that had been installed there. A line was built over the ridge from Seaside to connect the community with the Astoria-Seaside system. Rates, which started at 22.2 cents a kilowatt-hour, were sharply reduced.

Extensions of service in 1917 included the Washington communities of Buena, Union Gap and Touchet. In 1918, service was extended to Helix, Oregon, and Kahlotus, Washington. Rieth, Oregon, was provided with electric service in 1921, and in 1922 lines were extended to Fort Stevens, Oregon, and Donald, Washington. Pacific ran its lines to Pilot Rock, Oregon, in 1924, and the following year an extension brought service to the Ahtanum community in the Yakima Valley. In 1926 other Yakima area extensions included lines to Harrah, Parker, Tieton and Wiley City. Service also was extended to the railroad town of Wishram, near Celilo Falls. Dee, Tygh Valley and Mission, Oregon, and Lowden, White Swan and Whitman, Washington, also were connected to the system in the late 1920's.

Chapter 6

It Took Money, and More Money!

ONE OF THE FIRST major construction projects undertaken by
the young Pacific Power & Light Company was a transmission
line to connect the Walla Walla-Pendleton system with the
Yakima-Pasco system. This line ran from Walla Walla to Pasco.

But there were a great many more capital expenditures to be
made, as illustrated by these diverse examples taken as they
appeared among improvement requisitions ratified by the executive
committee of the Board of Directors on March 22, 1911:

Reconstruction of Naches Steam Plant on Naches River, Wash.	$ 48,675.00
23,000 ft. of cast iron pipe, gas distributing system at Walla Walla	24,412.00
One 16 Inch Carriage Underwood Typewriter G. Manager's Office, Portland	83.00
Erection of Gas Plant, N. Yakima	101,840.00
Reconstruction of the Hanford and Priest Rapids Transmission Line from 22.5 kv to 66 kv operation	49,420.00
Construction of 6600 v Transmission Line from Toppenish to Wapato	19,976.00
Construction of 66 kv Transmission Line, point on Yakima v Transmission Line, south of Richland to the town of Hanford	60,340.00
Erection of substation, Toppenish, Wash.	28,239.00
Construction of 6600 v Transmission Line, Sunnyside and Granger	12,825.00
Rebuilding of local distribution system, Walla Walla.	7,112.62
Blanket Requisition, expenditure to cover labor and material to make extensions and connections, probable new electric consumers, Pendleton, Oregon. .	2,637.03
Credit for sale of one scrap generator at Kennewick.	125.00
Two Torpedo body Hupmobiles, for Walla Walla Plant and North Yakima Plant	2,149.00
Construction of a 6600 v Transmission Line of 35' Poles from Coyote to White Bluffs	14,646.00
Priest Rapids, Beverly Transmission Line, 66 kv	56,805.00
Construction of concrete sidewalk along the north side of our office building, North Yakima	98.00
Provision for 5 Western Elec. portable telephone sets handling trouble on transmission line, North Yakima. .	44.00
Blanket Requisition, expenditure necessary for the cost of erecting two street lighting posts in the front of office, fixtures and furniture, Astoria, Oregon. . . .	184.20

Setting poles in the early years called for lots of coordinated muscle power, as exemplified by this Copco crew at work in an area south of Medford. The scene was reenacted thousands of times throughout the country as electric service was extended to community after community.

Grading streets in front of our lots in
Railway Addition to Freewater.................. 107.80
Construction of a 66 kv Pole Transmission
Line from Dalles to Hood River.................. 44,347.00

The total amount of these and other authorized expenditures acted upon at the meeting was $619,691.02.

One item acted upon by the Board on June 19, 1911, was $22,302 for 6600-volt distribution lines from Sunnyside to Outlook, Mabton and Grandview and for substation equipment at Sunnyside. Another was $46,171 for line extensions westward from Freewater.

Isolated systems serving the Dayton, Washington, area were interconnected with Walla Walla for the first time by a 66-kv transmission line calling for an expenditure of $80,390.

Approval was given to the construction of a brick substation at Richland, Washington, at a cost of $10,075, and the purchase of an 18-drawer index cabinet for the Company's addressograph equipment cost $25.

Minutes of the June, 1911, Board meeting showed that improvements and additions in the first 12 months of the Company's corporate existence totaled $957,295.97.

33

On November 11, 1911, the executive committee approved "extension of 2300-volt pole line to insane asylum at Pendleton, Oregon," at a cost of $2,070, and construction of a 6600-volt circuit from Waitsburg to Prescott, Washington, $15,028.

Committee approvals at the December 18, 1911, meeting ranged from $12.45 for a sidewalk at Dufur, Oregon, to $12,661 for reconstruction of the distribution system at Dayton. Extensions and connections to electric consumers in the Astoria district were approved in the amount of $4,195.15.

At the executive committee meeting on February 21, 1912, "The chairman read a telegram dated February 20th from Mr. Talbot, recommending the immediate extension of transmission lines into six new irrigation districts to take care of business which has already been contracted for, or can be secured at once. The estimated cost of these extensions was $47,000. . . . The Committee recommended that the President of the Company be instructed by wire to proceed with the work forthwith, sending formal Improvement Requisitions for approval in due course."

During the following month expenditure approvals included $2,355 for "equipment and extensions to lighting circuit for Astoria Centennial celebration" and $2,068 for a 3-phase power extension at Astoria to Uniontown.

At the July, 1912, Board meeting it was recorded that gross earnings for the preceding 12 months amounted to $1,198,355.93.

Construction expenditures of nearly half a million dollars were approved at the Board meeting January 16, 1913. Included in the list of projects were the following:

Mt. Hood extension, Hood River, Ore.	$ 7,209.00
Danger signs, Pendleton, The Dalles, Astoria	375.00
Extension county poor farm, N. Yakima	1,143.00
Street lighting system, Pendleton, Ore.	2,923.00
Substation, The Dalles, Ore.	18,229.00
Transformers, Naches Power Plant	3,896.00
Sanitary Toilet Cottage, No. Yakima	96.00
Transmission Line, The Dalles, White River	47,514.00
Distribution system, Adams, Ore.	1,813.00
Reconstruction, Street Railway, Astoria	14,991.00
Office Building, Sunnyside, Wash.	7,118.00

Purchase of a horse and wagon for use in Kennewick at a cost of $285 was approved by the executive committee in February, 1913, also reconstruction of the hydraulic works at the Hood River hydro plant at an estimated cost of $5,956.

34

Naches power plant was a major supplier of energy in the early years of the Company and had to be kept running even though it took great effort to keep ice from blocking the penstocks during a hard winter.

A meeting of the executive committee held in New York on June 16, 1913, recorded that S. Z. Mitchell "further presented for discussion the financial condition of Pacific Power & Light Company, and it was deemed advisable to wire Mr. Talbot to impress upon him and the officials of the Pacific Power & Light Company the necessity of increasing the Company's net earnings for the purpose of making the securities of the company marketable."

How familiar became the burden of that message!

Capital expenditures in the second half of 1913 included two secondhand Locomobile cars, one for the Walla Walla manager and one for Hood River, $100 for a single buggy and harness for the Naches power plant and $90 for the installation of bath and plumbing in the Company's house at Dayton. A motorcycle for the Lewiston office was purchased at a cost of $362.75.

Largest project in 1914 and 1915 was at Naches. The power canal was enlarged and relined at a cost of $486,907 and a 1,400-kilowatt generator installed at a point where the canal dropped from one level to another. This "Drop Plant" added approximately 25 per cent to the hydro production of the Naches development, which in 1915 produced more than 40 per cent of the Company's entire generation. More than $1,000,000 was spent on the program in the two-year period.

Chapter 7

Company Bulletin a Boon to Historian

START OF A COMPANY publication, *"The Pacific Power & Light Bulletin,"* in 1913 began to give a more comprehensive picture of the organization's activities than is available from the formal minutes of meetings of the Board and executive committee in the early years. These minutes, however, were invaluable for information not elsewhere recorded.

From the beginning, a lively phase of activity is reflected in *Bulletin* reports of efforts to gain new business. The November, 1913, issue, for example, carried the news from Walla Walla that 14 gas engines had been displaced with electric drive in irrigation pumping installations since the Company started business. The district had secured 1,249 horsepower of load formerly served by steam engines and 156 horsepower in mills previously operated by water wheels. Also, one small gasoline engine generating plant had been displaced by service from a power line.

Alertness of Yakima Manager George C. Sawyer in getting business was likewise favorably reported. "A few days ago," the story said, "Mr. Sawyer spied a gas engine on a dray driving toward the country. Mr. Sawyer followed the wagon and, catching up with it, introduced himself to the farmer. After a little talk he introduced the subject of 'Electric Motor vs. Gas Engine.' His argument proved so successful that within a short time the farmer turned around, carted the gas engine back to town, and when he finally turned back he had an electric motor tucked carefully away under the seat and a duplicate contract in his vest pocket."

Another service feat was reported from Pendleton, where, "during the Pendleton Round-Up, an interesting problem in supplying current for lighting the trains of Pullman sleepers which the railroad companies had there was solved successfully. It was necessary to get current at 65 volts, as the lamps in the cars are nearly all designed for this voltage." The story went on to describe an unorthodox hook-up of transformers to reduce 2200-volts to the level required by the parked Pullmans.

36

Flags with 48 stars indicate that this picture of Pendleton Round-Up street decorations was taken some time after the admission of Arizona to statehood on February 14, 1912. "Power & Light Co." sign is prominent and F. W. Vincent, PP&L manager, may well have been somewhere in the picture.

The late G. I. Drennan, who was Pomeroy manager in 1913 and later became the Company's field superintendent, was cited for his success in selling electric washing machines. Twenty per cent of the town's 368 lighting customers had electric washers, it was reported. "In other words, some 75 washers are in use at Pomeroy giving us a connected load in washers alone of 6.99 kilowatts. Fifty of these have been sold in the past 12 months. An average of four are placed each month."

One story about Drennan's success selling washing machines in Pomeroy, a town of only 1,600, became a salesman's classic.

The Thor washer sold by the Company was manufactured by the Hurley Machine Company, of Chicago, which was having a discouraging time trying to get established in the market. On a particularly gloomy day, when the Hurley management actually was contemplating shutting down its plant, a telegram came in from Pomeroy ordering a carload of Thor washers.

No one in the company knew anything about Pomeroy, Washington, or G. I. Drennan, but the order had a galvanizing effect.

"If somebody we don't know can sell a carload of washers in

37

a town we never heard of," declared Hurley's president, "something's wrong with us — not with the machine. We'd better find out how it's being done!"

That turned the tide, and Thor went on to become a respected name in the washer market for many years.

It was noted in the January, 1914, issue of *The Bulletin* that the same G. I. Drennan had narrowly escaped serious injury when a buggy in which he was riding lost a king bolt and collapsed, throwing him out of the vehicle.

The same issue told of electrical progress in Dayton, where, it stated, "up to the present time there have been a number of isolated lighting plants . . . but after several months of effort against this type of installation, Manager (H. A.) Mott has finally been able to replace practically all with electric service. To date a total of three gasoline lighting outfits, one kerosene and one isolated electric plant have been replaced."

A novel plan to promote the use of electric irons was reported from The Dalles in the March, 1914, issue of *The Bulletin*.

"During the latter part of the month," it said, "arrangements were made with the editors of the *Mosier Bulletin* and the *Dufur Dispatch,* both weekly papers, to offer a six-pound Hotpoint iron and a year's subscription to the paper for the price of $3.50. These papers are very enthusiastic and believe the inducement of a flat iron will help to increase their circulation."

Competition for lighting service had not quite disappeared in 1914. A *Bulletin* story from North Yakima related that "a Wizard gasolene gas lighting installation was placed by a Seattle firm in the Diamond Cafeteria. The city plumbing inspector learned of the installation and advised them that the work did not comply with the city ordinance covering gas piping and that it must be removed or replaced under his direction. In spite of their many remonstrances the inspector remained firm and the new gas lighting system left the city in disgust."

Sunnyside reported "considerable interest over the electric incubator window display in the Company's office. The actual demonstration of this incubator was successful, as 77 per cent of the eggs were hatched. As a result, the incubator was sold and many inquiries have been made for similar machines."

Earlier, Dayton had featured an incubator window display and

PP&L delegation at September, 1914, meeting of the Northwest Electric Light & Power Association in the Davenport Hotel, Spokane, included (seated, from left) C. S. Knowles, construction department; J. C. Martin, engineer; J. E. Shinn, construction superintendent; B. P. Baily, The Dalles district manager; L. A. McArthur, assistant general manager; and John V. Strange, Prosser manager. Standing (from left) are V. V. Vercoe, Sunnyside manager; George C. Sawyer, North Yakima manager; W. D. Conover, Federal Sign Company; J. B. Kilmore, Astoria manager; H. A. Mott, Dayton manager; D. L. Lewis, Pomeroy manager; A. S. Hall, Hood River; George D. Longmuir, Pasco-Kennewick manager; J. E. Davidson, vice president and general manager; J. C. Naylor, Goldendale manager; M. C. Osborn, contract agent, Washington Water Power; E. W. Thompson, Neptune Meter Co.; and H. S. Wells, new business manager. One individual at right was not identified in BULLETIN *issue that first ran the picture.*

had started a guessing contest on how many of the 120 eggs would hatch. The story said that 323 guesses had been received but failed to record the actual results. These apparently were favorable, for thirty electric incubators were reported to be on the lines in the Dayton area.

Walla Walla noted the sale of three electric signs in one month and the connection of a three-kilowatt X-ray machine.

From Toppenish came news that "The Wapato water system, which for the past few years had been operating by gasoline, was connected up on a trial installation of motor drive early in the month and proved so satisfactory that the council has authorized the signing of a five-year contract."

A new manager at Pomeroy continued the sales success of his predecessor, as indicated by the following: "A number of new residences of bungalow type are under construction at this time. All are being wired and, through the efforts of Manager (D. L.) Lewis with the architects, in several cases special outlets are being provided for connecting appliances."

A combined apple and electric cooking promotion was held in Walla Walla December 14 and 15, 1914. "The apple-cooking demonstration was given by Mrs. Elinor M. Redington . . . and was well patronized and created a great deal of interest. Mrs. Redington used an electric range for the demonstration and prepared apples in more than one hundred ways." The cooking show was staged on an OWR&N railway car that was on tour to encourage greater use of apples in the kitchen.

From The Dalles in 1915 came this report: "After having tried out an electric range for several weeks in the home of Mr. Hawley, of the building committee of the proposed Knights of Pythias Lodge apartment house, it has been definitely decided by the committee to install electric ranges in all apartments. This means there will be 26 or 27 ranges installed."

The Company helped promote an electrical exhibit at the 1915 Oregon State Fair. "This year," *The Bulletin* noted, "marked the first attempt of the Oregon power companies to make a display at the Oregon State Fair, and an excellent beginning was made. The show was modeled somewhat after exhibits formerly used by the Pacific Company in Washington fairs, and was housed in a large tent . . . churns . . . milking machines . . . washing machines . . . separators . . . grindstones . . . ice cream freezers . . . ensilage cutters and much other apparatus. A large electrically driven centrifugal pump showed what could be done by irrigators . . . a number of modern electric ranges . . . on one day over 6,000 adults visited the show."

But all was not gain in the progress of the electric business. In Oregon, Washington and Idaho prohibition became effective January 1, 1916.

Reviewing 1915 operations in the January, 1916, *Bulletin,* C. R. Young, secretary to the vice president and general manager, said: "Our loss in revenue from the saloon business, etc., will amount to at least $25,000 a year."

The Toppenish correspondent wrote: "The eight saloons here closed their doors on December 31, and two of them reopened as soft drink and confectionery stores. It is remarkable to state that all the bar-rooms were entirely sold out by 10 o'clock on the evening of December 31."

Editorially, *The Bulletin* took the situation philosophically. "We stand to lose some revenue," it said of the saloon closing. "However, if prohibition is going to give us a more physically fit and mentally alert and therefore more efficient citizenship we are not going to mourn our losses."

First reference to success in getting a builder to wire houses for electric ranges came from Astoria in July, 1916, when it was reported in *The Bulletin*: "The Hyland Homes Company is at present erecting seven or eight cottages at the end of our Taylor Avenue streetcar line. . . . We have been able to influence the architectural plans to the extent of having electric range circuits included, which will be some leverage in inducing future owners to use electricity for cooking.

Seriousness of the wiring problem as a deterrent to use of electric appliances was discussed in a feature article by Lewis A. McArthur in *The Bulletin* of September, 1916:

"It is probably true," he wrote, "that few central station men realize the great lack of appliance outlets in the average home. This is because an electrical man can generally find a way to put a few more outlets or appliance sockets in the house in which he lives and thus ameliorate a condition that the less fortunate householder finds it difficult to remedy.

"The writer believes that the two most important obstacles in the electrical appliance game are the lack of plenty of outlets and a common standard attachment plug . . . .

"Since the writer has lived in the house he now rents, he has put in several new outlets, all of which are used, and he has a number of appliances that he never uses because of the inconvenience of connecting them up. If this condition exists in the home of a man in the industry, how extensive must it be in the homes of those not interested in electricity.

"Only a short time ago I looked through a fine new house in Portland, of a type far above the average. There was but one appliance outlet in the house, and that was in the kitchen. The

A sudden cold spell in December, 1914, froze many water pipes in The Dalles. B. P. Baily, district manager, reported to The Bulletin *that this home-made rig was much in demand for thawing out pipes. The barrel on the hack was a water rheostat with a broomstick variable control. One secondary wire went to the kitchen faucet in the house, the other to the nearest fire plug or outdoor hydrant. A 200-ampere charge usually thawed out the service pipe in two to ten minutes. The bill was $3.00. One housewife wanted assurance that the treatment would protect against freezing in the future.*

lamp fixtures were so situated as to make it decidedly difficult to use any breakfast table appliances, or even reading or stand lamps, and a vacuum cleaner would have been almost out of the question. It seems incredible that such an electrical arrangement would be installed by an up-to-date architect. . . .

"The outlet system should be so planned that there will be outlets in sufficient number to permit the operation of a vacuum cleaner in all parts of the house, with a cord that is not unreasonably long. . . . The kitchen should have a total of at least three outlets in a medium sized family. . . . The dining room can probably be operated on two outlets, for the toaster and percolator are frequently on a single cord, splitting at the table. . . . In living rooms and libraries, there should be sufficient outlets to allow for the use of the cleaner, and above all, a handy place for a fan in summer.

"It is surprising how much light ironing will be done upstairs in a bedroom if only an outlet is conveniently located. Many small

42

utility irons are in daily use for light bedroom ironing, and the day of the single-iron house should be a thing of the past. Most houses should have two electric irons. One iron for each home is not saturation by any means.

"An outlet for a milk bottle warmer is almost a necessity in the bedroom where the baby is fed. The fan should not be neglected in the bedroom, nor the electric heating pad. . . .

"It will only be a question of time until more household electrical appliances will be on the market. Even now there is news of a small kitchen motor that will operate a grinder, a buffer, a cream whipper and an egg beater. The electrically operated dishwasher is already on the market. These are facts enough to show that the number of outlets should be on the increase."

One of the first, if not the very first, all-electric homes on the Company's lines was described in the October, 1916, *Bulletin* under the heading "The House Without a Chimney."

"Electricity . . . has made its first inroad upon the vocation of Santa Claus in Hood River," the story read. "There is one house in Hood River which Santa Claus will find it difficult to penetrate, and should he do so, will have to seek other access than down the proverbial chimney."

Then followed the description of a new operators' cottage of "bungalow type" just completed at Powerdale, which included "a kitchen 10′ x 13′, fitted with a Hughes No. 50 electric range and a General Electric water heater. . . .

"The heating of the house is accomplished by electric radiators of the power house type, and outlets are provided for the installation of such heaters as may be necessary."

Although the house was not insulated in the modern sense, it had a double floor and a layer of building paper between the outside walls and the sheathing "so that no stray ventilating currents are possible, thus rendering the house very easy to heat. . . .

"It is a building of which the Company may well be proud and it is built with a view to permanency and low upkeep cost."

In the last *Bulletin* issue of 1916 "Tam" McArthur authored another feature article, this on "Cost of Electric Cooking."

"Investigations made by the Pacific Company during the past year indicate that cooking electrically is not expensive as compared with results obtained with other fuels in the territory we serve.

"We have over 200 electric ranges operating on our system, and the average monthly cost is approximately $3 per range, a small sum compared with coal and wood and their disadvantages."

Makes of electric ranges in service were listed as follows:

Westinghouse-Copeman 86
Hughes 96
Hotpoint 3
General Electric 10
Simplex 6

    Total 201

Data developed by McArthur indicated that the average cost per month for electric ranges regularly used was $3.13.

It was also determined that 46, or 22.8%, of the range customers had electric water heaters at the time the study was made.

The article concluded by reprinting a letter received at the Yakima office from a happy housewife, who wrote: "I have used a Westinghouse electric range for sixteen months and would not like to keep house without it. Continuous use of this range has convinced me that I can do better cooking with less labor than I could upon any other kind of stove."

A subsequent review of the year 1916 described it as the best in the Company's brief history for the promotion of appliance sales. Eighty-four electric ranges and 20 water heaters were sold during the year, along with 45 curling irons, 504 toasters, 50 sewing machine motors and 2,027 electric flat irons.

Chapter 8

Rate Reduction Program Began in 1911

S ALES PROGRESS of the young company was abetted not only by the service improvements and extensions that called for a steady flow of new capital, but also by early electric rate adjustments.

On the Yakima-Walla Walla-Pendleton system electric rates were reduced in June and July, 1911, and initial steps taken toward bringing about more uniformity in schedules.

For residential service, the average reductions ranged from 19% for 15 kilowatt-hours a month to 25% for 100 kilowatt-hours. Reduction in the price of 250 kwh averaged 22%.

In terms of average billings, cost of the 15 kwh, for example, was reduced from $2.22 to $1.80, which brought the price per kilowatt-hour down from 15 cents to 12 cents.

Instead of paying an average of $12.30 for 100 kwh, the home user now got this amount of electricity for $9.26, a drop in average kwh price from 12.3 cents to 9.3 cents.

At the rates PP&L inherited, 250 kwh cost an average of $27.13, or approximately 10.8 cents per kwh. The new schedules cut such a bill to $21.25, or 8.5 cents per kwh. In the following year, a further reduction of 23% in the 250 kwh bracket brought the average bill down to $16.40, or a little over 6.5 cents per kwh.

The July 1, 1912, adjustment in rates also reduced and generally made uniform other brackets in the Company's residential schedules in the cities of Yakima, Walla Walla and Pendleton.

Rates in Astoria in 1910 already were close to the reduced schedule instituted east of the mountains in 1911, reflecting an early injection of S. Z. Mitchell's operating philosophy at the time the property was reorganized. In fact, for monthly use in excess of 15 kwh, the Astoria residential rates actually were slightly lower and no changes were made in the schedule until January 1, 1913. The price of 250 kwh was then reduced to conform with an adjustment that had been made in Washington a few months earlier.

At The Dalles, 1910 rates for household use were above the 1911 Yakima level for billings up to and including 40 kwh, and

45

Sales of electric appliances were pushed by the Company, starting in its very early years. Pictured is a two-oven, two-burner Copeman electric stove on the Wellman ranch in the Walla Walla district. The alarm clock timer hanging from the wooden frame was an extra. The electric washer in the corner was a Maytag. The year was about 1915.

below that level for larger consumptions. A July 1, 1911, rate adjustment for The Dalles cut the cost of 15 kwh from $2.25 to $1.80 and of 40 kwh from $5.00 to $4.40, and other rate adjustment in 1912 gave further reductions to the small users, of whom there were a great many, and effectively cancelled out the increases that had been made in the larger brackets of use. These adjustments brought about substantial uniformity of residential rates in The Dalles, Yakima, Walla Walla and Pendleton.

Cost of electric cooking was reduced 28% in 1915, when the cooking rate was cut from 5 cents per kwh to 4 cents, with a 10% discount bringing the new rate down to 3.6 cents.

At the same time a flat rate for electric water heating was made available where the water heater was on the same circuit with the range, and a two-way switch had been installed to allow only one or the other piece of equipment to be in use at any time.

An article by George D. Longmuir, Company manager for Pasco-Kennewick, in the April, 1915, issue of *The Bulletin* decribed an electric water heating unit that could be attached on the side of a conventional storage tank and told of tests made.

"It was found that starting from a cold tank, hot water was available in 15 minutes," he wrote. "By permitting the heater to run over night before washday, sufficient hot water was had to do the entire washing. . . .

"From February 12 to April 1 a meter on the tank showed a consumption of 636 kwh, or about 400 kwh a month, an average of 13.5 kwh a day, or an average use of the heater of 18 hours per day. During the same period the range used 97 kwh, or 62 kwh a month.

"Naturally the first thought would be that no rate within reason could be quoted on a heater requiring 400 kwh a month, but it is believed that a flat rate could be given, say at $2.50 per month, on a 750-watt heater, which would be in the neighborhood of .6 cent a kwh, it being understood of course that this be given only in connection with an electric range.

"An analysis of the earnings from 12 ranges in Pasco and Kennewick over a combined period of 100 range months, shows that we receive on an average from each range $39.00 annually. This is on a 5-cent rate.

"The average demand of the ranges installed is 2 kw and this represents the capacity of equipment necessary to take care of them. We receive, therefore, $19.50 per kw-year from electric cooking and if the same equipment will care for the water heater, and it will with the method of control (a two-way switch) as outlined above, a flat rate of $2.50 per month on the heater will give us an earning of $34.50 per kilowatt-year, and at the same time remove the chief obstacle in the selling of electric ranges."

Bear in mind that when the foregoing was written the hot water tank commonly stood beside a wood or coal kitchen stove, which had in its firebox a pattern of pipe to heat the inflow to the storage tank. Merely to substitute an electric range for the old solid fuel range left the householder not only without a source of hot water but also without a handy place to burn trash and combustible garbage. The electric water heater was a practical answer to the first problem, and an early piece of auxiliary equipment for an electric range was a matching trash burner to snuggle in beside it. The trash burner could also be used to provide heat for the kitchen during cool weather, which was a common function of a solid fuel stove in the days when central heating systems were few.

The Bulletin of July, 1915, in reporting the establishment of a combination rate for electric cooking and water heating did not describe the flat-rate water heating schedule but, from other evidence, it seems likely that the suggested $2.50 per month charge for a 750-watt heater, with correspondingly higher charges for larger units, was close to the actual rate.

There is no question but that the flat-rate water heating idea played an important part in the pioneering of both electric cooking and water heating. But once established, it was not easy to eliminate. More than 25 years later, customers on a flat-rate schedule were reluctant to give it up, especially if the insulation had, in some mysterious way, vanished from a water tank that was conveniently located in the bathroom and radiated warmth to take off the chill on a cold morning.

With the progress of market development, the promotion of flat-rate water heating service was followed in due course by a low metered rate for off-peak service. A time clock was installed to cut off the water heater during the evening peak hours, usually between 5 and 8 P.M. During the rest of the day the heater was under automatic thermostat control.

This method of control, too, served its time and outlived its usefulness. One drawback was that if service should be interrupted for any reason, all the electric control clocks were affected and had to be reset by a serviceman to get them back in step.

As more and more water heaters came into use, another problem gradually developed. During the hours when the water heaters were cut off by the controls, dish washing and other requirements would draw off hot water and, when the clocks closed the time switches, practically every water tank on the line would be calling for power. As a result, the highest peak of the day on a residential circuit often came not at the dinner hour but well after dinner at the moment when all the water heater control clocks snapped this load back on the line.

The eventual result was the development of rates that provided for 24-hour service to thermostatically controlled electric water heaters, the load having grown to the point where the natural diversity in customers' hot water requirements and living habits acted to level out the peak demand more effectively than an inflexible time control system.

48

Husum Power Company built this 75-kilowatt plant at Husum Falls on the White Salmon River in 1909. Initially it served 16 customers in the White Salmon area. When the property was acquired by PP&L in 1911, the little system had 12 miles of pole lines, 30 transformers and about 190 customers

These more advanced rate forms eliminated the need for two meters on the premises of a water heater customer, since combination cooking and water heating schedules included a block of low-cost kilowatt-hours adequate for most normal requirements.

In the 1915 period, however, a 28% reduction in the electric cooking rate and the initiation of flat-rate water heating marked a notable step in the promotion of electrical living.

49

Chapter 9

The World War I Period: 1914-18

THE 1914-18 world war I period was one offering many interesting sidelights on the problems and progress of Pacific Power & Light Company.

In the February, 1914, issue of *The Bulletin,* employees found an article "The Income Tax," by George L. Myers, reminding them that the 16th Amendment and Tariff Act of 1913 required affected citizens to file an income tax return on or before March 14. Single persons were entitled to a $3,000 personal deduction, it was noted, and married persons $4,000. The tax rate on incomes of between $20,001 and $50,000 was at the rate of 1%, an income of $50,001 to $75,000 was taxed at 2%, and so on.

The same issue reported that a committee investigating the possibilities of a Columbia River power project at Five Mile rapids near The Dalles had found that "approximately 300,000 horsepower can be developed."

The March issue said: "Construction work on the Celilo Canal continues to progress rapidly and the work to date is farther advanced than was expected."

Another news item informed readers: "Commencing the first of the month the Walla Walla Valley Railway will operate its cars to the State penitentiary."

Installation of a $3,889 fish ladder at the Company's Hood River dam was approved by the Board on April 16, 1914.

With the outbreak of war in Europe, the money market had been upset to the point that in August, 1914, the Board of Directors, to get needed construction capital, sold $107,000 of bonds to American Power & Light at 85% of par and accrued interest. American, in turn, agreed to pay Pacific such additional sums as might be realized from its resale of the bonds when conditions warranted. Uncertainties of the time were reflected in the minutes of the meeting. The chairman was given authority "to sell other bonds from time to time as necessary on the same terms."

In the transportation field, the Hill interests in the summer

*An estimated 10,000 persons gathered at the Great Northern Pacific
Steamship Company's terminal at Flavel on March 16, 1915, to celebrate the
inaugural voyage of the S. S. "Great Northern." Two special trains brought
a large Portland delegation, among them President Talbot and Treasurer
Nevins of PP&L. The Company built a transmission line from Astoria
to serve the new terminal. The "Great Northern" and its companion
"Northern Pacific" teamed up with SP&S steamer trains to give 30-hour
service between Portland and San Francisco.*

of 1914 were building a railway-steamship terminal at Flavel, west
of Astoria, and the Company was called upon to construct a
25,000-volt transmission line to serve the new facility. Nearing
completion at an eastern shipyard were two fast ocean liners, the
"Great Northern" and the *"Northern Pacific,"* to be the finest,
fastest ships in service on the Pacific coast. They were scheduled
to go into service between San Francisco and the Columbia River
early in 1915, to compete with Southern Pacific for Portland-
California passenger traffic, including visitors to the Panama-
Pacific Exposition which was then opening.

The Flavel power line construction job was described by J. C.
Martin, Company engineer, in a subsequent *Bulletin* article.

"The new line," he wrote, "starts at the 25,000-volt substation located at Pacific Power & Light Company's steam plant
in Astoria. . . . This substation receives current over a 25,000-volt
3-phase line from the Hammond Lumber Company's plant. . . .

"At Youngs River bridge occurs the first construction that is of special interest. The fact that the stream is navigable and that the river above the bridge is an anchorage for ocean going sailing vessels, made the construction of an overhead crossing practically impossible owing to the excessive height and cost of towers required. A submarine cable was the only reasonable solution and it was finally decided to use a cable across the bridge draw only, building a pole line along the bridge for the remainder of the crossing. Therefore, fifteen poles ranging in length from sixty to ninety feet were used for the pole line. Because of the depth of the water it was necessary to use a pile driver to set the poles. This made it possible to drive them into the river bottom far enough to secure a good hold.

"The cable is five hundred feet long, and is made up of three No. 2 B. & S. conductors each insulated with 5/32-inch of 30 per cent para rubber plus a lapped rubber faced tape, plus a 4/32-inch winding of black varnished cloth. The three conductors are assembled into a cable of suitable pitch and filled to circular cross section by jute fillers, impregnated with insulating compound. This assembly is then covered with 9/32-inch of black varnished cloth finished with a well lapped winding of rubber faced tape. Waterproofing is secured by means of a 5/32-inch lead sheathing. The lead is protected by a jute bedding and the cable armored with No. 4 B.W.G. galvanized steel wire. . . .

"The next interesting feature of the line is the Lewis and Clark River crossing. An overhead crossing was possible here as a 60-foot clearance between high water and the lowest wires was all that was required. The span is about 1611 feet in length and the towers are two-pole structures, each 135 feet high from foundation to top. It was necessary to splice the poles because of the impossibility of securing poles over 125 feet in length. . . .

"The line is framed to permit the installation of a future 2300 or 6600-volt distributing line. The substation at Flavel contains three 23000/2300 100-kw transformers. . . . This line will also serve power to the new Marconi wireless telegraph station located across Youngs River from Astoria.

"The construction of this transmission line adds about ten miles of 25,000-volt, 3-phase line to the system and opens up to electric service a considerable amount of new territory. . . . The

A 1914 Ford roadster with wire wheels would be too valuable a collectors' item today to be permitted to haul power poles on a trailer. But a Sunnyside line crew of the period was happy to enjoy the help of such a vehicle.

construction work took place during the rainy season and because of poor light conditions, it was hard to secure good photographs of the various stages of the work."

Electric service was ready when the *"Great Northern,"* first of the two steamships to be completed, arrived at Flavel on March 16, 1915, to be welcomed by an estimated 10,000 persons, many of whom had come from Portland on two special trains. Included in the throng were President Talbot and Treasurer Nevins of Pacific Power & Light.

Advertisements for the new train-ship service set forth that the "Steamer Express" left Portland every fourth day at 9:00 A.M. and reached Astoria at 12:05 P.M. The three-hour train trip down the river was made with the engine's whistle shrieking and bell clanging at every hamlet and crossroad. Arrival at Flavel was in good time for the passengers and baggage to be transferred on the dock from train to ship.

The ship sailed at 1:30 P.M. and was due in San Francisco at 3:30 P.M. the next day, providing 30-hour service from Portland. One-way first class fare was $20.00; round-trip $30.00. Tourist one-way fare was $15.00 and third class was $8.00.

Colorful as the service was, it lasted only a little more than two years. Following entry of the United States into World War I, the two ships were requisitioned by the government for the Atlantic transport run. One, the *"Northern Pacific,"* later ran aground on Fire Island east of the New York harbor entrance and could not be pulled off the beach. The other eventually was returned to Pacific Coast ownership and made many runs from San Francisco to Seattle under the name *"H. F. Alexander."*

A feature story in the June, 1915, *Bulletin* described the development of irrigation pumping on the Company's lines in the Columbia River area between Beverly and Wallula. There were 125 irrigation power customers in the district at the time. Eight were large installations, having a combined load of nearly 3,000 horsepower and supplying water to more than 25,000 acres of land. The various pumping plants were located on the Columbia, Snake and Yakima rivers, and distribution systems were extensive. The Northern Pacific Irrigation Company, for example, had 32 miles of main canals and eight miles of laterals serving 6,000 acres on a gravity system that took water from the Yakima River at Horn Rapids. It also had four miles of concrete canals connected with wood pipe lines supplying 4,000 acres with water lifted to higher levels at an 800-horsepower pumping plant.

In February, 1915, *The Bulletin* again mentioned committee studies of power potential at The Dalles, saying: "The engineers who conducted the investigation of the power possibilities of the Columbia River at Five Mile Rapids near The Dalles, reported that 480,000 horsepower could be developed at a cost of $50,000,000, but state that because of the great initial cost and the inability to secure a market for this large amount of power, the project would not be feasible as a commercial undertaking."

A serious problem for operators of street car lines during the period was the sudden burgeoning of the "Jitney Bus." This development was discussed by Dennis C. Pillsbury of the Portland accounting department in the March, 1915, *Bulletin*. Economy of the region temporarily was in the doldrums because of the war in Europe and no one really knows who started the jitney craze. Perhaps it was an unemployed workman, who happened to own a touring car and decided to cruise down the street ahead of the trolley with a "Downtown—5¢" sign on his windshield. At any

"Electricity on the Farm" exhibit by Oregon power companies was a feature of the State Fair at Salem in 1915. Pumping systems, feed grinders, electric stoves and the like were on display. Sponsors were Pacific Power & Light, Portland Railway Light & Power, Northwestern Electric, California-Oregon Power, Oregon Power, Yamhill Electric, Eastern Oregon Power and Tillamook Electric Light & Fuel Co.

rate, it wasn't long before half the automobiles in Portland had been turned into jitneys, or so it seemed at the rush hours. Passengers took it as a big lark, sitting on a stranger's lap or standing on the running board. There was always room for one more!

Effect of this unregulated competition on street car revenues was drastic, in more ways than one. Even after jitneys came under regulation and eventually disappeared, the idea of driving to work kept growing in its appeal, and more and more people were getting automobiles every day. And why not? Cars were getting cheaper.

In 1915, for example, the Company bought a Ford runabout for its irrigation agent at a cost of $545.00.

In 1916 the minutes of the July meeting of the Board of Directors showed approval of the purchase of a Ford automobile for $490.00.

In January, 1918, the Board authorized the purchase of a Ford for $470.00—the low figure of record.

For those interested in automobile operating costs, a report published in the February, 1915, *Bulletin* gave some detailed information. A tabulation showed that in a six-month period a Ford in the Pasco district had traveled 3,043 miles, averaging 18.4 miles per gallon of gasoline and 88 miles per quart of oil. At North Yakima a Locomobile had traveled 3,814 miles and averaged 9.4 miles per gallon of gas and 91 miles per quart of oil. A Franklin in the Yakima district went 3,743 miles in the period and ended up in the cellar with an average of only 7 miles per gallon of gas and 37 miles per quart of oil. It must be recalled, however, that the Franklin had its air-cooled engine under a beetle nose in the *front* end of the car instead of the rear!

Price of gasoline at the time was recorded as being 16.5 cents per gallon in Yakima and 22.8 cents in Pasco.

Weather was one of the standard subjects of news notes from *The Bulletin's* district correspondents. Often the reports had to do with local conditions, such as a lightning storm. The winter of 1915-16 was, however, something else.

The Bulletin for February, 1916, featured this summary of the problems:

"January witnessed the worst storm conditions ever seen on the Pacific Company's system. Continued snow and cold weather prevailed throughout our entire territory and presented a number of very difficult problems to handle.

"On January 12 congested ice in the Wapatox Canal caused a break in the structure, and from that time until early in February the power system was confronted with difficulties arising from ice and sleet troubles. Some of the power loads had to be dumped, but steam plants were operated at full capacity and practically no lighting customers suffered for any considerable length of time.

"Steam plants at Naches, Walla Walla, Kennewick, Waitsburg and Pomeroy carried full loads and relieved the situation materially. Toward the end of the storm coal supplies became badly depleted, because of the fact that the railroads were blocked, thus preventing the delivery of cars. However, we had sufficient to last until the weather moderated.

"Adding to the difficulties of the power department in keeping the various power plants in operation during the month, the Walla Walla River plant was put out of commission on February 2 by a snow-slide which filled up about 300 feet of open flume at the headgate, and a second slide carried away a trestle at station 154. The work of getting the plant back in shape was greatly hampered owing to hardships encountered in getting new timbers to the plant over the snow, it being waist-deep.

"Considerable trouble was also experienced at the Naches plant, which was shut down for a time on account of heavy ice jams forming about the forebays from snow blown into the canal.

"The situation at The Dalles was very serious, but the Company carried the load without interruption, due to the excellent work of all employees. At Astoria transformers of the Hammond Lumber Company burned out, thus making it necessary to hold off the dredging load. Service at Goldendale and White Salmon was maintained with difficulty and hard work.

"Trouble in other cities was as bad or worse than on our system. Power, lights and telephones were demoralized in parts of Portland, Spokane and Seattle. At Vancouver, Washington, all public utilities, including city water, were out of service except the gas system of the Pacific Company. At Gresham, Oregon, all electrical and telephone lines were out. Baker, Astoria, Ellensburg, Walla Walla, Spokane, Seattle and many other communities reported city water supplies interrupted or service and main pipes frozen and burst.

"The Walla Walla Valley Railway Company was forced to suspend operations several times during the storm."

From The Dalles, it was reported that the winter was the coldest experienced in the 43 years that weather records had been kept. On the night of January 13, 1916, the temperature dropped to 17 degrees below zero, "resulting in frozen water pipes and drains throughout the city. It has been possible to cross the Columbia River at this point on the ice for several weeks, not only on foot but with teams and wagons."

Snowfall at The Dalles amounted to five inches in the latter part of December, it was reported, "29.75 inches in January and 32 inches thus far in February, and it is still snowing."

Trains were blocked in the Columbia gorge, and *The Bulletin* correspondent noted: "From Monday morning, January 31, until Saturday noon, February 5, The Dalles has been without train service of any kind, all lines being blocked by the heavy snows. With the river filled with ice and all phone and telegraph wires down with the single exception of one of the latter, which was reserved for train dispatching, the town has been practically isolated. The first train to arrive from the west on Saturday consisted of nine coaches, which necessitated the use of three of the heaviest type of locomotives used by the O.W.R. & N. Co."

Pendleton received no Portland mail from February 1 to 7.

Astoria had 27.3 inches of snow during January, and had below freezing temperatures every day for two weeks. A 94-mile gale hit the coast January 25 "but due to the efficient work of our line crew the public suffered very little in consequence."

Compared with the Portland area, most of the Company's 1916 operating districts escaped the worst of the winter's damage. Initial heavy snow in Portland was followed by moderating temperatures and then a devastating "silver thaw." Power and telephone lines were crushed throughout the city. On top of the ice-encrusted old snow came a new snow cover. Schools were closed and many high school boys celebrated the vacation helping line crews dig telephone and power lines out of the snow and ice blanket that covered them, and dragging insulated duplex wire across the slippery surface to bridge gaps in telephone circuits.

It was a winter to be remembered, followed by a heavy June freshet on the Columbia when the snow began coming out of the mountains in a big way. The July, 1916, issue of *The Bulletin* reported, again from The Dalles: "Due to present high water conditions, river transportation is more or less demoralized, the only boat operating between The Dalles and Portland being the *Bailey Gatzert,* the most powerful boat on the river and the only one at present able to negotiate the rapids at Cascade Locks."

In Astoria, at the same period, crews were extending the Company's lines from Flavel to Hammond "and if the material required will arrive at the promised time we hope to have this in operation at the end of the month. The work of wiring up the residences and stores is in progress, and soon all the gasoline and acetylene lighting private plants will be relegated to the basement or attic."

With the World War I shipping pinch beginning to be felt by the allied forces in Europe, four schooners were reported to be under construction in the Astoria shipyards and plans for a shipyard at Warrenton were announced by a Spokane company.

One Company district after another was beginning to tell of men called to National Guard duty because of the 1916 situation on the Mexican border.

PP&L float won first prize in the 1913 Fourth of July parade at Walla Walla.

Atmosphere of the day was reflected in a June, 1916, *Bulletin* note: "On the night of June 3 a large preparedness parade was held in Portland and the Pacific Power & Light Company was represented by a section consolidated with the Portland Gas & Coke Company. About 200 men represented these organizations. H. M. Papst, general manager of Portland Gas & Coke, was marshal in charge of the 13th division of the parade, and Mr. McArthur of the Pacific Company in charge of the PP&L and PG&C section."

From The Dalles came word that Congressman N. J. Sinnott had introduced a bill in the House appropriating funds for the Army Engineers to investigate the much discussed dam site near Celilo Falls "and the practicability of establishing there a large plant for the production of nitrates, which in the event of war, would be used in the manufacture of explosives and in times of peace for fertilizing and other domestic purposes."

Personal items included such notes as: "John Boyson has purchased a self-starting Ford automobile" and "J. H. Siegfried, superintendent of power at Kennewick, is now the proud owner of a new Buick Six. The speed generative powers of practically all the jack rabbits within a 20-mile radius of Kennewick have been greatly developed since the purchase of this machine."

59

A 22-kv line from Warrenton to Seaside was completed in August, 1916, to interconnect the newly acquired beach resort power system with the Company's Astoria area facilities. Budgeted cost of the line and substation was $39,871.

From the standpoint of earnings, 1916 results were affected by $50,000 of extra expense due to the severe weather in the first quarter of the year and by the loss of several large power loads. The published review of the year, however, declared that the future was much rosier.

"The kilowatt-hour output for 1916 was about two and one-third million more than during 1915," a resume of the year stated in the January, 1917, *Bulletin*. "Our load has increased to such an extent that we have reached capacity and, should we not have obtained more power we would have been unable to furnish sufficient power during 1917. We expect to have our lines connected with our new power source by August or September of this year."

The added power source referred to was an interconnection with the system of The Washington Water Power Company under an agreement approved by the Pacific Company's executive committee on January 13, 1917. Construction of the tie-line from the vicinity of Pasco to Lind, Washington, about 62 miles northeast, was not accomplished on as optimistic a schedule as had been forecast, but it was completed and in service by November of that year to become the first of the many system interconnections that eventually grew into the great Northwest Power Pool.

The interconnection agreement provided for "reciprocal sale and purchase of waste electrical power and energy from time to time between the two companies," and the basic principles of the contract arrangement subsequently have been followed over and over again throughout the nation.

A utility having a temporary surplus of generating capacity sells to a neighbor who is short of power at the time, to their mutual benefit. One obtains revenue from energy that otherwise would be wasted. The other is able to delay making capital investment in power plant expansion until its system requirements are such as to provide a substantial load for a new generating facility as soon as it comes on the line.

News notes of early 1917 also included a sprinkling of incidents of local interest, such as this from Walla Walla: "On February 6, a Mr. Brewer was moving a house on Second Street, using eight horses in the work, when for some unknown reason the horses became unmanageable and ran away. Being firmly hitched to the house it is needless to say the spectacle was well worth witnessing. They ran approximately six blocks, striking two of our poles and snapping them off. After repairs were made and in answer to a letter from the manager, the gentleman called and deposited the sum of $25.00 to cover damages to the company property."

In April, 1917, Company people throughout the system were participating in various parades and drills following the entry of the United States into World War I. New urgency was being placed on the construction of ships, and the McEachern Shipbuilding Company had a yard going on Youngs River near Astoria with ways for construction of five wooden ships at one time. These ships were 250 to 275 feet long, 43 feet in width and 23 feet in depth. Each ship required about 1,000,000 board feet of Douglas fir in the building. Four hundred men were employed at the yard.

Of sidelight interest, this and other yards in the district had labor problems later in the year when workers presented demands for a closed shop and increased pay. Ship carpenters asked for an increase from $5 to $6 per day, and caulkers from $6 to $7 per day, with double time for Saturday afternoons.

Material for construction of airplanes as well as ships was being produced in Clatsop county, which was one of a number of areas along the coast supplying high quality spruce for wing spars and other structural sections.

Chapter 10

Other Notes on 1917-18 Period

UPON HIS RETURN from a trip east in May, 1917, President Talbot observed: "The declaration of war did not disturb general financial conditions as the situation had been discounted," but added, "it was a very disturbing element in the question of marketing new securities and the security business is more or less at a standstill.

"Investors are marking time," he said, "and I do not believe the the security market will become active again until after full disposition of the war loan is completed. Financial interests of New York I believe to be extremely patriotic in the way of taking government war issues and the government will find no trouble in placing them immediately. When these loans are absorbed I am under the impression the market for issues of new industrial, railroad and public utility concerns will become active again."

Talbot noted that he had traversed 27 states in the course of his trip "and found substantial prosperity almost every place. Of the southern states, Texas seems to be especially prosperous, due to the high prices of cotton and cattle."

Speaking of tourist travel, he said: "Many wealthy Easterners visited California this winter, and many preferred California to Florida. A great many expressed their regret at their inability to motor to Oregon and the Northwest.

"As soon as a good automobile road is established between Northern California and the Willamette Valley, I look for a large tourist travel to this district during the latter part of April and May. A good many people with whom I talked do not care to ship their cars for a short tour in this district but with good roads much of the California traffic undoubtedly will come here.

"The roads in California are getting to be extremely good, being the means of distributing hundreds of thousands of dollars throughout the state. The Northwest is suffering from a lack of purely tourist hotels, but those will come with good roads."

Appearing in the September, 1917, *Bulletin* was the first honor roll of Pacific Company employees in military service. There were 21 names on the roll, with almost as many different locations . . . The Presidio . . . Fort Stevens . . . Fort Sill . . . American Lake . . . Fort Leavenworth . . . Camp Green . . . and other familiar centers.

Prefacing the honor roll was: "We take real pride in publishing the following list of those who were in the employ of the Company but who have gone into active service with the Military or Naval Establishments of the Federal Government in waging our War in cooperation with our Allies against the Central Powers to bring democracy and political freedom to the World."

The same issue had an article by "Tam" McArthur on the subject "Electrical Power and The War." In addition to three ship-yards in operation and one under construction, he noted that the Pacific Company was serving 13 flour mills with a total daily output of 7,465 barrels and 21 canning or food processing plants. Refrigeration was also an important activity.

"At Hood River alone," he wrote, "the refrigeration plants have a capacity of 450,000 boxes, and at Zillah one big warehouse will handle 600 cars of perishables."

By October, 1917, the Second Liberty Loan campaign was in progress on the home front, and Pacific Northwest volunteers were beginning to move in full stream toward eastern ports of embarkation. A *Bulletin* note from The Dalles said: "On Friday, October 26, two long troop trains carrying 900 members of the Third Oregon passed through The Dalles on their way to the Atlantic seaboard. Their stop of an hour or more was enlivened by the usual festivities on the part of the local inhabitants."

Announced in the December, 1917, *Bulletin* was a new program to encourage customer ownership of the Company's 7% Preferred Stock. In addition to developing a new field for the procurement of capital, customer stock ownership plans were coming to be widely used in the electric industry because of the belief that local investor interest in the business not only would help promote use of its services but also contribute to broadened public understanding of the corporation's problems and purposes.

The plan to make preferred stock available to customers followed by two years the inauguration of the Company's first employee stock purchase program, instituted in 1915. Under this plan, any employee could subscribe for five shares or less of 7%

Antedating the Northwest Power Pool was the Company's first interconnection with The Washington Water Power Company, through a 62-mile, 66,000-volt line built by PP&L from Pasco to Lind. Here a construction crew is shown setting Pole No. 66 on July 9, 1917.

Preferred Stock at par value of $100 per share, with the privilege of distributing payments over a number of months. First payment was $5 per share and the remainder could be paid in monthly installments of $2.50 per share. Within a short time after this stock purchase plan was announced, 273 members of the Company's organization had signed to participate in the offering.

In a day of huge power networks, operating at 500,000 volts and covering vast regions, it is interesting to read sidelights on the Company's first interconnection with The Washington Water Power Company as recounted in *The Bulletin*.

In July, 1917, an article by J. C. Martin, Company engineer, described the specifications for the line and discussed some of the problems. Need for a 5000-kva synchronous condenser at Pasco, he said, "is made necessary by the distance of The Washington Water Power Company's generating plant from the operating center of our system. The length of the WWP lines into Lind and to the end of our line out of Lind is a little over 150 miles from the nearest Washington Water Power generating plant.

"Under no-load conditions on the line, the normal voltage maintained on the WWP system would produce considerable

64

voltage rise between their plants and the center of the PP&L system. As it is impossible to reduce voltage at our center of distribution by reducing the power plant voltage of WWP without seriously interfering with its service, it will be necessary to make use of the synchronous condenser equipment for controlling this voltage, and the eventual layout will be such that a constant difference of potential between the WWP plants and the center of distribution on our system will be maintained. Unless means of this kind were adopted, it would be impossible to tie the two systems together because of the variation in voltage."

After the line had been completed, the behavior of the line and incidental aspects of the construction job were described in the December, 1917, issue of *The Bulletin*.

"Construction news centers in the work being done on the Pasco-Lind transmission line and substations at Pasco and Lind. The construction crew under Mr. Shinn completed the 62 miles of line between the Pasco Reclamation Company's substation and Lind on November 11. A few minutes after the last insulator tie was made the line was charged from Kennewick to Lind. When the auto-transformer at Lind was placed on the line, trouble developed in one of its coils, so that it was necessary to dry out the other auto-transformer before the Lind load could be carried. The Washington Water Power Company's load at Lind was finally carried on our system November 16, and on November 18 the Ritzville load was also transferred to our system.

"One thing of considerable interest developed from the results obtained when the Lind line was charged. From the time this line was first considered it had been a matter of considerable speculation among those who are working on the design of the line as to what results would be experienced when the line was finally charged. Careful attention had been given to see that the instruments on both the panel at Kennewick and The Washington Water Power Company's panel at Lind were reasonably correct. When the line was charged it was found that the charging current amounted to a trifle over 14 amps. . . . The Washington Water Power Company's voltage at Lind was approximately 62,500 volts, and our voltage at Kennewick was 66,000 volts. The rise in voltage at Lind due to the charging current on the line amounted to only 500 volts. This was lower than was generally expected.

"At the time construction work was started on the Lind line The Washington Water Power Company had about ten miles of iron wire on their line between Lind and Little Falls. This was located just north of Ritzville. In order that the Company could obtain any reasonable amount of power from The Washington Water Power Company, it was necessary that this iron wire be removed and replaced with copper. . . . This involved not only the replacing of the iron wire with 1/0 copper, but also removing such poles as an inspection showed would be unable to withstand the strain placed upon them by the heavier conductors; also replacing a few more poles which with the new loading did not leave sufficient clearance between the conductors and the ground. . . .

"The substation work under the supervision of Mr. Knowles has made all the progress that could reasonably be expected under the circumstances. The substation at Lind is short several pieces of equipment, but was put in such shape that the load could be carried on it temporarily. . . . The synchronous condenser has been installed in its final location and will be ready for operation."

After all the work was completed, the inauguration of the intertie was celebrated at a dinner in Pasco on March 2, 1918.

Floods that occurred just before Christmas, 1917, and took a curtain call a week later were duly reported in *The Bulletin.*

"The trouble in the Yakima country was very serious. The head gates to the Naches canal were flooded with great quantities of logs and the wing-dam was taken out. During one steam run the water came up to the boiler room floor. Added to the troubles at Naches was the fact that the coils on two generators were damaged. . . . We had to make emergency connections with The Washington Water Power Company to save running steam.

"At Hood River the first flood before Christmas put several feet of water over the top of the dam, took out most of the fish ladder, practically all the head gates, about 150 feet of pipe line and one 6600-volt river crossing. At no time has the flood water receded enough to permit complete repairs . . .

"At White Salmon the high water took out the wing dam and head gates. It was necessary to anchor the power house with cable. We made an emergency connection with the Northwestern Electric Company and have been using that company's energy ever since while repairs are taking place at the Husum plant.

66

The turbine for Northwestern Electric's first steam generator in the basement of the Pittock block was hauled through the streets from the Portland waterfront by a 26-horse team December 28,1913. Sign on Ainsworth dock advertises steamship sailings to San Francisco and Los Angeles.

"The Tygh Valley power house operated in good shape throughout the trouble. The water was within 6 inches of the generator pits, and had it come up another half foot the plant would have been put out of commission. . . .

"The Fruitvale canal was damaged twice and a large gravel bar has been deposited in front of the head gates. This will have to be removed with scrapers.

"The weather conditions are now moderating and no further trouble is looked for."

Regardless of December floods, the New Business report for the year declared: "Considering the shortage of men in the Sales Department and the time spent by all employees in selling our stock, December merchandise sales were very good. For the calendar year just ended our total sales have amounted to about $220,500 as against $126,000 for the year 1916. . . .

"The most notable articles sold were 409 washing machines, 602 cleaners and 1919 ranges. . . . To maintain our 1917 record this year is going to call for greater efforts and closer planning than ever before. Are we there? We should say so!"

The first issue of *The Bulletin* in 1918 told of the reorganization of its staff. The editor, C. R. Young, sales manager, and an associate editor, Henry C. Edwards, both had left the Company and George L. Myers, secretary to the president, was named editor. Associate editors were listed as Barbara Crocker, file clerk; J. G. Hawkins, chief engineering accountant; William Maxwell Wood, assistant to the general manager; and J. E. Yates, engineer.

"The reorganization makes it opportune to reminisce," the announcement said. *"The Bulletin* was first published in January, 1913, four years ago this month. At that time it was published as the *Manager's Bulletin,* in mimeographed form. It had its origin with Harold S. Wells, at that time new business manager, and until November, 1913, its publication was confined entirely to his efforts. It was no light task for one person to edit and it was considerable work to mimeograph it, but very few pages having been printed, confined to the few articles that were accompanied with photographs. Mr. Wells' assistant in its publication was Alma Todd, his stenographer. Miss Todd attended to the clerical details and did the mimeographing work.

"At a meeting of the Efficiency Committee November 5, 1913, it authorized the printing of *The Bulletin,* changed its name from *Manager's Bulletin* to *Pacific Power & Light Company Bulletin,* and appointed Harold S. Wells editor-in-chief, and Lewis A. McArthur, then assistant to the general manager, managing editor, with the following associate editors: H. E. Manghum, secretary to Mr. Laing; J. C. Martin, engineer; George L. Myers, secretary to the president, and D. C. Pillsbury of the accounting department. The Efficiency Committee was a committee composed of the respective heads of the Accounting, Engineering, Legal and Operating Departments, to further co-operation with each other in promoting efficiency and economy in handling various affairs of the Company, and to render assistance and suggestions to each other and to the president in problems of general interest affecting the welfare of the Company, its members being Messrs. Davidson, Laing, McGee and Nevins.

"The Bulletin first appeared in printed form in its issue for November, 1913."

A second significant transmission interconnection with a neighbor system was authorized by the Company's Board of Directors

68

How and where Company car No. 6 got stuck in the mud and weeds is not recorded in the annals of 1919. This could have been the Model T that the Board authorized to be purchased in 1918 for a price of $470.00.

on January 16, 1918, when approval was given to the expenditure of $129,586 for a 7½-mile 66,000-volt tie line between Hood River and the 15,000-kilowatt Condit hydro plant of Northwestern Electric Company on the White Salmon River. From Condit, Northwestern had a 66-kv transmission line to Camas and Portland, its principal center of distribution.

Company Engineer J. E. Yates, describing the Hood River-Condit line in the May, 1918, *Bulletin,* noted that the new tie "makes possible the interchange of surplus power between any combination of three companies—Pacific Power & Light, Northwestern Electric and Portland Railway Light & Power Company," the latter now Portland General Electric Company.

"The crossing over the Columbia River has been made from a point on the Oregon side a little above Hood River, known as Stanley Rock," Yates wrote. "The rock is 126 feet above the high water mark and by using this rock considerable saving was effected in the height of the tower."

The line was suspended between one steel tower on the Oregon shore and a 220-foot tower on the Washington side, backed by a third steel supporting structure.

The new line was first charged on April 22, 1918, and put in regular service on June 2. Two 25-kv 6600-2200 transformers were installed at Condit to furnish emergency service for the White Salmon territory "should anything go wrong with the Husum plant," and Yates noted that the installation "adds quite materially to the reliability of the service which will be rendered to customers in the district."

Formal completion of the line was described from Hood River as "quite an epoch-making event. . . . Since this date we have been sending all of our surplus kilowatt-hours into Portland over their (Northwestern Electric's) lines to be mingled with those of that company and Portland Railway Light & Power Company in doing their bit in the shipyards."

Walla Walla was also doing its bit for the shipyards, according to a report from District Manager C. S. Walters in the same issue.

"Owing to the heavy demand for locust wood for shipbuilding purposes," he wrote, "a greater portion of the locust trees in the residence district in Walla Walla are being cut down and sold to the government and if the war continues another year, Walla Walla will have nothing on Pasco for lack of shade trees."

The Yakima district modestly reported a small contribution to the war effort, having again put into effect a special water rate for irrigating war gardens.

The spring of 1918 also saw the Company's general offices in Portland moved from the Spalding building at S.W. Third and Washington streets, where it had occupied space since 1910, to the Failing building at S.W. Fifth and Alder. The new quarters were shared with Portland Gas & Coke Company and the 12-story structure was given the name "Gasco Building." The Pacific Company and its sister utility occupied the basement, part of the first floor, all of the second and third floors and most of the fourth floor under a five-year lease. Remainder of the building was occupied by other tenants.

Describing the office of the president, *The Bulletin* said: "It is large enough to conveniently accommodate almost any delegation that may call upon the president, which was not the case in the old quarters."

The directors' room was "large enough to comfortably take care of a full attendance of members of the board" and "The assembly room is a new social feature, heartily welcomed by employees, although the women derive more benefit from the accommodations offered than the men. It is used constantly by the women employees as a lunch room, being fully equipped with lunch tables, gas range, cupboard, silverware, dishes, percolators and other accessories. One end of the hall is tastefully furnished in wicker and admirably serves the purpose of a rest and recreation room. Cheery chintz covered chairs, an inviting chaise-lounge, and magazine littered table promise to make this little corner a most popular retreat for femininity.

"The room is also to be used for meetings of employees, such as talkfests, entertainments, lectures, etc., an adequate supply of folding chairs being available to provide accommodations."

A committee of two, one from each company, "is to be appointed every two weeks to see that the lunch room is kept in good order." The first appointees "took up a collection of ten cents from each girl in both companies to supply tea, coffee, salt, pepper and sugar so the girls might have something hot with their lunches."

Chapter 11

Astoria Plant a Postwar Project

UNFORTUNATELY FOR THE HISTORIAN, the mounting stresses of World War I caused publication of *The Bulletin* to be suspended with the June 1918, issue, not to be resumed until March, 1920.

A proposal to establish a second interconnection with The Washington Water Power Company was approved by the Board in the spring of 1918. The minutes of the April 16, 1918, meeting recounted that Intermountain Power Company was building a 110,000-volt line from Washington's Long Lake plant to and beyond Lind to supply electricity to the Chicago Milwaukee St. Paul & Pacific railroad. Extra capacity in the line could be used by WWP to transmit power to the Pacific Company and increase delivery capability at the already existing Lind connection point.

To obtain the benefits of the additional line, PP&L purchased three 110-kv to 66-kv transformers and necessary switching equipment for its Lind substation and was able to get the tie completed in June, 1919, in time to be of important service during the irrigation season. The earlier tie with Washington's 62,500-volt line to the Little Falls plant was contined in service to make a triangular interchange of power possible.

A decision was reached in the summer of 1919 to build an entirely new steam plant at Astoria to replace the old Astor Street station and relieve the area's dependence upon power from a generator at the Hammond Lumber Company's mill. A new gas plant was included in the construction program. Site of the development was a 15-acre plot with 800 feet of frontage on Youngs Bay, west of the city.

The budget approved by the Board on April 16, 1920, provided $700,000 for the steam-electric station, $110,000 for the gas plant, $30,000 for new electric lines and $20,000 for new gas lines.

After building a waterfront bulkhead, 90,000 cubic yards of sand were pumped by dredge to fill the plant site. Building founda-

Company's Youngs Bay steam plant at Astoria was completed in mid-1921 but did not go into service until September 11, 1922, when the Hammond Lumber Company mill burned and cut off a power source upon which the area had drawn since 1908. The picture was taken in 1924 after installation of a dock and hog fuel conveyor.

tion rested on piling driven to below the water level. The structures were of reinforced concrete.

As described in the April, 1920, *Bulletin,* specifications were for "three Stirling water tube boiler units of 600-horsepower each, with superheaters, and equipped for burning oil, with space provided for future installation of Dutch ovens for burning hog fuel (saw mill residues). The generating equipment will consist of a 3750-kva, 11,420-volt, 3-phase, 60-cycle General Electric turbogenerator. Provision has been made for the extension of the boiler room to house additional boilers to provide steam for the unit.

"It is interesting to note that the turbine is designed for high pressure steam, using steam of 250 pounds pressure and 200 degrees superheat."

Today, steam pressure of 2,500 pounds at a temperature of 1,000 degrees is common in the industry.

The new gas plant was designed for two oil gas generators, one for general use and one for spare. "The generators are being bricked up on the inside to cut down their generating capacity to 15,000 cubic feet of gas per hour," it was stated. "It is estimated

73

that one of these generators in an eight-hour shift will generate a sufficient quantity of gas to last 24 hours."

At the Pasco substation during the same period, reference was made to the synchronous condenser installed when the first PP&L interconnection was established with Washington Water Power. "This condenser," the construction resume said, "requires a considerable amount of power to start and bring up to speed, so much, in fact, that when starting it interferes seriously with the regulation of the Pacific system. In order to improve these conditions a 150-horsepower, 2800-volt motor has been installed to bring the condenser up to speed."

Housing was short in almost every Company district following World War I. Money was tight and prices were high. In the summer of 1920 the Company had to accept an 8% interest rate on a new bond issue, the issuance of which "required a good deal of time and attention on the part of the Legal, Accounting, Engineering and Property Departments during the month of August."

The Lewiston district reported that "the high price of sugar has materially affected our gas sendout. Housewives are not putting up the usual amount of fruit."

To brighten the scene, the following local item appeared in *The Bulletin*: "Bill Till of White Bluffs reports that business is fine, and that they have a new newspaper in town, one which a traveling salesman dropped in front of the Cash Store."

And a precocious report from Pomeroy said: "The matter of a public aeroplane landing field in Pomeroy has been taken before the city council by the Commercial Club. Pomeroy is on the air line between Spokane and Walla Walla and if plans for a landing field are completed we will probably get the benefit of fast aerial mail service."

From Hood River a timely news item read: "Paving on the Columbia Highway between Wyeth and Hood River is progressing rapidly now with two shifts laying 1,000 feet of pavement a day."

Toppenish reported: "Cecil Root, our appliance solicitor, terminated his sojourn with us May 8. He is some salesman and sign writer. One of his signs, which resulted in the sale of many washing machines, read thus: 'Do not kill your wife with hard work. Let one of our electric washers do your dirty work!' "

At Dufur a 4,100-acre apple orchard, "reputed to be the largest in the world . . . expects a rather large crop and has contracted with a California orange packing contractor to pack its crop." The Dufur Orchard Company, owner of the development, "has to keep on its payroll about 100 during the winter time, and from early spring until late in the fall it has as high as 600 people to be fed and housed." Although the south slopes of the ridge north and west of Dufur were well suited for the orchard venture, it is remembered today only by the older residents of the community.

A decrease in one phase of the Company's business during 1920 was cheerfully reported after the end of the year. This was a decline in the number of electrical appliances sold by the Company.

"With improved business conditions," a *Bulletin* article said, "a number of new appliance dealers started up in business . . . and in every town the outlets for the sale of electrical appliances have increased to a marked extent.

"A few years ago the Company was the only appliance dealer in many of the communities in which it maintains offices and few of the local electrical contractors carried a representative line of appliances. Today every town along its lines of any size has an electrical store and the larger communities have several dealers specializing in all kinds of appliances for the use of electricity. Even hardware and furniture dealers carry washing machines and vacuum cleaners, as well as many other electrical devices. This is a condition the Company has encouraged through its policy of treating the merchandise business on a plane intended to make it self-supporting and as a result it is certain the number of appliances going into the homes of customers has greatly increased."

How rapidly prices changed in the period immediately following World War I is illustrated by the fact that in October, 1920, a Ford touring car for the construction department cost $963.00 compared with $470.00 in early 1918.

Chapter 12

1922: Radios--Powerdale--Astoria Fire

THE NEW ASTORIA GAS PLANT was completed in May, 1921, and took over the work of the old plant "which has done service since the time of Lewis and Clark." The electric plant was completed, except for clean-up, a month later but was not put on the line until September 11, 1922, when the Hammond Lumber Company mill burned. This cut off a power supply source which the Astoria system had drawn since 1908, when the availability of surplus energy from the mill made it possible to put the old Astor Street steam plant on a standby basis.

An August, 1921, *Bulletin* story also noted that the Company's street railway in Astoria had 5.7 miles of main line, operated six cars on a 10-minute schedule and hauled 100,000 to 150,000 passengers per month for a 5-cent fare, which was proving inadequate in that inflationary period. A request for approval of a 7-cent fare had been made in the fall of 1920 but it was January, 1922, before the request was granted.

A news note in the November, 1921, *Bulletin,* recounted that the Rotary Club of Astoria had lunch at the new electric plant. Fifty guests were present. Investment in the new facilities was reported to be approximately $1,140,000.

Another transportation facility the Company owned was the Walla Walla Valley Railway, which had its own share of financial problems in the new automobile age. At the December 5, 1921, meeting of the Company's directors, President Talbot reported that an agreement had been negotiated for the sale of the capital stock of the railway company to Northwestern Improvement Company for $650,000 cash, and the proposal was approved by the Board. The line still exists as a freight branch of Northern Pacific.

First mention of radio as an entertainment medium appeared in *The Bulletin* during 1922. The May issue said: "Now that Yakima has two large broadcasting and receiving stations the radio craze is beginning to affect every fellow in the office. Most of the boys here are working nights making the necessary apparatus to listen in on Seattle, Spokane and, of course, our own stations."

The November issue reported from Astoria: "A program of semi-classical selections was given out last evening by station KFBM, operated by Cook & Foster, the Astoria Hardware Company and the *Morning Astorian* for the benefit of the many radio fans in this vicinity. Station 7HD, Seaside, reported everything was coming in in good shape and modulation all that could be desired. It is planned to have a program every evening."

Radio receiving sets in that early period provided no load for an electric system beyond the extra lighting that might accrue while the hobbyist tinkered with his crystal set. Yet the demand for electricity was steadily growing. Company sales of energy in 1921 were nearly 10% greater than in 1920.

At the July 17, 1922, meeting of the Board, decision was made to go forward with a $1,291,000 hydroelectric development at the Powerdale site on Hood River. This decision followed negotiation of an agreement with Northwestern Electric to sell that utility 3,000 to 5,000 kilowatts for three years from a 6,000-kilowatt plant to be in service by May 1, 1923, and to deliver up to a maximum of 3,000 kilowatts as available for the next 22 years.

Describing the development, an article in the August, 1922, *Bulletin* said: "The generating equipment will be located in a permanent building a short distance below the Powerdale station in about the same location as the development started in 1913, which was discontinued on account of the financial situation incident to world war conditions.

"Water will be diverted from the river by a steel roller type dam, without storage, and conveyed to the turbine through approximately 1,000 feet of canal and flume and 14,000 feet of 10-foot wood pipe on concrete saddles. An effective head of 180 feet will be secured. The pipe line will utilize excavation of the lower end made in connection with the 1913 development. . . . The power house will be a handsome concrete building located just south of the Columbia River Highway bridge across Hood River."

The article also noted that "an interesting feature of the plan is the probable construction of a complete radio outfit for the purpose of communicating with the Portland office of the Pacific

Men and teams did much of the site preparation for the Powerdale
hydroelectric plant on Hood River in 1922. They were helped
by a steam donkey engine. Construction manager was H. H. Schoolfield,
Company chief engineer. J. E. Shinn was construction superintendent.
(Below) Powerdale plant as it appeared on completion. It was
dedicated May 10, 1923. Capacity is 6,000 kw.

Company and the Northwestern Company, as the latter company already has radio communication available."

H. H. Schoolfield, chief engineer of the Company, served as construction manager of the project, and J. E. Shinn was construction superintendent. George F. Mackenzie, later vice president and controller of the Company, was cashier for the project and D. R. McClung, president of the Company from 1958 to 1966, was a young engineer on the job.

The Powerdale development was further described as "the largest that has been made in the state of Oregon since the plant built by the Mt. Hood Railway & Power Company was constructed at Bull Run."

Extreme cold weather in December, 1922, and a big flood in January, 1923, handicapped construction for a period. A December snowstorm put two feet of snow on the ground and temperatures ranged between 10 above and 10 below zero for two weeks. The project correspondent reported that all buildings in camp "were adorned with enormous fringes of icicles" and chimneys were "belching forth large quantities of black smoke, denoting the main occupation of those fortunate enough to be confined to camp—keeping warm."

An overnight Chinook wind brought a sudden moderation in temperature on January 6 and resulted in the residents of the Powerdale construction camp "being awakened rather forcibly at 4 A.M. to the fact that unless something was done soon it might find itself floating down the Columbia. . . . Hood River had come up over its banks and completely flooded the camp, carrying out all bridges, and was traveling at a rate of about 20 miles per hour. . . . The pipeline bridge — a mere 50-ton steel structure — was washed down the river about 300 feet and came to rest upside down on an island. . . . One end of the mess hall caved in whilst the cooks were making breakfast for the flood fighters. . . . Noah had it all over us because he knew what was going to happen and we did not, so we had to carry all our valuables and not-so-valuables out of the office to safety and help move freight cars by hand and switch trains and fill sacks for the dam. Fortunately, before any of the buildings assumed the proclivities of the Ark the waters abated and the dove returned with the olive branch, leaving us fairly well messed up, but all here. It has been estimated

*Big Astoria fire of December 8, 1922, destroyed much of central
business area before it finally was checked by dynamiting buildings in
the path of the flames. Losses to PP&L included its district office,
power circuits in the fire area, gas lines where viaducts had
collapsed and a section of street car track.*

that the total damage due to the high water will run up to $30,000
or thereabouts."

In spite of these difficulties the plant was completed on schedule and "dedicated to useful public service" on May 10, 1923,
by Prudence Talbot, "small daughter of President Talbot, as she
opened the great Johnson valve, turning the water into the
wheel . . . and when a huge American flag was unfurled to the
May sunlight, the applause from the 500 throats and thousands
of hands of the eager watchers drowned the hum of the huge
generator."

Although construction of the Powerdale plant was a bountiful
source of news in the 1922-23 period, the most dramatic *Bulletin*
headline appeared on a double-page spread recounting the big
Astoria fire of December 8, 1922.

"COMMERCIAL DISTRICT IN ASTORIA, OREGON,
IS WIPED OUT IN DISASTROUS FIRE." it stated. "Company
Suffers Loss of Entire Underground Electric Distribution System,
Together With All Primary Feeders, Transformer Installations and
Street Lighting System—One and One-Eighth Miles of Gas Mains

and in Excess of One-half Mile of Electric Railway Track Destroyed. Office Burns but Records Are Saved."

The fire started about 2 o'clock in the morning and by noon had destroyed substantially the entire business district. Three of the streets paralleling the waterfront were supported by piling for a distance of four blocks and when the fire got into these viaducts they served as flues to carry the roaring flames the length of the district. Two of the streets that caved in took car tracks with them.

The Bulletin story of the conflagration told of members of the local force beginning to arrive immediately after the fire started.

"The electric current was first shut off to avoid unnecessary danger. Then a survey was made to determine the possibility of destruction of the Company's office."

Early opinion was that the wind would carry the fire away from that location, but as a precautionary measure "the more valuable records in the office were assembled and packed in boxes to permit hasty removal if necessary. By this time the fire had started south to Duane street and merchandise of all sorts from diamonds to automobiles were being piled in the streets or being conveyed to places of safety. Rain poured down in torrents periodically during the fire, drenching everyone; yet the heat was so intense that within a few minutes those within the fire area would be walking in a cloud of steam."

Within two hours the fire was moving westward toward the Company's office, and trucks were summoned to remove the records and such equipment as could be salvaged.

"By 5:45 A.M. the flames were raging across Tenth street and the heat had cracked the office windows. The show window caught fire and the heat became intense, but still the work of saving everything possible went on and at 6 o'clock the last truck had left the office. Fifteen minutes later Lineman Schmid, in defiance of the police, who had established the danger zone on Ninth street, one block west of the office, broke through the lines and warned Messrs. Baily, Dempsie and Dunlap, who were still in the building, that dynamite was being set off across the street. The four men left just a few seconds before a terrific explosion took place, which sent flying embers hurtling through the air and enveloped the entire building in a mass of flame and smoke. The building was not seen again."

The fire raged for ten hours, but even before it was under control at the east end "linemen were climbing hot poles at Eighth street cutting and tying in circuits so that the fire-swept area might be cut off without interfering with the service in the residential section," which had service restored by midafternoon.

Gas was turned on that night "as a result of the herculean efforts of Mr. Thomas and his crew, who had to cut and plug the ends of mains where the viaduct streets had fallen in. Just before 7:30 P.M. the Boy Scouts were sent out through the town warning residents that the gas would be turned on and for them to watch their stoves carefully until all air had been forced out of the mains.

"Street car service was resumed Saturday morning in the West end, temporary arc circuits were strung and arc lights hung to aid the guards in their duty of guarding the ruins."

A temporary office was installed in the old car barn "and while it is not strictly modern in its appointments it serves the purpose very well for the present."

On the scene in Astoria as soon as available transportation from Portland could get them there were Lewis A. McArthur, vice president and general manager, and R. M. Dooley and Ferry Smith, insurance men. Uninsured loss to the Company was estimated at $100,000.

Chapter 13

"Hog Fuel" and a Mobile Line Camp

TWO CONSTRUCTION PROJECTS described in 1923 issues of *The Bulletin* were the installation of "hog fuel" burning equipment at the Company's Youngs Bay steam plant at Astoria, to replace oil with saw mill residue, and construction of a transmission line from Pasco to Pendleton.

The Astoria steam plant was designed for possible modification to burn hog fuel, and early in 1923 a satisfactory fuel contract was negotiated and the conversion approved.

A *Bulletin* article by Assistant Chief Engineer Yates said: "The source of fuel supply is the mill of the Crossett Western Lumber Company at Wauna, Oregon. Since this mill is situated 26 miles up the Columbia River from Astoria, the first consideration is that of transporting the fuel. Four wooden barges will be required for this purpose, three of which are under construction. These barges are 120 feet long, 34 feet wide and have a fence 8 feet high surrounding the deck, which forms the fuel bin. Hog fuel is usually measured in units, one unit being 200 cubic feet. It is estimated that one of the barges when loaded will carry 200 units.

"The burning of this type of fuel requires special equipment, both for handling and for burning and, to be certain of a continuous supply, a quantity should be available as near the plant as possible. The plans for Astoria call for the creation of a dock 300 feet long and 80 feet wide surrounded by a 5-foot fence located between the bulkhead and pierhead lines and paralleling the present dock, which will be used for storage and for supporting the conveyor. Storage space for a 30 days' fuel supply is thus provided.

"Fuel barges will be unloaded at the pier with a clam shell bucket operated by an electric hoist. The bucket will discharge into a hopper, which in turn empties into the conveyor. The conveyor will elevate the fuel and carry it over the storage dock. . . .

"The successful burning of this type of fuel under boilers requires a special arrangement of the combustion chamber and it is necessary to have space to which the fuel is admitted and partially burned. This is known as a Dutch oven. Ovens of this character are being added to the boilers, each oven being 12 feet by 12 feet by 10 feet high and arranged with four fuel openings. These ovens will be lined with high grade fire brick. . . .

"Construction work has already started and it is hoped to have the installation complete by December 1. Present oil burning equipment will not in any way be disturbed, and will be used for emergency fuel.

"When completed this installation will be watched with a great deal of interest. The use of this type of fuel is limited to localities where extensive lumbering operations are in progress with a reasonable cut ahead and where operation moves along with some degree of regularity so that a constant supply of fuel will be available. Existing installations are not numerous and performance data for the design of the plant are very meager."

Construction procedure and camp facilities for crews on the Pasco-Pendleton transmission line job were described in the November, 1923, *Bulletin* by Harold H. Cake, then a young engineer with the Company, who in later life began a new career and ultimately became president of Equitable Savings & Loan Association in Portland.

"Visualize a barren, brush-covered, dust-colored range of hills interlined with canyons, dotted here and there with homesteaders' cabins, seared with winding single-track roads and you have a casual observer's impression of the country our new Pasco-Pendleton line is to traverse for the first 23 miles from Kennewick to Plymouth," he wrote.

"Take these same lifeless hills, sprinkle a line of poles every 250 feet or so, garnish with insulators and copper wire, season with Herman, Happy, Howard and Carl, shake well with Charlie Knowles and the result is as pretty an addition to the Pacific Company's transmission system as even G. I. Drennan could hope to criticize.

"Construction is progressing at an extremely satisfactory rate due to the above mentioned recipe, and it fairly seems as though the poles spring into place. The inhabitants of the country through which the line passes are greatly concerned about the construction work. Where are you now? How soon will you be in Oregon Are you making good time?, such queries are heard on every side. To

"Office wagon" on the Pasco-Pendleton transmission line construction job in 1923 also served as a recreation center. Jovial look of the participants in this game gives away the fact that the four aces held by Lou Happy, right, and the straight flush held by Howard Whitbeck, left, were set up for the photographer. Across the table are Otis Stephenson, left, and Gerhard Carlson. Each crew in the field had its bunk wagons, cook-house and dining wagon. Battery radios brought in music of popular orchestras from Chicago and way points.

even a layman the construction work is fascinating, while to those directly connected with the erection of the line it is a revelation in team work.

"When on September 10 authorization was given to start work, everything and everybody was ready. Two crews were organized. One consisting of pole diggers (with Herman in the lead), framing crew, erecting crew, two truck drivers, clerk and cook, all under the supervision of H. G. Carlson, immediately began to get the poles in the air, ready for the copper conductors. All material was hauled by truck well in advance of the workmen. The poles were carried directly to the holes by means of Ford trucks, while crossarms, wire, insulators, bolts, braces and the like were handled by a White and a Reo truck, one of which was kept steadily on the run between Kennewick and the scene of operations.

"After the crew had reached Zintel Canyon, five and one-half miles from Kennewick, they immediately took up quarters in their new improved Camp de Luxe, first located about midway between

85

Kennewick and Plymouth on the main highway connecting these two points.

"Listen to a description of these camps, you old-time construction men, and weep. Four large tent wagons were built, two for sleeping quarters for the men, one for a dining room and the other for a kitchen. Each bunk wagon has room for 12 men and in one is located the office, where the Chief Clerk keeps his accounts. The dining wagon has tables and benches built on one side, and the kitchen would be a delight to any housekeeper's eye. A fine wood range is located at one end, hot water is on instant tap, cupboards are large and numerous and there is a bed for the cook at one side. And, wonder of wonders, there is a radio set for each camp. A first-class long-distance set with loud speaker able to pick up anything from Schenectady west! Coyotes may howl, but the canyons of the Horse Heaven Hills will resound to the strains of George Olsen's Orchestra or that of the Edgewater Beach Hotel.

"The first crew is averaging about three-quarters of a mile a day and on October 2 moved their camp from the first location to Four Mile Canyon, so named because of the distance from Plymouth. By the time *The Bulletin* goes to press this crew will be in action somewhere near Hermiston on the Oregon side, having completed the second lap of the march on Pendleton.

"The second crew, under the supervision of Howard Whitbeck, consists of four linemen, a clerk, two truckmen, two teamsters and about ten groundmen. Starting nearly two weeks later than the first crew, they are now completing the line on the Washington side. It is their duty to lay out the copper along the ground, raise it over the crossarms and, by means of block and tackle, to pull the wire to the required sag. Once sagged the wire is securely tied to the insulators by means of short lengths of soft copper wire, and before the watcher realizes it another mile of high line is ready to be always at your service. The crew also has the job of installing guys on poles demanding them, although all anchors for these guys are placed in the ground by the hole diggers and erectors.

"This crew, as is the case with the previous one, started out in their portable camp, once their work had taken them past Zintel Canyon. The camps are moved from place to place by means of the trucks and two teams which are on duty with each crew.

"And finally we arrive at Umatilla, where Happy is in action, getting the foundations ready for the four large river crossing towers required for a span of 1760 feet. The two main crossing towers are 130 feet high and the two anchor towers 30 feet high. Three carloads of cement alone will be required in pouring the foundations and about 30,000 pounds of reinforcing steel will be placed therein to provide the required mechanical strength. So you see Happy has a decided job on his hands and we're afraid that, for once, he can't quite do it alone. But trust Happy! The towers will be erected on time even if all the drawings shouldn't happen to arrive from New York.

"Of course, this line has its innovations. They all have! A few of these new ideas are channel iron anchors in place of wooden anchors; steel double arming plates and double arming bolts in place of the old filler and space blocks; installation of a double armed structure every mile on a tangent of two miles or over with guys placed in four directions to steady the line in case of severe storms; and careful observance of additional electrical and mechanical strength at all corners and points of strain.

"So we see that our 1923 major transmission line is well under way with promise of completion in very good time, provided weather conditions permit and the radios work as they should. Very few setbacks have occurred and it is to the lasting credit of the entire Construction Department that the section of the line from Kennewick to Plymouth has been completed with dispatch and thoroughness."

The Pasco-Pendleton 66,000-volt transmission line was designed for the needs of Pacific's system and was built by PP&L construction crews, but it was financed and owned by an affiliated legal entity, Inland Power & Light Company. The $303,760 line was leased to and operated by Pacific at a rental based on actual cost of the facility.

All of Inland's stock except directors' qualifying shares was owned by American Power & Light Company and the officers and directors of the affiliate were staff members of Pacific or of the American family.

One reason for the organization of Inland on May 14, 1923, was that Pacific's 1910 mortgage did not provide for the sale of bonds in series as did later "open-end" mortgages. Subordinate

*Northwestern Electric Company's first generating station was the
Condit hydro plant, located on the White Salmon River a short distance
upstream from its confluence with the Columbia. Work on the
15,000-kilowatt project was started in 1911.*

bonds sold by the Company in 1920 and 1921 carried a rate of
8% and had the same 1930 maturity date as the senior issue. With
the money market as it was and with no let-up in Pacific's needs
for construction capital, it was deemed desirable to have a vehicle
through which the parent company might provide temporary
financing of projects, or hold an acquired property pending its
timely transfer or disposal, without bringing such properties into
Pacific's capital structure under an inflexible mortgage.

Chapter 14

Northwestern Electric Joins Family

THE PROPERTY acquisitions that had been made in the first dozen years of Pacific's existence had by no means exhausted the possibilities for the extension of its service area, and S. Z. Mitchell was imbued with long-range development plans for the Pacific Northwest.

A number of small, separate electric companies still existed in bordering territory. Other properties represented portions of scattered holdings of a company or group having limited objectives and resources.

In the larger picture were companies such as Northwestern Electric, Washington Water Power and Montana Power, each of which later was brought into the American Power & Light group.

In January, 1925, Inland Power & Light acquired a segment of the holdings of Washington-Idaho Water, Light & Power Company in and around Lewiston, Idaho, and Clarkston, Washington. This included the electric system serving the area and a water system at Clarkston. These properties were leased to Pacific and operated in conjunction with the Lewiston gas system, owned since 1910.

Power for the newly acquired electric service territory was obtained from several small hydro plants and from a connection with Washington Water Power near Lewiston. More power was needed and, in the spring of 1925, an agreement was made with Clearwater Timber Company for construction by Inland of a 10,000-kilowatt hydroelectric project in conjunction with a log storage pond on the Clearwater River at Lewiston. Plans were also approved for a 66,000-volt tie between Clarkston and the PP&L system at Pomeroy, and for a 110,000-volt link between Hanford and Taunton to increase capacity for power interchange between the Pacific and Washington Water Power systems.

These developments were encouraged by the fact that American Power & Light had just acquired Northwestern Electric Company through purchase of that utility's common stock, principally from

89

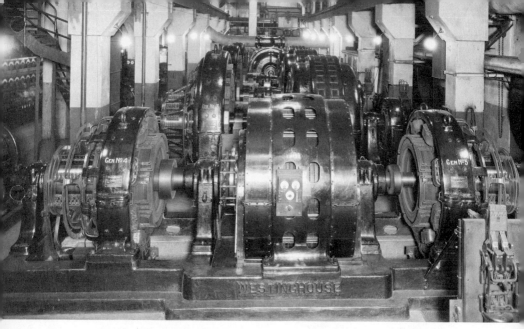

Motor-generators in Northwestern Electric's Pittock station supplied direct current to customers requiring it in the Portland downtown district. Principal uses in the beginning were for elevator motors, printing presses, arc lamp motion picture projectors, photo engraving and blue printing. Demand for dc service diminished with advances in alternating current equipment and in 1965 the remaining users were cut over to individual rectifier sets.

the Fleishhacker interests of San Francisco, and the long-range program was to integrate operations of neighboring systems.

Northwestern Electric had been incorporated July 14, 1911, by the investors then owning a paper mill at Camas, Washington. Its first activity was to provide added power for the paper mill by building a 15,000-kilowatt hydro plant at the Condit site on the White Salmon River, a short distance upstream from its confluence with the Columbia.

A companion project was the construction of a 66,000-volt transmission line down the Columbia River gorge to Camas. In the field heading this rugged job was L. T. Merwin, who later became vice president and general manager of the company and subsequently served as its president from 1936 to 1947, when Northwestern was merged into Pacific. Sharing his tent was E. F. Pearson, who in later years headed the Northwestern division after the PP&L merger.

The line was the first to be built through the gorge. There was no road along the north bank of the river. Much of the line material had to be brought by river steamer to various landings

90

along the way and hauled to the job by teams of horses, or carried by hand where the going was toughest.

While the project was under construction, Northwestern's backers late in 1912 succeeded in obtaining a 25-year franchise to operate in the city of Portland in competition with Portland Railway, Light & Power Company, the pioneer utility. Space was leased in the basement of the new Pittock block for a 7,000-kilowatt steam generating station, to back up power available from Condit in excess of the Camas paper mill's requirements. The Pittock station also was designed to supply steam heat service in the city's downtown business district.

The 66,000-volt Condit transmission line was continued from Camas into Portland, crossing the Columbia at Lady Island in the vicinity of Camas. Steel towers supported the crossing span. From an east side step-down substation in Portland, an 11,000-volt circuit crossed the Willamette River via submarine cable to tie in with Pittock.

Electric rate schedules introduced by Northwestern were below those of the established company, and it was some time before the new rates were met. Meanwhile, the young firm obtained a foothold. When the unique situation ultimately reached a point of stabilization, Northwestern had about one-third of the customers and business within the city, a ratio that long prevailed.

When Northwestern Electric came into the family in 1925, it had 34,500-kilowatts of generating capacity at three locations— the Condit hydro station, the Pittock station and the 15,500-kw Lincoln steam plant on the Willamette River south of the Portland core area. As noted earlier, the Northwestern system was interconnected at Condit with Pacific's mid-Columbia properties.

Revenues of Northwestern in 1925 amounted to approximately $2,500,000, obtained from 21,432 electric and 563 steam heat customers. The company had 65 miles of 66,000-volt transmission and 310 miles of sub-transmission and distribution lines, including 43 miles of underground in the Portland business district. In Camas, Washougal and Portland its operations dated from 1914, and its Vancouver, Washington, franchise dated from 1921.

By way of comparison, Pacific's revenues in 1925 were $3,545,000 from 42,250 electric, 7,249 gas and 8,741 water customers. Installed generating capacities on the two systems were nearly identical—35,550 kilowatts for Pacific compared with Northwestern's 34,500 kilowatts.

The installed generating capacity figure quoted for Pacific included a new 5,000-kilowatt turbo-generator that went into service at the Astoria steam plant on April 1, 1925, to add to the district's power resources.

This and other plant additions made on the system in the preceding year or two, together with progress in transmission links, had put the Pacific Company in a good position to serve new loads, and at a sales and service convention in Walla Walla in August, 1925, "Messrs. Talbot and McArthur spoke briefly of the growing necessity for sales activity on our system due to our increasing power surplus."

Topics discussed at the meeting centered on established devices such as vacuum cleaners, ranges, washers and ironers during the first two days, but a new household electrical appliance came into the spotlight on the third day. As reported in *The Bulletin*:

"Friday afternoon, the last session, was probably the one in which there was the most interest for everyone present. C. L. Lewis, General Manager, and E. S. Matthews, Sales Manager, Electro-Kold Corporation, had an electric refrigerating machine set up and put in operation and went quite thoroughly into the installation of these units. Mr. Matthews gave a very good talk on the machine from a sales standpoint and a lively discussion followed regarding various service questions which have arisen. It seemed to be the concensus of opinion that after having experienced a few growing pains with some few scattered units we can now look forward to a development of the household refrigeration business on our system, with the assurance of the best of co-operation and service from the manufacturers."

Electro-Kold units were made for converting domestic ice boxes to electric operation and for apartment houses and commercial installations. The compressor unit commonly was installed in the basement and connected by pipes with a freezing coil in the refrigerator.

Appliance sales reported in *The Bulletin* during 1926 showed only 71 refrigeration units sold on the system in that year, half of them in the months of May and June. By comparison, 481 electric ranges were sold.

92

In April, 1923, Northwestern Electric installed an 11-kv submarine cable across the Willamette River in the vicinity of the present Sellwood bridge, and it appears that a group of executives went along for the ride. Old Sellwood ferry appears in the background at its slip on the west side of the river.

In 1927 the sale of 122 refrigeration units was reported, not including a 26-unit apartment installation in Walla Walla, and 710 electric ranges were sold.

Early in 1928 the Company took on the new General Electric household refrigerator, the famous "monitor top" model with its hermetically sealed mechanism. However, the Company continued to handle the Electro-Kold line for apartment houses and commercial applications.

That year saw almost three times as many refrigerators sold as in 1927, and the 902 units sold in 1929 nearly tripled the 1928 record. Electric refrigeration had begun to catch on.

At the Company's general sales meeting in January, 1930, the area distributor for GE refrigerators said 300,000 of these units had been sold by the manufacturer in 1929 and that the sale of 450,000 was expected in 1930.

An electric refrigerator saved enough in expense for food and ice to pay for itself, he declared, noting that ice alone represented a cost of $3.54 a month or $42.48 a year to the average user. This was compared with a cost of $20.00 for 500 kilowatt-hours of electricity at 4¢ per kwh to run an electric refrigerator for a year.

Since most of the major electrical appliances sold in that period represented added use of electricity instead of replacements of old equipment, the rate of growth in average annual kilowatt-hour consumption by residential customers was remarkable.

In 1924 the average home on the Company's system used 393 kilowatt-hours. Only five years later, the figure had more than doubled, reaching 997 in 1929 and going up to 1,170 in 1930.

Average price received by the Company for this service was dropping in a similarly spectacular fashion. From approximately 7.7¢ per kwh in 1924 it went down to 3.5¢ in 1929, a decrease of 50 per cent.

No other period in the Company's history shows a sharper growth curve, or a steeper drop in average price for residential service.

The period also saw the introduction of plug-in radio receivers powered by 110-volt current. This was a development that required pioneering, as did another new device, the electric clock.

The March, 1929 issue of *The Bulletin,* reported that 132 AC radios had been sold on the Company's system in the month of January, 17 of them to employees.

The same issue stated that "time equipment has been installed on the Pacific Company system so that Telechron clocks may be used satisfactorily."

The story said that only 19 electric clocks had been sold in January "so we must regard this activity as an experiment, since we have had no experience in the sale of Telechrons and were hardly ready to intelligently promote such a sale."

Advent of talking motion pictures was noted the following month in a news item from Bend. "The talkies are coming to town," the district correspondent wrote. "A Vitaphone installation in the Capitol Theater of Bend is projected for the first of April."

In May, 1929, notes from Yakima included this: "Daily air passenger service between Spokane, Yakima and Portland by Mamer Flying Service was started May 15."

The Yakima items also said: "A new broadcasting station, KIT, is now on the air and is causing quite a bit of excitement."

A story in the Condon, Oregon, *Times* of September 23, 1927, also reflected the growing public interest in radio. "POWER CO. CLEARS AIR FOR BIG FIGHT," the headline read.

94

"Practically all radio interference caused by the power line was eliminated this week by Ellis Van Atta, radio expert for the Pacific Power & Light Company, who came here in an automobile with a specially equipped radio and tested every portion of the town," it reported. "Static discharge in the bushings of the transformer caused by a bare wire which was touching the porcelain was found to be the cause of the considerable disturbance apparent for the past week.

"Static had been bad in town since the new power was connected up and when George C. Sawyer, general sales manager, was in town Saturday the situation was brought to his attention. He immediately wrote to Van Atta at Walla Walla asking him to come and look over conditions before the Tunney-Dempsey prize fight Thursday, as many were anxious to get the returns. He arrived Monday and by Tuesday evening had practically all power line interference eliminated."

The "new power" referred to in the story was a transmission line built into Condon by PP&L to bring 24-hour service to the community. A September 16, 1927, story in the Condon *Times,* quoted exactly, said on completion of the line: "The service replaces a part time service from a diesel engine which has surprised the town with lights in the past."

Public Service Building was tallest in Oregon when completed late in
1927. It stands on the site of the old Failing home. Two subsequent additions
brought the wings up to the twelfth floor level. Portland Gas & Coke
Company's customers' office and appliance displays were on the
street level at the right. Northwestern Electric had similar display space
for electrical equipment on the opposite side of the lobby. The PP&L
operating and engineering staff was on the sixth floor.

Chapter 15

Public Service Building Erected

SOON AFTER THE ADDITION of Northwestern Electric to the family, plans were initiated for construction of a headquarters office building adequate to house that company's staff along with those of Pacific Power and Portland Gas & Coke. The latter two had occupied leased quarters in the Gasco (Failing) building since 1918 and Northwestern's offices were in the Pittock block.

The building site chosen was the west half of the block once occupied by the Failing family home, on S.W. Sixth Avenue between Taylor and Salmon streets.

President Talbot closed a deal to buy the property "by long distance telephone" on November 23, 1925, *The Bulletin* noted. A year later plans for the new "Public Service Building" had been perfected by A. E. Doyle, architect, and L. H. Hoffman had started construction on the 15-story and penthouse structure, "the tallest in Oregon!"

The cost of the building was $1,500,000. Its utility company tenants moved into their new quarters over the week-end of December 17-19, 1927, and formal opening ceremonies were held on January 3, 1928. Mrs. Guy W. Talbot raised the flag atop the building and a dozen homing pigeons were released to carry messages of greeting to utility companies in Seattle, Tacoma, Spokane, San Francisco and Los Angeles.

"New Edifice Enchanting to Visitor's Eye" read a headline in the Portland *Telegram* on January 2, 1928, over a story which began: "Thousands who have marveled at the Arabian nights and reveled in the magic touch of Aladdin's lamp will visit the new Public Service Building Tuesday where they may view the work of the modern genii, science."

The north half of the ground floor was used by Northwestern Electric for electric appliance displays and sales, and the south half was devoted to Portland Gas & Coke Company's appliance displays, sales and customers' counters.

Much has changed since November 1, 1926, but a power shovel excavating a building site still holds the attention of passers-by. This was shortly after the start of work on the Public Service Building, looking north along S. W. Sixth Avenue. The Corbett home in the next block was still occupied. Beyond, to the left, is a glimpse of the Portland Hotel.

A month before the building was opened it was reported that 85 per cent of the space had been taken, including a large part of the six floors available to non-utility tenants.

The operating staff of Pacific Power & Light occupied initially the sixth floor of the structure, and executive offices of the three utility companies were on the fifteenth floor.

Although the north and south wings of the new building went up only three stories, the foundations and structural steel were made adequate to carry a height of twelve stories, and such enlargement subsequently came about in two steps. The wings were built up to five-story height in 1947 and seven more floors were added in 1957.

Title to the building is now held by New England Mutual Life Insurance Company, which purchased the structure in 1950 and entered into a long-term lease-back arrangement with PP&L.

98

Chapter 16

Property Transactions in the 1920's

A HIGHLIGHT SKETCH of Company events in the 1920's must include at least brief reference to a number of property transactions that took place during the period.

The Company, for example, had owned and operated the Vancouver, Washington, gas system since 1913, when it acquired the entire capital stock of Vancouver Gas Company from American Power & Light. In the following year a pipeline connection was made across the Columbia River to bring in gas from the mains of Portland Gas & Coke Company. The small gas manufacturing plant in Vancouver was then closed down. This gas system was sold to Portland Gas & Coke in 1924.

Also in 1924 the Board of Directors authorized the Company's officers to take such action as might seem proper regarding the discontinuance of service and disposal of property of the Astoria street railway since, in the management's judgment, "there was no reasonable prospect of making this service self-sustaining."

Arrangements subsequently were made for a bus company to take over the responsibility for local transportation and the last run of the streetcars was on June 30, 1924.

Water systems the Company had acquired with electric properties in Pasco, Prosser and Yakima were sold to the respective cities in the 1923-1926 period.

Decision was reached in 1928 to dispose of all gas systems then owned by the Company. An agreement was negotiated with Union Utilities, Inc. to sell for $1,700,000 the gas properties at Astoria, Pendleton, Clarkston, Lewiston, Walla Walla and Yakima and the transfer was effected about February 1, 1929. These properties subsequently were operated for a number of years as Northwest Cities Gas Company.

The Company's eastern Washington neighbor, Washington Water Power, came into the American Power & Light Company group early in 1928, when the latter firm acquired control of the Spokane utility through the purchase of its common stock.

99

Two years later the electric and water properties owned by Inland Power & Light in the Lewiston-Clarkston area, and leased to and operated by Pacific, were sold by Inland to Washington Water Power and integrated with that company's operations in the nearby Moscow, Idaho, and Pullman, Washington, communities. The sale included the Lewiston hydro plant, built during Inland's ownership of the property.

On the other side of the picture, Pacific acquired substantial service areas in eastern and northeastern Oregon during the period.

The Company's 1927 annual report noted that "during the years 1926 and 1927 interests associated with your Company purchased electric power and light and water properties in Idaho and Oregon, including the properties of Grangeville Electric Light and Power Company, Ltd., Enterprise Electric Company, Sherman Electric Co. (whose properties included those formerly owned by The Heppner Light & Water Company and the Condon Electric Company) and the municipally operated properties at Arlington and Ione, Oregon. In 1927 the management of these properties and of Deschutes Power & Light Company, another associated company, were unified with that of your Company."

The Grangeville operation was combined with Lewiston and was included in the properties subsequently sold to Washington Water Power.

Enterprise Electric Company, organized in 1911, was the outgrowth of electric service ventures in Wallowa county, Oregon, dating as far back as 1900. First manager under Pacific Power & Light operation was R. L. Forsythe, whose association with electric service in the area went back to 1904.

Principal power supply for the Wallowa valley in 1926 came from a 1,000-kilowatt hydro plant built in 1921 at Wallowa Falls above the head of Wallowa Lake. An old plant at Joseph near the outlet of the lake was replaced by a new 1,250-kilowatt hydro unit put into service November 2, 1929.

A story in the Company *Bulletin* of December, 1929, covering the Joseph plant's dedication, included considerable information about the history of electric service in the area. It said:

"According to the transcript of proceedings in the adjudication of water rights in the Wallowa River and its tributaries, the first recorded filing for the appropriation of water was made by J. A.

Masterson in 1873 for irrigation, domestic and stock use. With this and subsequent filings by heads of pioneer families is interwoven the history of the development of the Wallowa country, so appropriately called the Switzerland of America. Of equal interest is the history of hydroelectric development.

"There are four towns in the Wallowa valley — Joseph, Enterprise, Lostine and Wallowa — and each town had its own lighting plant in the early stages of electric lighting.

"The first electric plant in the valley was established in 1900 in Joseph by F. D. McCully, banker, miller, and merchant. It consisted of a 30-kilowatt inductor alternator driven from a line shaft in the flour mill. This served the needs of the town after a fashion until 1909, when a modern plant (for that time) was installed, consisting of a 400-hp water wheel directly connected to a 225-kva generator. This was supplied with water through a 4,000-foot wood stave pipe line three feet in diameter under a 125-foot head. This plant continued to operate until June, 1927, when it was practically worn out. The final touch came when a large piece of iron broke loose inside the wheel casing and ripped all the vanes off the water wheel runner. This ended the career of this plant which at one time was the pride of the whole valley.

"Next came a 30-kw plant, which was installed at Spring creek, about a mile south of Enterprise, in 1901, to supply the town of Enterprise. This plant was installed by a Portland contractor with a view of selling it to the city upon its completion, but for some reason the city fathers were not convinced that it would be to their best interests to get into the business and did not buy the plant. It was, however, soon sold to a man by the name of William Makin and operated by his son Fred for a year or so.

"Soon the generator was moved from Spring creek to a power site in the city which had formerly been used as a planing mill and was in charge of a son-in-law of Mr. Makin until it was burned in a fire that destroyed the planing mill building. Another generator was installed in the Enterprise flour mill, operating until the planer site could be rebuilt. When this was done the plant went merrily on its way for another span of a few months. In July, 1904, another fire occurred and wiped it out again. The owners decided it was too much trouble to run an electric plant and were about to abandon the property.

Advertisement on the Madras stage office in the early days of Central Oregon development urged travelers to get irrigated land free under the Carey Land Act of 1892. "Apply to local agent or The Deschutes Irrigation & Power Co., Bend." Productive farms have replaced juniper and sage, and PP&L serves 3,000 customers in the Madras area.

"About this time a young sprig of 16 conceived the idea that this would be a good business to get into and talked his father, E. J. Forsythe, into buying the wreck. A new 60-kw General Electric generator was installed soon after on the same site and operated until the fall of 1905, when it was moved to a new site constructed during the summer of 1905, about a mile west of town, where a 230-hp water wheel had been installed. This was considered quite a plant and it continued to supply the needs of the city until 1911, when an investor from Portland by the name of George Jacobs purchased the property and operated it until June, 1912. It was then sold to W. C. Sivyer and Son of Spokane, Washington, and the Enterprise Electric Company incorporated.

"The first plant in the town of Wallowa was installed by the Wallowa Mercantile and Milling Company in 1903 and consisted of a 15-kw, 220-volt, direct current generator driven from the flour mill shaft. About the year 1907 a larger alternating current unit was installed with a larger water wheel, both of which were purchased secondhand from the company supplying LaGrande and which had formerly been in use at the Odell plant on the Grand

102

Ronde river a mile or so west of LaGrande. A number of distribution transformers were obtained from the same source, all of which are still in operation in Wallowa.

"This plant was bothered with ice troubles in the winter months and was often out of service for several weeks at a time. In June, 1911, the Wallowa plant was purchased by George Jacobs of Portland, Oregon, who had also purchased the Enterprise property. A year later both were sold to the W. C. Sivyer interest of Spokane, who immediately started construction of a 11,000-volt transmission line from Enterprise to Wallowa by way of Lostine. This line was finished in November, 1912, and the two plants ran together as necessary to supply both towns, as well as Lostine, which had also come in under this ownership with the abandonment of their small plant. In 1916, additional power was needed and a deal was consummated whereby the property of the Joseph Light & Power Company was taken over by the Enterprise Electric Company and the 11,000-volt transmission line extended from Enterprise to Joseph, tying in with the Joseph plant, which had more power than was needed at that point and in addition was fortunately situated so that it did not freeze in cold weather. These three plants continued to supply the needs of the valley until 1921, when the Wallowa Falls plant was established, after which the Enterprise and Wallowa plants were shut down and the Joseph plant held as an auxiliary until it was wrecked in 1927.

"A small direct current plant was installed in 1902 in Lostine and continued to supply that community in a haphazard way until November, 1912, when the supply was taken from the 11,000-volt transmission line between Enterprise and Wallowa."

In central Oregon, the properties acquired were those serving Bend, Redmond, Prineville and Madras, which had been brought together in 1926 in the name of Deschutes Power & Light Company, incorporated in 1904. An antecedent company in Bend was the Pilot Butte Development Company, incorporated in 1900.

The Bulletin of January, 1929, said that the Bend plant "was originally started by the Drake interests, who also at that time owned and operated a system of irrigation canals. The Drake development began about 1904 with the building of an irrigation canal through what is now the city of Bend and on which it built a hydro plant for the furnishing of electricity."

103

A meeting of PP&L district managers and staff representatives in Hood River on October 18, 1922, helped boost a washing machine sales campaign then in progress and gave opportunity for a picture of many old timers. Included in the photograph, from left, are: George C. Sawyer, John V. Strange, George Mackenzie, S. E. Skelley, V. H. Moon, Henry Anderson, W. D. Myers, J. B. Kilmore, Howard Cooper, F. W. Vincent, R. J. Davidson, J. C. Campbell, J. E. Yates, J. A. Russell, G. I. Drennan, Fred Florine, R. B. Bragg, W. T. Neill, C. S. Knowles, B. P. Baily, R. M. Freeman, J. G. Hawkins, Pat Kean, John Gest, J. H. Siegfried, W. A. Lackaff, Berkeley Snow, G. L. Corey, George L. Myers, W. H. Till, L. A. Safford, C. S. Walters, Roderick McRae, W. A. Dunlap and Lewis A. McArthur.

Later owners developed an 1,100-kilowatt hydro plant still in service on the Deschutes River near the center of Bend. Subsequently they built a steam generating station at the Brooks-Scanlon saw mill, which in time was sold to the mill company and the utility became a buyer of energy from the generator. Emergency power was obtained on occasion from the Shevlin-Hixon mill.

In 1926 the Bend property and those of Des Chutes Power Company came into the ownership of Pacific associates. The Des Chutes Company served Redmond, Terrebonne, Prineville, Madras, Metolius and Culver from a small hydro plant at Cline Falls on the Deschutes and a 1,200-kilowatt plant at Cove on the Crooked River. Formal transfer of all these properties to Inland Power & Light came in 1928.

Growth of the area, spurred in part by the large expansion of irrigation, is reflected in the increase of electric customers on PP&L lines from 4,823 in 1928 to nearly 15,000 in 1967.

Ownership of Sherman Electric Company was acquired by interests associated with Pacific in 1926 and the properties were placed under the Company's operation at that time. These included lines serving the communities of Moro, Wasco and Grass Valley. In 1927 the electric properties serving Condon, Heppner, Arlington and Ione were added to Sherman Electric and in 1928, shortly before the Sherman company was formally taken into Inland Power & Light, the electric system at Fossil was acquired.

When organized in 1920, Sherman Electric had originally proposed to build a generating plant on the John Day River but this project was abandoned in favor of building a transmission line from Dufur to obtain power at wholesale from the Pacific Company to supply the towns of Wasco, Moro and Grass Valley, each of which had been served by small local plants.

Electric service in Wasco dated from 1916. In Moro, the city in 1904 issued $2,500 in bonds to install two 25-horsepower gasoline engines and one 110-volt direct current generator. Lighting service was furnished only from 5 A.M. until daylight and from dark to 10:15 P.M. In 1921 the distribution lines were sold to Sherman Electric.

The city of Grass Valley bought a 20-horsepower gasoline engine and a 15-kilowatt dynamo in 1905. The residence meter rate initially was 16 cents a kilowatt-hour. Service was supplied on the same morning and evening schedule as prevailed in Moro. Along about 1915 rates had to be increased, and in 1922 the city sold its system to Sherman Electric.

First service in Condon was provided by Condon Electric Company in the fall of 1905, at a meter rate of 25 cents per kwh. Energy was supplied from a 50-kilowatt generator driven by one 25-horsepower and one 50-horsepower gasoline engine. This property was sold to Sherman Electric early in 1927.

The Heppner Light and Water Company began supplying that community with power from a small steam generating station early in 1893. In 1911 two new 125-horsepower boilers were installed to operate a 50-kilowatt and a 100-kilowatt generator. The Heppner company later built an 11,000-volt line to Ione, where a small city system needed power, and a distribution system was built at Lexington. Residence rates in 1920, after an increase was granted to offset operating losses, began at 25 cents a kwh.

Service was first furnished in the Fossil community by the Fossil Milling Company on December 1, 1923. The plant installed was a 75-horsepower semi-diesel engine with a 40-kilowatt generator. It was operated from sundown to midnight. The plant was destroyed in January, 1928, and the community was without electric service until Pacific crews were able to connect it with the Sherman system.

Arlington first had a city system constructed in 1914, supplying electricity at a meter rate of 15 cents per kwh. In 1922 the city purchased a 100-horsepower diesel engine and generator for $5.000. The entire electric system, which was direct current, was sold on February 9, 1927, for $7,000. The old system was scrapped and a new system built and connected to the Sherman transmission lines.

During 1927 a 22,000-volt transmission line was built east from DeMoss Springs, between Wasco and Moro, to Ione to link up the Heppner system, and branch lines were extended north to Arlington and south to Condon. The small generating plants in these communities were then shut down.

In a resume of 1927 activities, *The Bulletin* noted that "reduction of approximately 25% from the old prevailing tariffs was made to the consumers on the Sherman Electric Company system through the residential and commercial lighting and the power schedules. On the old Deschutes Power Company system at Prineville, Redmond and Madras, a reduction of approximately 15% in rates was made to the residential and commercial lighting consumers. . . . Obviously these reductions were graciously received."

The Company continued to operate in the Heppner, Condon and Fossil areas until 1963, when these lines were conveyed to the Columbia Basin REA under state-approved agreements made to resolve service area boundary questions.

The Inland Company in 1926 acquired from Puget Sound Power & Light Company the electric properties serving Rainier, Oregon, and Woodland and Kalama, Washington. A small hydro plant on the Kalama River supplied that area and also Rainier, the latter via a submarine cable across the Columbia River. These properties were leased by Inland to Northwestern Electric.

In 1930 Inland acquired the properties of Ridgefield Light &

106

*Arrow points to office of Northern Idaho and Montana Power Company
in Kalispell as it appeared about 1912. The property today is the location of
PP&L's district office and telephone center for the Flathead valley.
Northern Idaho and Montana was one of the companies acquired
by Mountain States Power when the latter began operations in 1918.*

Power Company, serving a portion of Clark County, Washington. These properties also were leased to Northwestern Electric, which had been selling power at wholesale to the Ridgefield company.

Inland in 1928 acquired the Yakima Central Heating Company, supplying steam heat in the city's main business district. The present boiler plant was installed in the basement of the Chinook Hotel in 1951 when that structure was in process of completion.

Another Inland acquisition in the period was the Black Rock Power & Irrigation Company, purchased as of December 2, 1926.

Predecessor of the Black Rock company was Hanford Irrigation & Power Company, incorporated November 13, 1905. This company built an electric distribution system in 1910 to serve the town of Hanford, Washington, developed by the corporation as a part of its irrigation and land promotion plans in the area which in World War II became the site of a huge secret development to produce warhead material for atomic bombs.

Power to pump irrigation water from the Columbia near Hanford came from a 2,100-kilowatt hydro plant at Priest Rapids some distance upstream. A small wing dam and diversion canal

107

brought water to the power plant at the foot of the rapids. The power plant and pumping station, developed by the Priest Rapids Irrigation District, were connected by a 22,000-volt line.

The irrigation project did not do well, one reason being that land in much of the Hanford area would not hold water because of the porous subsoil. In 1915 the Hanford company was sold to an individual at a receiver's sale and deeded to a new company, Black Rock Power & Irrigation Company. Hanford became an isolated village and in 1926 the electric lines were sold to Inland. The transmission facilities, which had been under lease to Pacific, became a link in the PP&L system and the substation was enlarged to become a transmission center. These facilities completed a 66,000-volt loop between Yakima and Pasco, via Hanford, and the Hanford substation was the point at which the Pacific Company's 110,000-volt connection with Washington Water Power at Taunton was reduced to 66,000 volts.

When the Hanford area was taken over by the government for its then mysterious World War II use, the Company's distribution lines were taken with the lands and its transmission facilities replaced in kind. Not until after the first atomic bomb was dropped over Japan did it become known what was going on in the remote buildings that had been erected far behind the security gates.

The power plant at Priest Rapids was operated by Pacific under lease from the irrigation district for a number of years, an arrangement which was continued by the War Department after the property was taken over for its purposes. The plant was eliminated with the construction of the present Priest Rapids hydroelectric project, a development envisioned many years earlier by engineers associated with S. Z. Mitchell, but then ahead of its time.

A side event of the late 1920's was a proposal announced in January, 1928, for the merger of Northwestern Electric Company into Portland Electric Power Company, as it was then known. Under the Northwestern franchise, any sale or transfer of its properties in the city had to be approved by the city and a special election subsequently was set for April 9, 1928, by the city council at the request of the companies for a popular vote on the plan. A rate reduction estimated at $300,000 was promised if the merger could be effected. Press clippings of the period indicate the plan

PP&L long operated under lease the pioneer Priest Rapids power plant on the Columbia River, built in 1908 by Hanford Irrigation & Power Co. to supply pumping power for an unsuccessful irrigation development in the present AEC reservation area. A small diversion dam and two-mile canal served the 2,100-kw plant. Photo was supplied by Si Yeager, Yakima, once an operator at the plant, which was retired in 1955 to make way for the present hydro project.

had the general approval of officials but little appears to have been done to explain in detail to the voters the merits of the proposition. Nor had definite plans been made for the status of the affected employees. Thus the adverse 2-to-1 vote on the proposition should not have come as a surprise.

The Company's 1910 bond issue matured in 1930 and at that time a major refunding and financing program was worked out in cooperation with American Power & Light. One result was to bring into Pacific's ownership the distribution properties of Inland Power & Light that had been operated under lease, and to make the Inland corporation itself a wholly-owned subsidiary of Pacific. The only properties that continued to be held in Inland's name were a large new hydro project under construction at the Ariel site on the Lewis River and the small hydro plants at Wallowa Falls and at Cove on the Crooked River.

Chapter 17

Lewis River Development Started

STUDIES of the power potential of the Lewis River, which joins the Columbia about 25 miles north of Portland, were started by Northwestern Electric. That company obtained a preliminary permit from the Federal Power Commission covering the Yale site as early as 1922. Subsequently the project was deferred because system interconnections gave access to additional power to meet the needs of the day. Later, after Northwestern became affiliated with Pacific and the Inland Company had acquired several electric systems in the general area, the latter undertook to carry forward the Lewis River program.

Toward the end of 1928 Inland filed with FPC for a preliminary permit for a comprehensive Lewis River development and, in August, 1929, received a permit for the "Ariel" and the "Basket" or "Yale" sites, which were about equal in power potential.

After more study, it was decided to go ahead with the Ariel site first. Ariel was 12 miles downstream from Yale and that much closer to the rail head at Woodland. Fewer miles of road improvement would be required to get supplies and equipment to the project, and a later development at Yale could share the benefit of this work. A license to build at the Ariel site was applied for and was received before the end of the year.

In assuming its Lewis River construction role, Inland acquired from Northwestern all of the latter's interests in the area, including substantial holdings of reservoir lands.

As described in Pacific's 1930 annual report: "The dam at the Ariel development is to have a total length at the top of 1,240 feet. At the lowest elevation it is 73 feet below sea level, and the top of the parapet is 240 feet above sea level, giving the dam a total height of 313 feet, while in thickness it ranges from about 20 feet to approximately 96 feet." Initial installation at the project was a 45,000-kilowatt generator, with provision made to permit the future addition of up to three more units.

110

First known as the Ariel project, Merwin dam on the Lewis River
was taking definitive shape at the time of this construction photo, October
31, 1930. In clearing the site to bed rock, workers found a pot hole in
the old river course that went down 73 feet below sea level and held a
boulder "ground like a marble." Crest of the dam is 240 feet above sea level
and a full reservoir gives 188 feet of head on the turbines.

Some may be curious why this major project for its day was started only a matter of weeks after the 1929 stock market crash. As will be pointed out later, the market break came a number of months before the Company's business began to show significant decrease in growth. Moreover, a long-continued drought in the latter part of 1929 had curtailed the operation of a number of hydroelectric plants and resulted in a shortage of power in some parts of the Pacific Northwest. The Pacific Company, its own resources buttressed by power purchase contracts, had been able to ride through the drought and meet customer requirements, but the situation was far from being comfortable. *COP. II*

One step toward assurance of power supply was the construction of a large hydroelectric project having substantial reservoir capacity, such as the 12-mile lake that would be created behind a dam at Ariel. Another important step was to add to system interconnections for the exchange of power and energy.

Pacific's lines in the Hood River-The Dalles area were interconnected with the Northwestern system at Condit and the Yakima-Walla Walla-Pendleton system was interconnected at three points with Washington Water Power. But there was a 75-mile gap between Yakima and the Company's mid-Columbia system. Unless this was bridged, the new plant at Ariel could not send power east when required to meet needs in the upper Columbia area, nor could the Portland area draw power from Spokane, for example, in case of need.

Plans were made, therefore, to construct a 110,000-volt transmission line from the Company's substation at Union Gap directly across a rugged stretch of country to the Condit point of interconnection with Pacific's mid-Columbia system and Portland.

In telling about the line at a meeting of Company district managers in April, 1930, H. H. Schoolfield, chief engineer said: "This line will be the most rapidly built of any line constructed by the Company."

To expedite the location of a right-of-way, an aerial survey was made of the route. This appears to have been the first such power line reconnaisance to have been made by the Company. Ground survey parties began their work in February, 1930, when, to quote a later *Bulletin* story, "most of the hills were still covered with several feet of snow."

It was necessary to carry in all supplies for the survey parties on pack horses. Twenty-six men, seven horses and one packer were required for the task, which was completed in the middle of April.

Six construction camps then were established along the route at points accessible via the Mt. Adams road. A story in the *Bulletin* reported: "One supply truck makes daily trips with food and other goods, visiting each camp on alternate days and hauling approximately one-half ton of food from the headquarters at White Swan. . . . The creeks in the vicinity of the camps are nearly all dry during the summer months and it is necessary to haul water for as great a distance as fourteen miles, with a total of 1800 gallons used every day. An average of 200 men are employed in various lines of work. . . .

"In Toppenish canyon, which is probably the worst part of the line, it was impossible to drive trucks or tractors down the steep sides of the cut and even horses, of which there are two in use, could not traverse the soft shale walls. In this place it was necessary to haul the 3200-pound reels of copper cable for 38 miles over a circuitous route to gain five miles along the right-of-way and the seventy-foot poles had to be carried by hand for one and a half miles along the precarious path."

112

Spillway at Merwin dam got a major test on December 22, 1933, when a flood far beyond any previous record swept down the Lewis River. Air view was taken the day after the crest had passed. Flood washed out a steel bridge just below the plant and backwater reached into the power house.

From Union Gap the right-of-way followed a straight line for 17 miles. In the whole line there were only five angles, the largest less than 20 degrees, and since these largely cancelled themselves the 75-mile line as a whole went as the crow flies.

Field work was started at the Yakima end on April 21, 1930, and the line was tied through to the west 128 working days later. It was placed in trial service in November, and *The Bulletin* of that month said "up to 10,000 kw of power have been transferred from this system to the Northwestern Company system.

"Five large operating companies have successfully operated in parallel — Montana Power, Washington Water Power, Puget Sound Power & Light, Pacific Power & Light and Northwestern Electric companies having been solidly tied together and operated in parallel without difficulty for several hours at a time."

The initial 45,000-kilowatt generator at the Ariel hydro development was placed in commercial operation January 1, 1932. It was connected with the Northwestern Electric system at Vancouver and Portland by a 110,000-volt circuit constructed for the purpose.

Because of the plant's close association with the Northwestern system, an agreement was made with that company for operation of the facility. Cost of the Ariel development at the time was about $8,600,000.

Chapter 18

Growth Kept Up After '20 Crash

As THOSE WHO WENT through it can recall, the "Great Depression" came on gradually over a period of months and did not occur overnight after the 1929 stock market crash. In fact, there were many who felt that the tumble in stock prices mainly reflected a purging of over-extended speculators, and were confident about the basic economy.

The Pacific Company's 1929 revenues showed a 4% increase over 1928. Electrical appliance sales totaled $1,072,605 compared with $792,072 in the preceding year. One hundred miles of rural distribution lines were built during the year and the Company created the positions of Agricultural Agent and Illuminating Engineer "to build up uses of electrical energy for rural and illuminating purposes and to assist customers in the most efficient and economical applications of electrical power."

The 1929 annual report noted: "In the latter part of the year equipment for the mechanical operation of customers' accounts was installed in the general office. This change has made it possible to supply customers with their statements with greater speed, neatness and uniformity and with a saving in labor costs."

The report also said that "among new uses of electric power which have been developed by the Company within the past few years are stationary spray plants, apple washing and wiping machines, solution-vat heating for apple washing, bulk grain handling, electric hot beds, sterilizers for milk cans and electric drinking water heaters for dairy and poultry farms. . . .

"Recently your Company has joined with other electrical power companies in the Pacific Northwest in the construction of an experimental high tension line for the Oregon State College for the purpose of studying radio interference. . . .

"Economic conditions throughout the Company's territory during the year compared favorably with those of 1928. The lumber output in some of the territory was heavier and the salmon pack and wheat crop about equal to those of the previous year, while the production of fruit and produce was somewhat smaller, although better prices increased the value over that for similar products in 1928. About one-half of the wheat crop had been marketed at the close of the year at a price ranging from $1.05 to $1.15, the remainder being held for better prices. The ability of the wheat growers to hold so large a portion of their crop without evidence of distress to themselves or to their bankers is an indication of the prosperous conditions prevailing in that industry. From present indications the outlook for 1930 is favorable."

Operating results in 1930 appeared to justify this optimistic point of view. Revenues showed an increase of 6% over the previous year. Kilowatt-hour sales increased 5%, with residential use climbing from 997 to 1,178 kilowatt-hours for the year.

Residential rates were modified to permit the installation of up to five-horsepower, single-phase motors in conjunction with domestic service, at the regular domestic rate, compared with a previous two-horsepower limit. Also, "a new commercial cooking rate was established to enter the highly competitive field of heavy duty cooking and baking."

Sixty miles of rural line extensions were built in 1930 to serve 362 customers. The annual report for the year also stated: "Of unusual interest was the construction of about nine miles of distribution lines built primarily for airway illumination, and serving three beacons, seven airway border lights and intermediate landing field installations."

Appliances placed in service by customers included 1,373 electric ranges, 1,005 water heaters, and 910 refrigerators.

"There was an increase of more than 12% in the number of rural customers," the report said, "a greater percentage of increase than that of any other class of business. The Company is making vigorous efforts in an organized manner to stimulate among farmers the use of electricity where adaptable and contributing to more efficient farm operations and domestic convenience and comfort."

Although over-all operating results in 1930 presented a rather good picture, there were certain signs of weakness in the economy. The September, 1930, *Bulletin,* for example, carried a report from Astoria that "depression in the lumber market" was causing shortages of hogged fuel for the Youngs Bay steam plant, and that the plant had started burning oil.

White River Falls, about 35 miles south of The Dalles, provided a 137-foot head of water for the Tygh Valley power plant built here by the Wasco Warehouse Milling Co. in 1901 and acquired by PP&L in 1910. The 2,250-kw generating station was retired in 1969 and Company lands in the vicinity given to the State of Oregon for park purposes.

Earlier in the year the Company's manager at Bend had been quoted to the effect that new business for the year "must be secured in the main from existing users because industrial growth at the present time is more or less at a standstill."

The October, 1930, *Bulletin* carried an operating department note that system revenues in August had been 3.5% over the same month of the preceding year, adding: "This showing was made in the face of the generally conceded business depression pervading the country."

In the following month the magazine included a photograph of sacked wheat piled high at Pomeroy "due to the warehouses being practically filled with 1928 and 1929 crops, which made it necessary to pile a large portion of this year's crop outside."

The tone of articles in the *Bulletin,* however, remained generally optimistic, and kept strong emphasis on the need to go out and sell the benefits of electric appliances.

The Company's $6 preferred stock also came in for a sales push, with 5,316 shares being sold in a five-day campaign early in 1931. Proceeds were used to finance necessary construction.

116

Yet there were notes of caution voiced along the way. The operating department, after noting the March, 1931, sag in service revenues, said: "This prompts us to wonder if too much optimism has been reflected in considering effects of the current business depression on Pacific Company business."

Further, the period was one of political as well as economic difficulties. In the 1920's public ownership of power began to be espoused by agile and zealous disciples throughout the nation. Their attack on the utilities tended to be loudest in hydroelectric areas like the Pacific Northwest. The utility industry's sometimes inept efforts to defend itself were subjected to political scorn in Federal Trade Commission hearings.

In Oregon and Washington the public ownership push centered on the idea of getting legislation to enable rural areas to establish power districts as the farm counterpart of municipally-owned systems. Five years of agitation resulted in power district initiatives being on the ballot in both states at the 1930 general election. In objective, they were similar. In detail, they differed in one respect, at least. The Washington initiative permitted power district boards to issue revenue bonds in unlimited amount on the commissioners' own motion, without reference to the people. The Oregon initiative provided for a popular vote on bond proposals, whether general obligation or revenue bonds.

In each state the sponsors of the initiative laid great stress on the idea that their proposals were merely enabling acts, that they did not obligate anyone, and that the proposals were aimed to benefit rural areas in need of electric service.

The Washington initiative carried by a vote of 152,487 to 130,901. In Oregon, the vote was 116,916 to 84,022. Thus the public utility district, or PUD, laws got on the statute books of the two states.

Chapter 19

Depression Brought Multiple Problems

THE POLITICAL pressures being brought to bear on the utilities in that period combined with an emotional demand for lower electric rates in a time of falling commodity prices to create many difficulties for corporate budget balancers.

The Pacific Company put into effect reduced rates for residential and commercial lighting on July 1, 1931, resulting in an estimated saving to customers of $115,000 in the last half of the year. Use of electricity by residential customers increased to 1,318 kilowatt-hours during the year, up 121 kwh from 1930, but average kilowatt-hour price received for the service declined 6%.

Total operating revenues for 1931 increased about 1%, and net went down 1%. Additions and improvements to the Company's facilities, excluding Inland's plant construction program, amounted to $840,000.

Capital expenditures by Inland Power & Light in 1931 exceeded $2,800,000, and brought the Ariel hydroelectric project to completion at the year-end. To finance this work and other property additions the Pacific Company sold $3,500,000 of 5% bonds during the year.

Line extensions continued to be built into rural areas and 621 new electric customers were added to the system in 1931.

D. B. Leonard, then agricultural agent, estimated the Company was serving between 7,000 and 8,000 rural customers at that time. At a meeting of Company district managers and sales representatives he told of studies being made on the system to determine the extent of farm utilization of electricity to increase production efficiency.

"Our problem is to help the farmer reduce his costs so as to increase his margin of profit and encourage a higher standard of living," Leonard said. "What we do to build up the prosperity of the farmer helps to make for our own prosperity and that of everyone else." The comment was sound and constructive, but the immediate problem of most farmers at the time was to hold down the margin of loss.

U. S. Department of Agriculture statistical reports show that average wheat prices in the country dropped from $1.30 a bushel at Minneapolis in 1929 to 82c a bushel in 1930 and 71c in 1931. In 1932 there was a further sag to 61c.

Pear prices slid down from $1.65 a bushel in 1929 to 36c in 1932. Potatoes dropped from $2.18 a hundred pounds to 62c. Eggs went from 30c a dozen to 14c. Average value of a sheep on the farm was $10.71 in 1929 and $3.44 in 1932.

In the circumstances, it is not surprising that the Company's 1932 annual report showed an operating revenue decrease of 13% from the prior year, "reflecting a decline in practically all classes of electric service, particularly to commercial and farm customers."

The report noted that the decline in revenues "was offset only in part by retrenchment in operating expenses, notwithstanding the inauguration of many economies, including a reduction in salaries and wages. Increased taxes offset to some extent the economies effected. Net revenue from operation declined 19%."

Construction expenditures "were maintained at a minimum and were confined to extensions and additions necessary to secure new business and assure adequate service. The major construction item was a 35-mile rural extension to serve ultimately 160 customers in Clatsop County."

These were sparse words to describe one little facet of the full-scale depression that had swept across the nation, and there was little of comfort in the day to day business news as the Company went into 1933. Bank closures had become epidemic. The national administration was in process of change. Business and personal credits were stretched to the breaking point.

Problems of the time bore heavily on many shoulders, and one who felt the nervous and physical strain was Guy W. Talbot, who had headed the Pacific Company since its beginning in 1910.

At a meeting of the Board on February 25, 1933, he presented a letter asking to be relieved of the "increasing cares and responsibilities of his office, which have been greatly aggravated by current business conditions." His health and strength had been affected to such a degree, he told the Board, "as to compel me to ask to be relieved from active duties as soon as possible."

119

Talbot said it had been his hope and that of other directors that John A. Laing, vice president and general counsel for many years, might accept the presidency in the event of his retirement. Laing, however, had expressed the desire to remain as counsel and adviser "and at the same time maintain a substantial contact with the general practice of law, rather than to become completely involved in executive responsibilities."

The letter of resignation related that "subsequent inquiries and consultations among our directors and advisers have disclosed the opportunity to secure for the presidency of our Company the services of Mr. Paul B. McKee, formerly vice president and general manager of The California Oregon Power Company, and for the past seven years president of Empresas Electricas Brasileiras (Brazilian Electric Company). Those of us who are acquainted with Mr. McKee and his record as a utility executive believe him to be exceptionally well equipped to act as president of this Company, and it is a great pleasure to me to recommend him unqualifiedly to the Board for election as my successor."

Talbot's resignation was accepted by the Board "reluctantly and with deep regret" and with "the grateful thanks and appreciation of the Company for his twenty-three years of outstanding and successful leadership."

On Talbot's motion, McKee was elected a director of the Company and thereupon named president. The minutes then recited that McKee "entered the meeting at this point at the request of the Board and was cordially greeted by the directors."

McKee likewise was named president of Northwestern Electric and Portland Gas & Coke companies.

Born in San Francisco on October 11, 1891, McKee was graduated from Stanford in 1914 with a degree in electrical engineering. He, as captain of the track team, gained athletic fame by winning the tie-breaking run-off of a sprint event to give Stanford victory in an historic meet with the University of California.

He went to work for The California Oregon Power Company in 1914 and in 1920 was made vice president and general manager of that company, a post he held until 1927. In that year he was chosen by Sidney Z. Mitchell to go to Brazil on behalf of American & Foreign Power Company, an Electric Bond & Share

120

Paul B. McKee, president of Pacific Power & Light Company from 1933 to 1958 and Chairman of the Board from 1958 to 1965.

subsidiary, to serve as president of Empresas Electricas Brasileiras, with headquarters in Rio de Janeiro.

McKee spent six busy years traveling throughout Brazil and acquiring for operation and development a group of utility properties in that nation. It was an assignment demanding resourceful leadership and a talent for building and maintaining good public relations, qualifications which were obviously in demand for the challenging new task in the Pacific Northwest.

121

Chapter 20

Business at Low as McKee Joins Team

So FAR as the Pacific Company and most of its customers were concerned, 1933 marked the low point of the depression, and the first letter to preferred stockholders bearing McKee's signature was one dated May 1, 1933, transmitting a dividend payment at one-half of the regular rates.

The letter reported that for the 12 months ended March 31, 1933, the amount available from earnings for preferred stock dividends was $10,888 less than the full requirement, and that for the quarter ended March 31 such earnings were actually less than the amount required to pay one-half of the regular quarterly amount. This meant that part of the payment had to come from previously accumulated surplus.

It was pointed out that no dividends had been paid on the Company's common stock since 1931, and that the unpaid portion of the preferred stock dividend was cumulative and had first claim on future earnings.

On August 1, 1933, another dividend was paid on the preferred stocks at one-half the regular rate. In his letter McKee said: "The downward trend of gross earnings . . . has not entirely stopped, but there are some encouraging signs. The decrease for the month of June, as compared with the same month of last year, has been smaller than any other monthly decline in 1933. There are other indications of an upturn in general business conditions which should begin to reflect themselves in improved earnings for the Company. The Directors therefore felt justified in again paying the one-half dividends although not earned from actual operations in the past three months. . . .

"Every effort is being made to further reduce operating expenses and increase earnings. On June 1 an additional reduction of 10% was made in the compensation of all officers and employees having a base rate of pay over $150 a month. This salary cut will result in an estimated annual saving of about $25,000. The

Company is taking care of all its current cash obligations and has no outstanding bank loans and no early bond maturities.

"On the other hand, the Company is faced with new and increased taxes. Beginning September 1, 1933, a 3% federal tax upon revenues received from residential and commercial sales of electricity will be levied upon the Company. This tax has heretofore been paid by the customers. Further, commencing August 1, 1933, we will have the additional tax burden in the State of Washington of the state sales tax of 3% upon our residential, commercial and industrial sales of electricity. It is estimated that our operating expenses will be increased to the extent of approximately $140,000 per annum by reason of these additional taxes.

"The National Industrial Recovery Act recently enacted by Congress imposes a tax of 5% upon the receipt of dividends by any person other than a domestic corporation and requires the payor corporation to deduct this tax from any dividends paid and remit the amount to the government. This tax continues until the first day of January succeeding the year in which the President of the United States declares the United States budget is balanced as defined in the act, or declares that the 18th amendment to the Constitution is repealed, whichever is earlier. Your current dividend check . . . is therefore for the amount of the dividend declared less this 5% tax."

For the record, this tax had the unique distinction of being short-lived. Repeal of the prohibition amendment was proclaimed December 5, 1933!

The sag in revenues continued unabated through the third and fourth quarters of 1933 and net was insufficient to permit any dividend payment on November 1. In fact, for the calendar year the Company's balance of earnings after depreciation charges amounted to only $77,104 compared with $506,579 in the previous year. The greatest revenue loss was experienced in commercial business, which in two years decreased more than one-fifth, followed by a 17.6% decrease in farm revenues.

Even though the Pacific Company, in common with most other utilities of the nation, was hard pressed to keep from going in the red, the political mood of the day was to make the utilities a whipping boy, and the wielders of the lash commonly were indiscriminate in their targets and vitriolic in their accusations.

In Washington, D. C., an assault on holding companies was being organized in the halls of Congress, a flood of new regulatory provisions were being drafted, and agencies such as the Federal Power Commission were beginning to develop new concepts of accounting.

Reaction of state bodies to the political hue and cry was reflected in the following paragraph from the Company's November 1, 1933, letter to preferred stockholders:

"The Company is now engaged in making an exhaustive detailed inventory of its physical properties to satisfy orders of the regulatory commissions in Oregon and Washington. . . . Your Company also has pending at this moment a number of rate investigations and valuation proceedings in Oregon and Washington which require the attention of the officers and personnel of the organization in order that the interests of the bond and stockholders may be protected."

The considerable cost of making such inventories and valuations was pointed up in the Company's 1934 annual report. An increase of $145,569 over 1933 in operating expenses other than taxes was attributed almost entirely to such regulatory expense in the amount of $144,433.

124

Chapter 21

1933-41 Period Was Tumultuous

THE PERIOD from 1933 to 1941 could well be described as the most tumultuous in the Company's history, although even more critical hazards were to be faced in the five years following a temporary respite during World War II.

One high priority task was to build back revenues lost in the depression. Every issue of *The Bulletin* (reinstated in 1934 after a two-year lapse) was filled with news about sales campaigns in which every member of the organization was sought to be enlisted to help put the Company's power surplus to work. Management, at the same time, had the demanding job of trying to direct operations in such manner as to bring some reasonable portion of the revenue gains down into net income in order to provide a return to investors and protect the Company's credit standing.

These were important responsibilities, but a vastly more complex and vexing problem facing the Company was one of survival as a private enterprise against repetitive attacks by public ownership zealots of the day.

Persons then active in the Company recall the period as one of intensive guerilla warfare, in which the ideological adversary often was egged on by political opportunists or by mercenaries who had quickly calculated the thousands of dollars to be made in fees and commissions if the electric companies of the region could be sliced up for transfer into ownership by many small political entities.

Intensity of the struggle is evidenced by the fact that from 1934 to 1941 there were 84 elections held in Washington and Oregon on the question of establishing public utility districts, or PUDs, and eight or ten more involving municipal ownership propositions.

The standard public ownership theme was built around the public works projects started by executive order in 1933 at the Bonneville and Grand Coulee sites on the Columbia River. These federal dams were evangelistically proclaimed to mean "free power for nothing at no cost to the taxpayers if only you vote for a PUD and bust the power trust." Seldom did a platform speaker put the message in so few words, but that was the gist of it.

To simplify this narrative, it perhaps is best to deal first with the business progress of the Company in the immediate post-depression years and then take up the story of how it approached its other problems.

The early months of 1934 brought some improvement in the Company's revenues but not until the second half of the year did significant gains begin to be recorded. The full year's revenues were 12% above the 1933 depression low, and earnings in the latter months were sufficient to make possible the payment of a preferred stock dividend at the regular rate on November 1. At that time, unpaid cumulative dividends amounted to $8.75 a share on the 7% preferred stock and $7.50 a share on the $6 preferred, which was the equivalent of five quarterly dividends.

An increase of 6% in revenues occurred in 1935 and net income was adequate to meet current preferred dividend requirements. As a sidelight, the 1935 annual report noted that, in spite of business gains, revenues still were 5% less than they had been in 1931, while the Company's taxes were 43% greater.

A major construction project in 1935 was a 16-mile, 66,000-volt transmission line from Ariel to a point near Kalama, where it connected with a similar line built by Washington Gas & Electric Company. This made possible the sale of seasonal surplus hydro power from the Lewis River plant to reduce steam generation on the WG&E system then serving Longview.

Interestingly, the September, 1935, Company *Bulletin* reported an unusual steam operation on the Company's own system to keep electric service going in Heppner, Oregon, during a fire-caused transmission line interruption.

Ray Kinne, commercial agent at Heppner, and L. D. Rasmussen, lineman, were credited with having rounded up kindling to get a coal fire started under the boiler of the old power plant that once served the community.

"By 3 P.M. August 13 they had a head of steam in the boiler, opened the throttle and let 'er roll," the story said. "For 23 hours the old reciprocating Corliss engine ground out the kilowatt-hours. A high demand of 105 kw was registered between 11 A.M. and 12 noon August 14. Low demand was 30 kw.

126

"Total number of kilowatt-hours generated in the period was 1,380, to produce which the boys shoveled approximately 8½ tons of coal. That's an average of about one kwh per 12 pounds of coal. Modern steam plants average one kwh per 1.45 pounds.

"But they kept Heppner from being without electric service."

Improvement in business continued through 1936, a year in which 3,408 electric customers were added to the Company's lines. Construction included 166 rural extensions to serve 522 farms. The Company made electric rate reductions amounting to $275,000 annually in Washington and Oregon and another Washington rate reduction early in 1937 brought total savings to customers within a 12-month period to nearly $400,000.

On December 24, 1936, the Company also was able to take a first step toward clearing up unpaid cumulative dividends on its preferred stocks, when a payment covering two-fifths of the accumulation was made to 5,196 stockholders.

In 1937, a year in which revenues showed a 10% growth, the Company connected its 10,000th farm customer in the course of building 102 miles of rural line extensions to reach 533 new customers. The 10,000th farm was the home of Mr. and Mrs. John G. McGuire, on Russell Creek southeast of Walla Walla. A pioneer wheat farmer, McGuire had lived on the 160-acre farm since it was bought by his father in 1862 at a price of 1,500 bushels of wheat. A *Bulletin* story about electrification of the farm related that McGuire was three years old when his parents crossed the plains from Iowa by wagon train, taking six months for the journey. The original log cabin on the property, it stated, "is still preserved within the walls of the present house. Siding was nailed over the logs when the cabin was enlarged and the only indication that the comfortable dwelling contains a cabin is the depth of the window and door frame in that part of the house."

Prior to construction of the Russell Creek line the McGuires had for some years operated their own gasoline-powered lighting plant, a once popular adjunct of well-to-do rural homes.

Chapter 22

The Long Road to Inland Consolidation

IN JUNE, 1937, the Company applied to the Federal Power
Commision for approval of the proposed consolidation with
Pacific of its wholly-owned subsidiary, Inland Power & Light Company, in the interest of corporate simplification. This plan for the
liquidation of the Inland Company had first been submitted to and
approved by the Oregon Public Utilities Commissioner and the
Washington Department of Public Service, and it appeared at the
time that the step could be accomplished simply and expeditiously.

However, that was not to be the case. As summarized in a
Company report two years later: "A hearing on the application
was held before the Federal Power Commission on July 19, 1937.
No evidence or showing in opposition to the proposed transfer of
facilities was produced at the hearing, but on December 14, 1937,
the Commission announced its denial of the application.

"Following denial of application for a rehearing, the companies filed a petition for review of the Commission's order in the
United States Circuit Court of Appeals for the 9th Circuit. In their
petition, the companies pointed out that the Pacific Company,
with its Inland Company affiliate, is essentially an operating company and that the proposed consolidation is in line with the declared simplification policy of the Public Utility Act of 1935, and
they maintained that the Commission's order denying the per-
mission sought was wholly arbitrary and without any evidence to
support it.

"The Federal Power Commisision filed a motion to dismiss
this review on the ground that a so-called negative order of this
character was not subject to court review, but the Court held unanimously that the order was reviewable. On April 19, 1939, the
Supreme Court handed down a decision sustaining the Circuit
Court of Appeals for the 9th Circuit and upholding the right of
the companies to a court review of the Commission's order. Justice Frankfurter wrote the Supreme Court's opinion, to which there
was no dissent."

Ten-thousandth farm connected to PP&L lines was that of John G. McGuire, Walla Walla valley pioneer, which began receiving service in April, 1937. Enclosed within the siding of the wing to the right is the family's original log cabin home. The Company built 102 miles of rural lines in that year and brought electric service to 533 new farm customers.

To carry the story through to its conclusion, the Circuit Court then considered the case on its merits and on May 8, 1940, rendered a decision setting aside the Commission's order and returning the case to the Commission for further consideration. A rehearing was held by the Commission on October 9, 1940, and after the lapse of more than a year that body issued an opinion and order on December 9, 1941, authorizing the consolidation.

The consolidation plan was then placed before the Securities and Exchange Commission, which held a hearing on the matter on April 2, 1942, and subsequently gave its approval.

The five-year effort culminated with completion of the consolidation as of May 1, 1942. The Company's annual report for that year noted: "The entire business and properties of the Pacific Company are now in a single corporate ownership."

The outcome was one that could be regarded with modest pride by John A. Laing, general counsel for the Company, who carried the case through the Appeals Court and the Supreme Court, because the latter's decision established a legal landmark. The basic question at issue was whether or not an appeal could be taken from an order of an administrative branch of government which said, in effect: "What you propose to do is lawful and won't hurt anybody but we do not choose to say 'Yes'."

Going back to other corporate developments, the Company in 1938 and 1939 showed continued growth and on August 1, 1939, brought its preferred dividend payments up to a current basis. In 1939 the third rate reduction in three years was made with a $200,000 cut in rates to benefit customers, and a payment of 20 cents a share was made on the common stock, the first such distribution since 1931. Rural line extensions in the 1938-39 period totaled 142 miles and brought electricity to 765 farms.

In 1940 the Company built 154 miles of rural lines to serve 616 customers and also brought into its system two small distribution companies. One was Hermiston Light & Power Company serving 850 customers adjacent to Hermiston, Umatilla, Echo and Stanfield, Oregon. The other was Knappa-Svensen Electric Company serving 340 customers in an area adjoining the Columbia River east of Astoria. Each of these systems had purchased power at wholesale from the Company.

The Company's fourth major rate reduction since 1936 was made in 1941 in the amount of $486,000. This meant that in a five-year period the Company's rate adjustments had brought annual savings of $1,000,000 to customers.

The year saw a slowdown in rural line extensions, however, because the national defense program had placed limitations on construction materials. It also saw the Company discontinue electric appliance sales.

The 1941 annual report said: "As public acceptance has been established for various electrical appliances, the Company progressively over a period of years has been limiting its own direct merchandising efforts and putting more and more emphasis upon dealer coordination activities. Early in the fall of 1941, with curtailment of appliance manufacture in prospect, the Company announced its complete withdrawal from the direct sale of major electrical appliances. This step had long been planned, and one of the impelling reasons for taking it at this time was to assist dealers by making available to them all of the limited supply of equipment that might be obtained from manufacturers."

Extent to which electrical appliance dealer outlets had developed throughout the system was well indicated by the fact that these dealers handled 93% of the $4,979,000 volume of appliance purchases by the Company's customers in 1941.

Note was also made of the fact that the Company's direct taxes for the year had passed the $1,000,000 mark.

Frontispiece of the 1941 report was a reproduction of a wartime Company advertisement showing a service flag with 72 stars over a heading which read: "A Flag Like This Brings War News Close to Home."

The historian, checking back on milestones in the 1933-41 period of the Company's life, can find himself looking quizzically at once familiar numbers and asking: "Did we really make so much business progress in those years?"

That is because the sharpest personal memories of the time relate to the major policy problems facing the Company and to the intermittent fighting in the hedgerows rather than the workaday tilling of the fields.

Yet the impressive fact is that during this period Company revenues grew from the 1933 depression figure of $3,615,000 to a 1941 total of $6,793,000. Net income increased from a slim $77,-104, alarmingly close to red ink, to a more respectable figure of $740,000. Preferred stockholders received payment in full for the unpaid dividends that had accumulated on their shares. Number of electric customers served increased from 49,097 to 73,079. The Company built more than 500 miles of new rural lines and added 4,400 electrified farms to its customer total. Construction expenditures in the period amounted to approximately $5,000,000, mostly for distribution facilities. Local, state and federal governments received from the Company $6,793,000 in direct taxes. Customers of the Company enjoyed electric rate reductions that brought them annual savings of $1,000,000.

Ability of the Company team to rack up such a record despite many distractions reflected the spirit in which the organization approached its problems and sought to turn them into opportunities, to use one of Paul McKee's favorite adages. It also reflected a concern that. "If we want to save the Company, we'd better prove to investors and the public that it's worth saving!"

Chapter 23

Bonneville Start Posed Policy Question

A POLICY DECISION that had to be made in the early summer of 1933 concerned the Company's position with respect to the federal dams at the Bonneville and Grand Coulee sites on the Columbia River.

An announcement that President Franklin D. Roosevelt favored construction of a dam "on the Columbia River between Portland and the mouth of the Snake River . . . designed primarily for navigation, with power as a by-product" appeared in Portland newspapers on July 13, 1933.

"The site of the dam," said an *Oregonian* dispatch from Washington, D. C., "would be selected by army engineers where it would be most practical in view of the ultimate complete development of the river. This was all indicated today by the president to Senators McNary and Steiwer in a three-quarter-hour White House conference."

On the following day an *Oregonian* story was headed "Roosevelt Stand on Dam Cheered—All Oregon Hails News of Columbia Plan—Chamber Visions Victory. . . . Amadee M. Smith, president of the Portland Chamber of Commerce, expressed high pleasure that President Roosevelt was evidently acting toward fulfillment of an effort the chamber has had under way for 40 years. . . ."

Also on July 14, 1933, the Portland *News-Telegram* had a story headed "River Power Plan Backed by Utilities," in which Paul B. McKee, president of Pacific Power and Northwestern Electric, and Franklin T. Griffith, then president of Portland Electric Power Company, both were quoted directly in an interview by Mel Arnold.

"As a citizen of Oregon, I am in favor of anything that will benefit the Pacific Northwest without imposing too great a burden upon it," McKee was quoted as saying.

"I am confident that the government will not confiscate the investment of the 40,000 to 50,000 citizens in the northwest who have purchased securities in public utilities which will be affected by the development.

"All I ask is that the government dispose of the power in a businesslike manner."

In the interview, McKee pointed out that the peak load of the interconnected electric systems of the Pacific Northwest at the time was only 600,000 kilowatts, or less than half the installed capacity of 1,400,000 kilowatts.

The reporter wrote: "Both executives refused to condemn the president's proposal to build a dam." He interpreted their position to be: "If the government will stand the tremendous expense, which private capital cannot bear, and wait until a sufficient market is developed, private interests may benefit."

Griffith stated: "It would be folly for the government to make the very great investment necessary for navigation if it did not also provide for power development. With improving business activity it is reasonable to assume that the existing surplus will be consumed, and that in time the output of a federal plant on the Columbia River will be absorbed."

A week later the Portland papers reported that General Charles H. Martin, Congressman from Oregon's third district, had received word in a letter from Lieut. Col. Thomas M. Robins, division head of the Army Engineers in San Francisco, that the Bonneville site was being recommended for the dam.

On July 28, 1933, announcement was made that President Roosevelt had approved the Grand Coulee development "as a part of the immediate public works program."

Some weeks were to elapse, however, before the Bonneville project received an official go-ahead. A dispatch in *The Oregonian* of September 7 said that Harold L. Ickes, Secretary of the Interior and Public Works Administrator, had had on his desk for two weeks the Army Engineers report on Bonneville without calling it to the attention of the president.

The story said: "After being informed by *The Oregonian* correspondent that Secretary Ickes has had the engineers' report on the Bonneville project for two weeks without calling it to his attention, President Roosevelt this afternoon sent for Ickes. The president appeared surprised that the recommendation of General Lytle Brown, chief of engineers, had been completed and submerged in the files of the public works administrator, as the president had notified Ickes in July that he wanted action. Saying he wanted to examine the report, the president reached for his desk pad and jotted down a notation."

General Martin and Senators McNary and Steiwer kept pressing for approval of the project and on September 29 Mr. Ickes announced formal approval of an allotment of $20,000,000 to start Bonneville, then estimated to cost $36,000,000.

Plans for the big work relief project were rushed ahead and first crews were on the job in November. One of the initial steps was to get power via submarine cable to Bradford Island, which was to serve as the construction base. This job fell to Northwestern Electric, which had lines adjacent to the Washington abutment of the dam.

As reported in *The Oregonian* of November 16, 1933: "Swiftness of the current of the Columbia River at that point made a ticklish operation of what ordinarily is a routine job for the underground crew and elaborate precautions were taken to insure that laying the cable would go through without a hitch.

"Two 3000-pound ship anchors were laid out upstream from the cable barge and when all preparations had been completed, the barge was swung in a 1000-foot arc from mainland to island with the aid of lateral cables running from each shore to winches on the barge. Standing by to hold the barge steady in case of emergency was the tug *Cruiser* of the Hosford fleet.

"S. B. Clark, superintendent of the underground department of Northwestern Electric, supervised the job. A considerable group of spectators gathered to witness actual laying of the cable, one of the most interested being O. L. LeFever, general superintendent of the power company.

"Approximately $100,000 is being invested by Northwestern Electric to supply construction power at the damsite and at the town of North Bonneville, according to Mr. LeFever. . . .

"At the point of crossing the Columbia is 1000 feet wide and from 25 to 32 feet deep. A ten-mile current makes navigation difficult. Sixteen hundred feet of heavily insulated steel-armored submarine cable was used."

The cable, incidentally, could never be salvaged after it had served its purpose. It had become inextricably wedged among huge

*Construction power for the Bonneville project was supplied by
Northwestern Electric Company, which laid a submarine cable from the
Washington shore to Bradford Island on November 15,1933. Work on
the dam was just getting under way. The picture shows the job
as it looked January 16, 1935. Power demand reached 5,000 kilowatts.*

boulders on the river bottom. All that could be done was to cut
it off and surrender possession to the river.

The general policy statement made about Bonneville by Paul
McKee in July was amplified by him in a story published in *The
Oregonian of* October 8, 1933.

Quoting from the story: "Continuation of the unity shown in
Portland during the campaign for the Bonneville project on the
Columbia River was advocated yesterday by Paul B. McKee . . .
as a means of advancing the industrial growth of this city in the
years to come.

" 'This is one of the few times in the history of Portland when
there has been 100 per cent unity,' Mr. McKee declared. 'Let us
preserve that unity and turn it to further use in bringing about a
bigger and better city where all may share in the benefits of
industrial development. We have won the Bonneville project, which
everyone wanted; let us now lend our unified efforts in seeing this
dam through to completion. . . .

" 'If the federal government will sell the power at low enough
rates, it is possible that some large industries of a kind not operat-

135

ing here now may be attracted. This company has already publicly evidenced its definite desire and expectation to cooperate actively in efforts to bring industries here, also to utilize as much of this power as it can upon a proper economical basis.' "

This theme was reiterated by McKee in a signed article published in the Portland *News-Telegram* of January 6, 1934. In it he said:

"A carefully planned, aggressive program of regional advertising that will sell industrialists on the idea of locating in the Portland area is the most important step to be taken toward bringing about utilization of Bonneville power for the best interests of all our people.

"Our big job now is to tell the world about all the natural advantages of the Columbia basin, and to tell the story so convincingly that investors of private capital will decide that here is the place for them to build their great electro-chemical and metallurgical plants. . . .

"Regardless of how low a price the government sets on Bonneville power, we must compete for industries with other regions to be served by Boulder Dam, Muscle Shoals and other developments, including the huge privately financed hydroelectric projects on the Saguenay River in Quebec. The fact that present generating facilities, here and elsewhere, are well in excess of present requirements means we are thrown into serious competition with areas that normally would not figure in the picture.

"Every one of these other regions had its own special inducements to offer new industries, including not only low cost power but proximity to major consuming markets. We of the Pacific Northwest believe we have unique advantages to offer here, but it is up to us to prove it."

McKee warned of danger that "political opportunists and some sincere advocates of public ownership may distract our people, including the many thousands of local investors in the so-called privately-owned utilities, with issues that will divert effort from the fundamental task before us, and at a time when concerted action should be the order of the day.

"Let us keep our eyes fixed upon the goal of real industrial progress," he said, "toward which all of us can work with common mind. Imagination is required, imagination, courage and faith

136

in the future of our community, but if we work with unity of purpose we may be confident of success."

Many civic organizations shared these views and were working vigorously for area development. On the other hand, old line public ownership spokesmen commonly regarded Bonneville and Grand Coulee as instruments they might use to drive the existing electric companies to the wall and provide a substitute power supply source for homes and farms. So far as industrial growth was concerned they took the position that "cheap government power" would solve all problems. This was something of a paradox since the states of Oregon and Washington already had the lowest domestic electric rates and the highest home use of electricity in the nation, although lagging in development of manufacturing and processing.

To help implement its own policy, the Pacific Company early in 1935 added an experienced industrial development salesman to work with B. P. Baily, industrial engineer. An immediate venture was to begin gathering information for a directory of manufacturers operating in the Company's service area. The first edition of this directory listed more than 200 manufacturing and processing companies, producing 60 commodities. It was arranged for convenient reference by purchasing agents and the first 1,000 copies went out to a list of prospects throughout the nation.

Some casual observers had a tendency to discount the Company's activities in the development field as a public relations gesture. This in no way discouraged McKee, who untiringly preached that "good citizenship is good business."

His basic philosophy was well expressed in a radio talk given in Walla Walla at the time of the Company's 1935 sales conference there in mid-February. What he said was keyed to the rapid expansion of green pea canning in the Blue Mountain country:

"That is a fine example of what a new idea may mean to a community. Here is a new industry that is bringing literally hundreds of thousands of dollars into this region. Many factors have contributed to its development, to be sure, but basically the whole thing goes back to the man who first got the idea that peas for canning might profitably be grown in the upland country of eastern Washington. This man experimented with various varieties of peas. He tested out the suitability of different types of land.

"The results were favorable. The idea was so good, in fact, that in a remarkably short time 35,000 acres of land has been put to new use. Where the soil formerly lay idle between crops of wheat, it is now producing. The farmers have benefited. The laboring men have benefited. The grocer and the butcher have benefited. And because all these have benefited, we of Pacific Power & Light are benefited.

"We have a product that must be sold relatively near the point of production. If you people here in Walla Walla raise vastly more fruit and vegetables and grain than you are able to consume, you put it in cans, or in sacks, and ship it away to other places, where there is a market.

"But we can't can kilowatt-hours. We have to sell them right here. And we can't sell them unless you can afford to buy not only the electrical energy we produce but also the ranges, the refrigerators, the water heaters, the motors, the lamps and all the other useful and convenient appliances that one must have if he is to increase substantially his use of electricity. . . . Our own progress depends upon the progress of the community."

Understandably, the "Can't Can Kilowatts" theme rolled up a lot of mileage in the years to follow.

Chapter 24

Customers Receive Position Statement

AS THE BONNEVILLE project reached the power generating stage a basic statement of policy regarding it was made by the Company and mailed to all customers.

Congress on August 20, 1937, had passed an act providing the form of administration for the Bonneville project and the manner in which power should be sold. Operation of the navigation facilities, fishways and power house was delegated to the Army Engineers. Activities relating to the transmission and sale of power were assigned to an administrator to be appointed by the Secretary of the Interior. On October 11, 1937, Secretary Ickes named as administrator J. D. Ross, superintendent of Seattle City Light.

Provision was made in the act for the sale of power to private utilities, industries, and public agencies, subject to the requirement that 50% of the available power should be reserved for public bodies until January 1, 1941. It also specified that public bodies should have preference at all times in the disposal of power.

Much was made of the public preference clause by advocates of public ownership in their drive to organize PUDs throughout Oregon and Washington. They made it sound as though formation of a PUD was essential to the enjoyment of the blessings of Bonneville and Grand Coulee. Such assertions impelled the Company to make the following detailed statement, signed by Paul B. McKee as president and dated October 15, 1938:

" 'What about Bonneville power?' " is a question often asked members of the Pacific Power & Light Company organization now that the dam is completed and the federal government is beginning to build transmission lines.

"Because this timely question is one of importance to the Company and to its customers, Pacific Power & Light Company desires to state again its consistent policy with respect to Bonneville Power. In brief, the Company's policy is this:

"To purchase such amounts of Bonneville energy as can be

utilized advantageously in its system, and to pass on to its customers any savings that may result.

"The Company recognizes that Bonneville is a reality. It also recognizes that it shares a responsibility to put Bonneville power to productive and beneficial use.

"The Bonneville rates established under the Act of Congress do not discriminate between utility companies and public agencies. Pacific Power & Light can buy Bonneville power at wholesale to meet every probable need of present or prospective power users at the same rate as any other eligible distributing agency.

"How much energy the Company may be able to purchase from Bonneville in the near future, we cannot foretell. Existing hydroelectric plants will, of course, continue to be used to the extent of their efficient capacity. This is to be expected under any form of ownership of the Pacific Power & Light Company system. The investment is already in these plants, and no businesslike management will allow them to be abandoned and lie idle.

"The Company is prepared to operate its own sources of power in coordination with Bonneville in whatever manner may prove most economical, and to use Bonneville power wherever available to carry increases in its own growing load.

"Furthermore, Pacific Power & Light Company gives these positive assurances:

"(1). That its present low electric rates will become still lower in the future, as the use of electricity is further developed and more and more customers purchase the electrical appliances necessary for its utilization.

"(2). That the full facilities and experience of the Company will be put behind community efforts to secure new power-using industries, create new markets and increase payrolls.

"(3). That the Company will continue actively to promote a sound program of business development, to the end that use of electricity be stimulated and the average price per kilowatt-hour thus be steadily reduced.

"(4). That present high standards of service will be maintained and that the constant effort will be to make the Company's service even better. The Company regards the rendering of prompt, efficient and courteous service as an increasingly important utility function.

"(5). That the Company will continue to push the rural electrification program that has already brought electric service to 11,387 farms in the agricultural areas it serves.

"(6). That the Company and the members of its organization will continue to work for the agricultural, commercial and industrial development of this territory.

"To make the record clear and complete, the Company also calls attention to the following facts:

"Pacific Power & Light Company must stand on its own feet. It is not subsidized directly or indirectly by the taxpayers. On the contrary, the Company carries its full share of the growing cost of maintaining local, county, state and federal governments.

"The rates, practices, finances and bookkeeping of the Company are under the strict regulation of the Washington Department of Public Service, the Oregon Public Utilities Commissioner, the Federal Power Commission and the Securities and Exchange Commission.

"The Company's rates are now among the lowest in the United States, and it has developed a very high average annual use of electricity.

"The Company knows that the continued satisfactory operation of its taxpaying, publicly-regulated business depends on its continuing to furnish superior service at favorable rates.

"Pacific Power & Light Company makes this statement directly to its customers at this time so that there may be no misunderstanding about its position with regard to the problem of distributing Bonneville power."

At the time of this policy statement, first Bonneville power to be distributed to electric users was flowing from the project into the interconnected lines of Northwestern Electric and Pacific Power & Light, with some of the energy passing into the system of Portland General Electric Company. This had begun in July, 1938, under an agreement with the Bonneville Power Administration on a temporary and experimental basis.

One purpose in making a connection between the Bonneville power house and Northwestern's 66,000-volt transmission line from Condit to Portland was to provide a practical test of how the new plant would operate in parallel with electric systems serving the region. The government's own transmission line program was just getting under way so this arrangement offered the earliest test opportunity. No difficulties in the interconnected operation were reported by the engineers for the companies.

A subsequent agreement made with Bonneville in December, 1938, provided for Northwestern to take a minimum of 2,500 kilowatts from the federal dam to December 31, 1939, or until such earlier date as the government's Bonneville-Vancouver transmission line might be completed.

The common endeavor of the Pacific and Northwestern companies was to work as constructively as possible in their business and engineering relationships with Bonneville, even while field agents of the federal establishment were open participants in the public ownership guerilla warfare that was being carried on against the vigorously resisting private electric companies of the area. Strange as this might seem, it was wholly consistent with the companies' position from the beginning that all should unite to help make the federal power developments a "plus" for the region instead of merely displacing existing capital investments.

Company people, for example, helped the Aluminum Company of America find a suitable site in 1939 for establishment of a reduction plant near Vancouver, to use power purchased directly from the government.

In 1940 the Pacific Company executed a contract with Bonneville for the purchase of 1,500 kilowatts at Astoria from a transmission line being built by the government, including in the contract an arrangement whereby the Company would deliver energy on Bonneville's account to a Rural Electrification Administration project which could not be served by Bonneville directly. Compensation for this service was measured in kilowatt-hours on a mutually satisfactory exchange basis. Several other similar REA service arrangements were also entered into by the Company to promote efficient use of available facilities.

A Company report to stockholders dated August 15, 1941, said: "In view of the present and prospective demands made by the national defense program upon both the private companies of the Pacific Northwest and the government projects, an unlimited co-operative and coordinated pooling of all available power is clearly indicated as the way to obtain maximum use of the region's resources. . . . Engineering studies indicate that the Pacific North-

142

west's power supply can be enhanced more than 100,000 kilowatts by such coordinated operation of public and private facilities and reserves without the installation of new generating facilities."

A year later a Company report commented: "The demand for power in the Pacific Northwest has increased tremendously with the establishment of large aluminum plants and other war industries on the Columbia River, and the greater part of the output of the Bonneville and Grand Coulee projects is going directly into these industries. The forecast is that the output of additional generating units under construction will be similarly absorbed as rapidly as those units come into production."

It was further noted that the Company "has entered into a system interconnection and power interchange contract with the Bonneville Power Administration and is cooperating fully . . . with the other power systems of the region in a program of voluntary coordination of all power facilities, to the end that every possible kilowatt be made available to the war effort."

The program so referred to was the Northwest Power Pool, described in the Company's 1942 annual report as "one of the most outstanding power pools in the country, extending across five states and including scores of power plants and several thousand miles of transmission lines. . . .

"Under the direction of a committee of engineers, the flow of power between the systems is so controlled as to make the most efficient use of their combined generating and water storage resources. Each of the members is represented on the operating committee, which has functioned smoothly and effectively.

"This voluntary pooling of facilities has added materially to the region's dependable power supply, and at almost negligible cost. It represents a type of cooperative program long advocated by your Company as the constructive way of dealing with all phases of the Pacific Northwest power problem to the mutual benefit of all concerned, in time of peace as well as in time of war."

Chapter 25

Dark Clouds Dimmed Outlook

O UTLOOK for the survival of private electric companies in the Pacific Northwest was far from bright in the late '30s and early '40s. Public ownership promoters were riding high, with many zealous ideologists uncritically welcoming the support of political opportunists and money-hungry adventurers.

In the Tennessee valley, Wendell Willkie's electric companies had been brought to their knees by the TVA and their properties sold into public ownership.

New Yorkers who thought of the Pacific Northwest as being somewhere in the upper Mississippi basin still had heard of big federal power developments out that way and, without thinking much about it, tended to assume everything there was or soon would be in public ownership.

Others, like a man on the investment committee of an eastern insurance company, thought all the timber in the Pacific Northwest had been cut and that the region was headed for economic oblivion. He got this idea because he had an interest in an axe-handle plant. Sales had been dropping off in the Northwest, and he wasn't aware of the extent to which logging was becoming mechanized.

It was encountering such misconceptions that prompted Paul McKee to put his advertising staff to work in 1939 preparing an attractive and comprehensive book "RIVER OF THE WEST— A Story of Opportunity in the Columbia Empire" to be sent to leading eastern financiers and industrialists. Published jointly by Pacific Power and Northwestern Electric, the book came off the press in 1940 and elicited many favorable comments.

The then heads of certain holding companies, including American Power & Light, were not immune to bearish views about the future of private power in the far Northwest. On the one hand, they saw their companies being pushed toward complete or partial dissolution under the court-contested terms of the Public Utility Holding Company Act of 1935. On the other hand, they were being subjected to the blandishments of public ownership middlemen, like the ebullient Guy C. Myers, whose offering-price formula added capitalized tax savings into the total amount they felt a tax-free public body could afford to pay for a property. To anyone whose faith in the future was wavering, such a computation could produce a figure that looked tempting, for the moment.

The first two Bonneville administrators made no bones about their belief that companies like Pacific would be swept away by a public ownership tide. This opinion was coupled with interpretations of the Bonneville Act and the policies of Interior Secretary Ickes as mandates to work for public ownership, even to the extent of taking local groups by the hand and helping organize PUDs where none existed.

J. D. Ross, first head of Bonneville, felt the practical way for a public body to proceed with utility acquisitions was to offer the controlling stockholders an attractive price for the property. It was he who introduced Guy C. Myers to the Pacific Northwest, having found the agile financier useful at an earlier time when selling a municipal revenue bond issue.

Possessed of disarming geniality and easy self-confidence, Myers found the Washington PUD law ideal for his way of working. PUD commissioners could issue any amount of revenue bonds on their own motion, without need for a popular vote. There was no prohibition against the private sale of PUD bonds or the payment of commissions to the middleman who arranged the deal. This was in contrast to the basic Oregon law, which required all public bonds to be sold to the best and highest bidder, forbade the payment of fees or commissions in connection therewith and provided for all PUD bond issues to be submitted to popular vote.

Dr. Paul J. Raver, the Illinois professor and regulatory staff member who was named BPA administrator following the death of Ross early in 1939, did not embrace the Ross-Myers approach. Instead, he preferred the idea of electric system acquisitions by Bonneville Power Administration, directly or indirectly as the legalities might dictate. A never-attained ambition was to persuade Congress to establish an autonomous Bonneville authority having, among other things, the arbitrary power to take over utility properties, keep the generation and transmission facilities it wanted and sell the distribution lines to public bodies and cooperatives.

145

*Mirror Pond in the heart of Bend, Oregon, is formed by the Pacific
Company's power dam on the Deschutes River. Many pleasant homes
front the pond. A piece of property adjacent to the plant recently was
contributed to the community for further park development.*

One example of the desired legislation was the 1942 Bone-
Smith bill to set up a Columbia Power Administration. Witnesses
heard in favor of this bill over a three-week period included Dr.
Raver, Secretary Ickes and other public power figures, after which
the hearing was recessed and the bill died in committee.

A great financial shot-in-the-arm for the public power movement of the period came through the early appointment of many
of the faithful to the Bonneville payroll when the federal agency
was being set up. Federal pay checks provided the meal tickets,
government cars provided the transportation, government printing
presses ground out literature to be spread along the way, and
government photographers were busy making movies of the glam-
orous river developments.

Prominent among the political appointees was Dr. Carl D.
Thompson, long-time executive head of the Chicago-based Public
Ownership League of America. He was carried on the Bonneville roll as a consultant. On occasion he gave the Bonneville headquarters office as his address in letters written on League sta-
tionery, which showed J. D. Ross as a vice president of the organ-

ization. One such letter, soliciting the support of a citizen early in 1939, spoke of his mission as follows:

"As you know, the Public Ownership League has been a pioneer in the promotion of public power districts. We have worked in close cooperation with J. D. Ross, now Administrator of the Bonneville Project, for more than twenty years. Now that he is at the head of this great federal project, we are more than ever interested in cooperating with him. As a matter of fact, I am now in Portland helping in this work in a general way and incidentally, along the same lines, endeavoring to stimulate our public ownership organization throughout the Northwest and Pacific States."

Appointed by Ross to head the Bonneville information division was Stephen B. Kahn, co-author of a laudatory biography of Senator George W. Norris and an organizer and executive committee member of the People's Power League, a group seeking to get up steam for public ownership in Oregon.

Bonneville field representatives included Fred Chamberlain, secretary of the Washington State Grange, spearhead of the PUD movement in that state, and Morton Tompkins, overseer of the Oregon State Grange and a vice president of the People's Power League. Also placed on the payroll were Byron G. Carney, a vice president of the Oregon Commonwealth Federation and an executive committee member of the Clackamas County Public Ownership League, and Frank Fitts, once a Seattle city councilman, who was close to Mr. Ross.

Named electrical engineer for Bonneville was R. W. Beck, a former City Light associate and a former secretary of the Washington Public Ownership League. Immediately prior to his appointment, Beck had been making a valuation study for the Nebraska PUDs, for whom Guy C. Myers was acting as fiscal agent. After Ross' death, Beck set up in business as a consulting engineer and was often retained to make feasibility studies in connection with PUD bond issues negotiated by Myers.

An early project of the People's Power League was the promotion of a sprawling PUD covering parts of seven northwest Oregon counties. This came to vote in April, 1938, after a campaign in which the League's affiliates in the Bonneville administration took an active part. Much of the pro-PUD publicity material bore the earmarks of early Bonneville publications, and about a

(Top) First western track team to invade the east was the 1895 group from the University of California. Champion in the heel-and-toe walk event was L. T. Merwin (right), shown here with Walter Christie, veteran trainer, at a team reunion in 1935. Merwin was vice president and general manager of Northwestern Electric Company from 1920 to 1936 and served as president from 1936 to 1947. (Below) A. S. Cummins (left) was chairman and president of The California Oregon Power Company from 1941 to 1961. A. W. Trimble (right) was president of Mountain States Power Company from 1950 to 1954, and served as vice president for finance of PP&L from 1954 until his retirement in 1970.

week before the election it was conceded by the administrator that 15,000 copies of one piece of literature had been run off on a Bonneville duplicating machine "outside of regular working hours." This piece bore the name of the People's Power League. In spite of the aggressive campaign made by the sponsors of the PUD, the proposal was defeated by a substantial majority.

A number of PUD proposals were on the ballot in Washington and Oregon at the November, 1938, election. About ten days before the election, Ross announced so-called Bonneville "objective rates," which were strikingly low and dramatically featured in a handout sheet produced by the BPA publicity staff. It just happened that the handout contained convenient blank spaces which PUD sponsor committee could fill with copy of their own to give a definite impression that the speculative Bonneville rates would be put in immediately if a PUD was formed. Literally thousands of these sheets were so over-printed and scattered broadcast in the Pacific and Northwestern territories where PUD elections were being held.

The more sophisticated over-print jobs were done on a press in red. Others were mimeographed. Big type at the bottom of the sheet identified the publisher as "United States Department of the Interior—Bonneville Power Administration." Somewhere else, among the amalgamated blocks of copy, careful scrutiny would reveal in small print the name of the local coat-tail committee.

One area that got a special dose of such "cut price" literature was Clark County, Washington, which in 1936 had rejected a PUD proposal by a 2-to-1 vote. The big push in 1938 resulted in formation of a PUD by a vote of approximately 9-to-7.

Promises of Bonneville transmission lines and substations were also a factor in the 1938 PUD elections, although not always immediately effective. As early as March of that year a mass meeting at The Dalles was told by Administrator Ross that a line would be extended to that community by way of Hood River as soon as survey and construction crews could get under way.

In July, 1938, Secretary Ickes announced approval of a PWA allocation of $10,750,000 for Bonneville transmission lines and substations, with $569,000 said to be earmarked for a line to The Dalles. In early September, Ross called for bids on transmission line cable for this line. A Portland newspaper story reported: "The

Bonneville chief explained that the 45-mile line to The Dalles was only the initial construction and that the line would be extended to adjoining areas as rapidly as the people get ready to receive the power and funds become available."

On September 13 Bonneville announced that survey crews had been put in the field. On September 28 the administrator announced that power would be ready in 18 months. On October 1 there was an announcement about the low bid on cable for The Dalles line. On October 11 the award of a contract for 13,968 insulators was announced. On October 14 the administrator announced that bids were to be invited for poles for the line. On October 27 the state PWA office announced presidential approval of nearly $700,000 for clearing Bonneville right-of-way, including the line to The Dalles. On November 1 Ross announced the exact route of Bonneville lines and invited bids on $750,000 of switching apparatus. One of the circuit breakers included in the list was stated to be for a substation at The Dalles.

On November 8 the voters of The Dalles and adjacent areas, seemingly content with idea that Bonneville power was coming to the community but unwilling to embark on a PUD venture, rejected the PUD proposal by a vote of 1,597 to 1,902.

On November 23 Administrator Ross announced a re-allocation of ear-marked funds. The sum of $400,000 from the allocation for The Dalles line was to be held in abeyance, although he said that the line would be built as far as Hood River, where the city was asserted to be "ready to sign a contract" and, although this was not mentioned in the release, where a PUD group was preparing to bring a district proposal to vote at a special election a few months later.

Ross simultaneously announced that a planned $800,000 substation for Yakima on the Bonneville-Grand Coulee circuit was being eliminated because the people of that county had also rejected a PUD. The substance of his declaration to the press was that "Bonneville would not waste funds building lines to areas where people voted down public distribution of power," a statement that was quite clear in its implications.

Throughout this period, Ross was discussing privately a program for the purchase of Puget Sound Power & Light Company and for substantial parts of the Pacific and Northwestern Electric

150

systems. Guy Myers, as fiscal agent for a number of Washington PUDs formed in earlier elections, was flitting to and from New York, seeking to promote the acquisition programs.

The death of Ross on March 14, 1939, after a short illness, removed a principal character from the public power stage, but not before the script and the supporting players were sufficiently well established to make difficult any policy change by Frank A. Banks, a career man with the Bureau of Reclamation, who was appointed acting administrator.

At a special election in the Hood River valley on June 19, 1939, a PUD was formed in the rural area, even though the city of Hood River voted adversely on the proposal and thus was excluded from the district. The PUD sponsor group at The Dalles promptly petitioned for a second election on their proposition, which was set for August 15.

On July 7 Acting Administrator Banks was quoted in the press as saying the Bonneville line to The Dalles would be built as comtemplated if the proposed PUD was formed and applied for power. On July 11 Bonneville deposited funds in federal court to "speed acquisition of right-of-way" for transmission lines, including 8.68 miles on the proposed circuit to The Dalles. On July 28 a condemnation suit was filed in federal court for an easement on land across part of Wasco county for the Bonneville lines.

On July 30 the acting administrator told Wasco PUD sponsors: "Early this month I promised Wasco county that the Bonneville administration will build a 110,000 volt transmission line to The Dalles if your proposed district is formed and applies for power. I repeat that promise today."

At a meeting called by the Wasco PUD sponsors on August 12, three days before the election, Charles E. Carey, chief consulting engineer of Bonneville, told the audience, in effect, that BPA would build the line to The Dalles only if the PUD were approved. Sharing the platform with him were Dr. Carl D. Thompson and Stephen B. Kahn of the Bonneville staff.

This time around, the body politic decided to grab the brass ring before it was snatched away again. They reversed their earlier decision. Two days later the acting Bonneville administrator was quoted as saying: "By forming a people's utility district, Wasco county is taking proper steps to receive the full benefit of low-cost Bonneville power for homes, farms and industry."

One more similar incident might be related to illustrate the breadth and depth of problems faced by the Company in that troublesome period. This occurred in the fall of 1940, when a third attempt to form a PUD in Yakima county was under way. Although fairly early in the regime of Dr. Raver as BPA administrator, it was almost a year after he had accepted the extra-governmental task of undertaking to negotiate the purchase of certain PP&L properties for a group of PUDs.

A Bonneville administrative order on September 15, 1940, reorganized the agency's System Planning & Marketing Division to include a "Systems Acquisition Staff . . . responsible for making valuation studies, financial analyses, and for conducting negotiations in connection with the acquisition of power facilities. . . ."

On October 7, 1940, a letter signed by Charles E. Carey as Acting Chief of the System Planning & Marketing Division was addressed to the committee spearheading the Yakima county PUD campaign, and copies were given broad circulation in the area.

The letter said that BPA had studied "in considerable detail" the valuation of electric properties in the county and had reviewed the earnings.

A PUD, the letter stated, could be operated under the Bonneville standard resale rates, with rates to the consumer cut an average of 38%, and could meet all costs and bond interest charges "assuming that the system would be acquired at a reasonable figure in relationship to the physical value of the property."

The pivotal paragraph in the Carey letter said this (emphasis supplied): *"In our studies we have assumed that the purchase of these properties would be part of a system-wide acquisition of the Pacific Power & Light Co., in which the Bonneville-Grand Coulee Power Administration or a corporation sponsored by the Administration would acquire the Company's generating plants and major transmission lines, and the Public Utility Districts would acquire the distribution and other properties.* In Yakima county, the Condit-Union Gap transmission line, the Union Gap substation, the Naches and the Naches Drop generating plants, and one of the transmission lines between the Naches plant and Yakima, under the assumption made, would be acquired by the wholesale

152

agency. The Federal Government or this wholesale agency would also assume responsibility for maintenance of the irrigation canal serving the Naches generating plant."

Attached to the letter were tables of existing and prospective rates to customers, an "appraised cost new" statement covering the properties to be acquired by the proposed PUD, amounting to $4,685,965, and a map showing properties "Bonneville or Wholesale Agency to Purchase" and "Yakima County to Purchase."

Calculations made by the Company indicated the Bonneville assumption regarding the PUD's cost of getting into business was about $3,000,000 less than would be required on any basis other than the hypothetical situation outlined. The big "if" in the seductive promise of a 38% rate cut was: "*If* we can get our hands on the property and sell a piece to you for 38% less than you would pay at retail!"

Bonneville had no legal authority to buy Pacific Power & Light or any other existing electric system. There was no basis in law for it to sponsor a private corporation set up as an acquisition device. If any such a corporation were formed, non-profit or not, specific Congressional action and appropriation would have been required before Bonneville could buy from it the properties so invitingly catalogued in the Carey letter.

But facts like this attracted little public interest in the heated election campaign. "The United States Government says electricity will be 38% cheaper if we form a PUD, so let's give it a try," is probably as good a way as any to describe what was going through the minds of a small but deciding block of voters.

The PUD was created by a vote of 18,832 to 17,389. A change of 722 votes out of the 36,221 cast on the issue would have reversed the outcome!

The 1940 elections marked the farthest advance of the PUD organizers. In subsequent years there were many attempts to establish new districts, both in Oregon and Washington, but none was successful. Most concentrated push of the post-war period came in 1946, when ten PUD formation elections were held in Oregon. In three counties such proposals were put forward and voted down twice within the year.

Because of a legislative change in dates of PUD commissioner elections, two of the three members of the original board in

Yakima county had to stand for re-election in November, 1942. Their "tax, spend and get going" program had included an abortive start on the construction of duplicate power lines in the Yakima city area, in the face of critical wartime shortage of line materials. The 1942 election found the candidates for re-election out of office, and two conservative-minded men in their place. This marked a long-lasting second thought on the part of a majority of the voters of the county.

Elsewhere on the Pacific Company's system, the situation as of the end of 1940 was mixed. PUDs which subsequently became inactive were in existence in a portion of central Oregon, the rural section of the Hood River valley, a small area east of Astoria and a rural portion of Columbia county, Oregon.

County-wide PUDs had been formed in 1934 in Benton and Franklin counties, Washington, in 1936 in Cowlitz county and in 1938 in Clark, Klickitat and Skamania counties.

An attempt to form a PUD in the city of Portland had been defeated 2½-to-1 at the time of the May, 1940, primary election and ten other PUD proposals were likewise defeated in the state during the year. Of the five districts formed in Oregon in 1940, two subsequently became inactive and one eventually was dissolved by popular vote after unsuccessful efforts to persuade the people to pass a bond issue. Two acquired isolated electric properties from a small utility that was being liquidated by its owners. The Bonneville administrator acted as negotiator in these transactions. The same firm sold another separate property to the Skamania county, Washington, PUD, which, in the fall of 1941, went on to file condemnation suits resulting in awards of $32,000 for Pacific's fringe distribution lines on the east edge of the county and $68,000 for Northwestern Electric's distribution in the small community of North Bonneville. These properties were taken over in April, 1942.

The Klickitat PUD on October 7, 1942, filed suit in a state court to condemn the Company's distribution lines in that county. On petition by the Company, the suit was removed to federal court, where it lay until the PUD finally brought it to trial in 1946.

Commissioners of the Benton PUD passed a resolution on November 9, 1942, purportedly authorizing condemnation of the Company's properties in that county, but no suit actually was filed until three years later.

154

Chapter 26

Cold War Had Many Phases

F OR A PERIOD during the demanding days of World War II
there was a seeming lull in open guerilla activities on the
part of the public ownership troop, but there was no let up in the
strategists' pressure on the electric companies.

One form of pressure was applied by Bonneville through proposed conditions in power sales contracts. Portland General Electric Company, for example, faced an early demand that it agree
in a power contract on an over-all base price figure for its properties. For all practical purposes, the proposed conditions would
have given any existing or prospective public body an option to
negotiate purchase of any desired portion of the property at a
pro-rata of the "gun-point" price. An immediate target was PGE's
distribution system in Vancouver, Washington, sought by the Clark
County PUD. Significance of such a contract weapon in the hands
of a Bonneville administrator who was doubling in brass as a negotiator is apparent. PGE refused to acquiesce.

Another example involved the efforts of BPA to get properties
for the Tillamook, Oregon, PUD. In a letter to the chairman of
the district, Dr. Raver said: "I want to state that one of the specific
conditions which must be met before the Bonneville Power Administration can enter into a contract with Mountain States Power
Company is that the company must in good faith enter into negotiations with the Tillamook County People's Utility District for
sale of the company's properties in Tillamook to the PUD."

These PUDs, it should be noted, had full authority of law to
acquire by condemnation any properties they needed, no matter
how unwilling the owners might be to sell, and the conditions in-
sisted upon by Bonneville were patently extralegal. Prolongation
of contract discussions did, however, help keep breath in claims
that communities should vote for public ownership to get "cheap"
power. Also, the more uncertain a company's future power supply
could be made to appear, the more pliable the management and
stockholders were expected to become.

Threats of building duplicate distribution lines to compete with private companies in key areas represented another form of pressure tactics. In several instances the local agencies through which such threats were voiced ultimately found themselves so far out on a political limb that wasteful duplication actually took place.

In this connection, a statement made by Bonneville Administrator Raver at a meeting of PUD commissioners in Goldendale, Washington, on December 5, 1939, was significant. Represented at the meeting were districts that had asked him to serve as their negotiator in efforts to buy Pacific Power & Light properties.

A dubious member of the commissioner group asked the administrator whether there was any assurance that negotiations for the purchase of the properties could be successfully consummated.

Dr. Raver's answer was that "experience showed that methods could be used to force the sale of utility properties."

Also of interest is a portion of the testimony given by E. L. Bennett, one of the first Yakima County PUD commissioners, at the June, 1942, hearing on the Bone-Smith bill to set up a Columbia Power Administration having authority to take over utility company properties. Speaking for the bill, Bennett related that "our boys" had gone to New York with Dr. Raver to negotiate with Howard L. Aller, president of American Power & Light, for the purchase of PP&L.

"Our last price was $33,000,000," Bennett told the committee. "We wired him and we said: 'Either give us a reply in 15 days or we will be compelled to take such other measures as are necessary.'

"In other words, we, as an association in southeastern Washington and northeastern Oregon, had in our minds to begin suits of condemnation in every district, all of them to start on the same day, covering the entire system . . . if we had to do it. Then Mr. Bone came with the bill, and naturally, we are going to wait until we see what legislation comes out of it."

In passing, it should be recalled that the threat of competition against PP&L had already been used by Bennett and his associates on the Yakima PUD commission. Bonneville had built a stub transmission line and had a substation planned for construction at the edge of the city of Yakima and, early in 1942,

156

the PUD had attempted unsuccessfully to get county and city franchises or permits to build a duplicating line to take over some of the Company's existing customers. Criticism of this as a wasteful use of copper in time of war was shrugged off by a PUD spokesman with the quoted comment that "one mile of line isn't going to break the government."

The 1941 report of the Yakima PUD, issued in February, 1942, also told of conferences Dr. Raver had held with Pacific's holding company and, "when it appeared that an impasse had been reached," went on to tell of the district's steps toward building duplicating lines.

"Administrator Raver advised Mr. Aller of the American Power & Light Company that the various public utility districts were, like the Yakima PUD, pushing forward on programs for establishing themselves in business on a competitive basis," the report stated. "He suggested that in the interest of good business management the American Power & Light Company might wish to reopen negotiations."

The Clark County PUD initially was put into business through arrangements made between Bonneville, the Federal Public Housing Authority and the Vancouver Housing Authority. The deal was consummated in the early months of World War II. Bonneville built a line to the shipyard housing project site and installed metering equipment ahead of the Housing Authority's own distribution system. The PUD became the technical serving agency, although its sole function in the beginning was to read the Bonneville meter and bill the housing project. Annual profit to the PUD from this arrangement was estimated at $50,000 a year, more than enough to pay for the first piece of line it bought a year later from the Housing Authority. Northwestern Electric, which served the area, was allowed no opportunity to bid for the business.

At that time the Bonneville administrator was acting as negotiator for the PUD and had been discussing proposals to purchase the Clark county properties of Northwestern and Pacific Power. In an earlier period the PUD had entered into an unannounced contract with Guy Myers to negotiate for these properties, with Myers' fee to be based on a percentage of any bond issue required to finance the purchase. This arrangement was brought to light by an inquisitive Vancouver newspaper and the contract with Myers was not renewed at expiration.

One of the points stressed by Dr. Raver in more than 50 pages of testimony in favor of the 1942 Columbia Power Administration bill was his need for a vehicle with legal and financial authority to acquire electric company systems as a whole, and there was no question that the proposed CPA would have had such authority!

In speaking of his efforts to negotiate with the heads of the companies owning the common stocks of Pacific and of Puget Sound Power & Light, Dr. Raver told the Congressional committee that these executives wanted to know how the aspiring purchasers could effect system acquisitions, legally and financially. He could give no definite answer. Understandably, this was frustrating.

None of the senators or representatives sitting on the committee took the opportunity to ask why drastic changes in the Bonneville act should be proposed to help a volunteer negotiator effect the liquidation of private electric companies in the Pacific Northwest.

Such an inquiry could have been prompted by recollection of an earlier statement made by PUD Commissioner Bennett: "I appointed this negotiating committee. Personally I called Dr. Raver up and asked him if he would act on this committee as an adviser and as a sort of a head of the committee. He said, 'I will *in my private capacity.*'"

A committee member did ask Dr. Raver how long he thought it would take to consummate the deals on which he was working.

"If this legislation passes, we ought to complete the Puget Sound deal and the PP&L deals in six months' time," was the answer.

In the 769 pages of the printed transcript of the hearings the bracketed word "Laughter" is appended to only a few exchanges of words.

One is at the point where Kinsey M. Robinson, then president of The Washington Water Power Company and a witness against the bill, was being needled by Senator Bone. Robinson was telling about a five-year rate reduction program he had instituted shortly after he became president of WWP in 1938. The senator was seeking to link these reductions with public ownership elections.

Robinson conceded that in 1941 there was a municipal owner-

158

ship election in Spokane "and I just took the 1941 reduction program and 1942 and put them together."

Senator Bone sharply demanded: "That was in the midst of that fight?"

"Well, senator, would you have waited until after the election?" was the good natured reply.

Senator John H. Overton, committee chairman, allowed a spontaneous outburst of laughter to run its full course before rapping for order.

Hearings on the Columbia Power Administration bill were recessed on June 19, 1942, subject to the call of the chairman. That turned out to be the end of it.

But for a number of weeks thereafter opposition to the proposal continued to crop up as more residents of the Pacific Northwest began to realize the ramifications of the bill.

An impartial public opinion survey sponsored by several of the electric companies of the region, including Pacific, and intended for presentation to the committee when hearings were resumed, showed little public appetite for legislation of this nature.

One question asked in the survey was: "Do you think this proposed Columbia Power Administration should or should not be given authority to buy or condemn and take over every electric power company in Washington and Oregon?"

Those who had an opinion on this question were almost 2 to 1 against giving a CPA such authority—46.1% to 24%—and sentiment was more than 5 to 1 opposed to a change in the Pacific Northwest power set-up during the war.

Another question brought a response of nearly 11 to 1 in favor of having the question of public ownership decided by the vote of the communities directly affected, instead of by Congress.

The survey also revealed that 78.6% of the people interviewed considered their electric rates reasonable.

When it became evident in the fall of 1942 that the CPA bill had no prospect of getting further attention by the Congress, a new scheme was developed by ringleaders of the groups most ambitious to turn Washington into a 100% public power state.

This was in the form of an initiative to the Washington legislature, approaching from another direction some of the major objectives of the Bone-Smith bill. It would have authorized public

159

utility districts, by mere resolution of their commissioners and without a vote by the people, to form so-called "joint commissions" having broad powers to acquire and operate utility systems. Further, the "joint commissions" would have been empowered to unite into "authorities," which would be twice removed from the control of people residing within the individual member districts.

There was flurry of editorial protest throughout the state when the sponsors of the initiative let it be known that they planned to solicit signatures at the polls at the 1942 November election. The state's attorney general held, however, that since the proposal was not currently on the ballot such solicitation of voters did not constitute electioneering in a manner specifically prohibited by law.

An initiative to the legislature is an uncommon procedure in Washington. The measure proposed cannot be amended in any way by the legislature, and if final action is not taken on the bill, it automatically is referred to the people.

Initiative 12, as it was numbered, was passed through the 1943 legislature, with the senate voting to refer it to the people for final decision at the 1944 general election. The resolution to refer, however, was indefinitely postponed when it went to the house.

The initiative included a purported emergency clause, which, the sponsors asserted, kept it from being subject to referendum. The State Supreme Court unanimously held that this clause was invalid, and in a short time a total of 125,000 signatures was obtained by the committee sponsoring the referendum, or four times the required number. The bill was certified to the 1944 general election ballot as Referendum 25.

While a vote was pending on the Washington power company take-over proposal, Guy Myers saw a possible opportunity to exercise his talents as a fiscal agent in Oregon.

A PUD had been put to vote in May, 1940, in an area covering the greater part of the properties of West Coast Power Company along the Oregon coast from Newport to Reedsport. It was defeated by a substantial majority of all the votes cast.

The PUD advocates then proposed creation of a much smaller district, essentially within the Newport city limits where the earlier vote had been favorable to PUD. This maneuver was successful.

The new postage-stamp district, with Dr. Raver acting as negotiator, got an agreement from the liquidating owners of West

160

Coast Power to sell to the PUD a distribution system extending about 100 miles along the coast. An $850,000 bond issue to finance the purchase was passed early in 1942. The deal was tied in with the simultaneous sale of West Coast's little system in the Clatskanie, Oregon, vicinity to a PUD that had been formed there.

Much of the property involved in the proposed Newport transaction was outside of the boundaries of the district, to such an extent that it was felt necessary to bring a friendly suit to establish the authority of the PUD to acquire the system.

The courts held that the Oregon PUD law, as it then stood, placed no restraint on property acquisitions, no matter how far-reaching. The decision of the Oregon Supreme Court was issued on February 2, 1943.

It was not long thereafter that Guy Myers began to exercise his powers of persuasion on the directors of the small PUD that had been created in 1939 in the rural portion of the Hood River valley. He got the PUD board to adopt resolutions submitting a $175,000,000 revenue bond issue to the voters of the district at a special election called for January 7, 1944, and giving him an "Advisory Agent" contract under which he could have received as much as $1,860,000 for his services.

An extraordinary contract arrangement was dictated by the fact that Oregon law does not permit payment of commissions on public bond issues.

There was calculated audacity in the launching of a $175,-000,000 bond scheme during wartime in a rural district having barely 1,500 power customers. The sheer magnitude of the deal had a hypnotic effect of its own, and not a few were inclined to chuckle over the idea of being in center stage for the take-over of PP&L, Northwestern Electric, Portland General Electric and any other power company in Oregon that could be handled within the generous limits of the proposed bond authorization.

The biggest task that opponents of the Myers' scheme had in the pre-election campaign was to convince citizens that the game would be played with real money. It took a lot of hard work, and even then the proposition got 552 votes, or 39% of the 1,417 cast at the mid-winter election.

The loophole in the Oregon PUD law that had attracted Myers to Hood River was closed by the next legislature. The amendment then passed prohibited a PUD from acquiring electric utility properties located in municipalities and other areas outside the district boundaries (with minor exceptions), without first obtaining the consent of the voters residing in the outside areas involved.

In Washington, the 1944 power fight centered around Referendum 25. Electric company acquisition schemes more or less marked time until their various sponsors found out whether or not the electorate would give them a quick and easy method of realizing their ambitions. The Referendum 25 campaign saw an open battle between the electric companies operating in the state and the backers of a measure to liquidate them.

The super-PUD proposal was rejected by voters of Washington by a count of 297,919 to 373,051. More votes were cast on the proposition at the November 7, 1944, general election than at any previous statewide election on a power issue.

Defeat of the bill soon was followed by a number of PUD condemnation suits, which, although not filed on the same day, were reminiscent of the threats that had been voiced earlier.

The Clark County PUD started the parade with a suit filed on April 6, 1945, against Pacific and Northwestern Electric as joint defendants. Then along came the Cowlitz, Benton, Franklin and Klickitat county districts, two of which had made preliminary gestures toward condemnation three years earlier. The Northern Wasco PUD began to talk of starting to build a competing system in The Dalles.

On top of this, there came the organization later in the year of electric co-operatives to threaten duplication of Pacific's distribution lines in the Hood River valley and in the Walla Walla area, plus the incorporation of Interstate Electric, Inc., as the announced vehicle for the acquisition of the entire Pacific Power & Light system.

The November 19, 1945, issue of the *Pacific Northwest Co-operator,* a co-op house organ, described Interstate Electric as "an innovation in cooperative organization whereby a group with proposed maximum capitalization of $22 (twenty-two dollars) plans to bargain for purchase of a $30,000,000 corporation."

Interstate Electric, the story said, "is the name of the young 'David' which public utility districts, REA cooperatives and privately financed electric cooperatives are sending forth to buy out

162

'lock, stock and barrel' in one transaction all properties of the Pacific Power & Light Company in Oregon and Washington."

President of Interstate Electric was Charles Baker, also president of the infant Walla Walla Electric Cooperative and long-time head of Pacific Supply Cooperative, a wholesaler to farm consumer cooperatives.

The Walla Walla *Union-Bulletin* of November 4, 1945, reported on the preliminary organization meeting of Interstate Electric at Pasco and quoted Baker as follows: "We expect to offer the Pacific Power & Light Company a fair price at the outset, but in the meantime we will not cease our efforts to condemn properties for public utility districts or to set up competing cooperatives. And the longer we are forced to negotiate and develop competing agencies, the less we feel their properties are worth."

A statement made by an Interstate spokesman following the preliminary organization meeting said: "Primary purpose of Interstate Electric, Inc., will be to negotiate with American Power & Light Company on behalf of the local PUDs and cooperatives for the purchase of Pacific Power & Light Company. Under an order of the Securities and Exchange Commisision, American Power & Light, a New York holding company which holds 94 per cent of the voting stock of PP&L, is required to sell Pacific Power & Light. Distinguishing features of Interstate Electric, Inc., are that each of its stockholders will represent a local power agency, and that it is organized on a completely non-profit basis."

A detailed contract form prepared for submission to participants specified that the maximum price Interstate would be authorized to pay for the Pacific system was $34,480,000. This sum, however, among other things, was to include "All reasonable expenses incurred from and after January 1, 1945, by Principal and by similar local agencies in connection with condemnation suits or competitive programs with Pacific Power & Light Company." This meant that the cost of building competitive lines, for example, would be deducted from the offering price to the Company.

The contract stated that in the operation of the properties the agent (Interstate) "shall retain all employees of Pacific Power & Light Company that are reasonably required to operate such properties; provided, that it shall employ none of the Company's officers; and provided further, that such employees as it does employ

*Company's first airplane, a four-place Waco, was acquired in 1944.
Pictured (from left) are George T. Bragg, then vice president and general
manager; Herbert Jonas, advertising staff, Yakima; and Tom McAdam,
pilot. One rule-of-thumb operating guide called for a least an 8,000-foot
ceiling over Toppenish Ridge en route to or from Yakima so as to be
able to glide to a possible landing strip if the engine failed.*

must be efficient and loyal to the purpose of Agent and Principal,
and agencies similar to Principal." Form of the loyalty oath requi-
site to continued employment was not spelled out.

Published reports about activities of Bonneville staff members
in the organization of the Walla Walla Electric Co-op and Interstate Electric resulted in Administrator Raver being asked to
appear before the Securities Sub-Committee of the House Committee on Interstate Commerce, whose chairman, Congressman
Lyle H. Boren, had become interested in the activities and techniques of Guy Myers and others seeking to transfer private electric companies into public ownership.

Apparently to give supporting background against which Dr.
Raver could testify on January 29, 1946, the president of Interstate Electric addressed a letter on January 22 to the chairman of
the committee, asserting the purity of Interstate's intentions.

Pacific Power had already made a hard-hitting public statement about what it bluntly termed the "blackjack" tactics of Walla
Walla Electric Co-op and Interstate Electric and, on February 11,

164

1946, after studying the statements that had been made to the Congressional committee, President Paul B. McKee addressed a detailed rebuttal to the chairman for the benefit of the record.

The text of his letter included much information of historical interest, and quotations from it follow to convey some feeling of the urgency of the problems facing the Company in that troublesome time.

"The future of Pacific Power & Light Company as a publicly-regulated, fully taxpaying public service enterprise is, of course, sought to be threatened by the Interstate Electric promoters," McKee wrote, "and I believe the record should include some pertinent facts not otherwise disclosed to the committee, although well known to anyone at all familiar with the situation.

"Both Dr. Raver and Mr. Baker seek to picture Interstate Electric, Inc., as a quasi-public organization or 'co-operative,' fairly representing the electricity-using public in the territory served by Pacific Power & Light Company.

"The fact is that Interstate Electric is organized under the private corporation laws of the State of Oregon, although its headquarters, for all practical purposes, are in Walla Walla, Washington. . . . The state constitutions of both Oregon and Washington specifically prohibit any municipal corporation from purchasing stock in a private stock corporation. This applies to public utility districts, which are defined by law as municipal corporations. . . .

"No public utility district, therefore, can buy stock in Interstate Electric, or cause stock to be bought on its behalf in the name of an individual, without violating the basic state law. None of the public utility districts claimed to be represented by Interstate has the slightest lawful voice or interest in the corporation, which Dr. Raver ingenuously described as 'a pure legal fiction and a device to accomplish an end.'

"The minutes of the meeting of the Clark County, Washington, Public Utility District commissioners held on December 13, 1945, contain this illuminating reference to Interstate: 'Manager George Hibbert reported on the meeting of Interstate Electric, Inc., held at The Dalles, Oregon, on November 23, 1945, and advised the Commissioners that *he had personally subscribed and paid for one share of stock in the cooperative, in view of the ques-*

165

tion of the District's legal right to purchase such stock.' (underscoring added.)

"The REA co-ops claimed as participants in the Interstate scheme may be the direct owners of stock in the corporation, but that is unimportant. The important fact is that these REA co-ops represent only their own customers, now receiving electric service from government-subsidized lines, and largely residing in their own distinct service areas. By no stretch of the imagination can these REA co-ops be considered as representing the customers served by Pacific Power & Light Company in adjacent areas. . . .

"Distinct from the REA co-ops is the Walla Walla Electric Co-op, created at the instance of the Interstate Electric promoters to give them a semblance of representation in the Walla Walla community. . . . This county has emphatically rejected two proposals to form a public utility district, and more recently cast a strong vote against a state public power measure. As in other similar situations, the strategy now is to try to bring about a hybrid form of 'public' ownership through corporate 'legal fictions' over which the people have no control. . . .

"The Walla Walla Co-op has no franchise to operate in the City of Walla Walla, and under state law any franchise application must be submitted to a vote of the people for their approval or rejection. Instead of submitting their proposal to such a test, the Co-op has been trying, unsuccessfully thus far, to persuade the city commissioners to give them a 'permit' to operate . . .

"Our Walla Walla district is the second largest on the system, with 9,424 customers. Adjoining it is the Dayton, Washington, district, with 2,734 customers, where public utility district proposals have been voted down three times—in 1936, 1938 and 1940. Immediately south of Walla Walla is our Pendleton, Oregon, district with 5,978 customers, in which there have been no public ownership elections.

"In Yakima county, Washington, we serve 27,780 electric customers. A public utility district was formed in Yakima county by a small margin of votes in 1940, after having been voted down in 1936 and 1938. The 1940 election result was influenced by a widely circulated letter given to the PUD sponsors by one of Dr. Raver's staff members in his official capacity. . . .

"At the time the district was formed, three ardent public

166

ownership advocates were elected as PUD commissioners. They promptly levied special taxes to finance preliminary steps toward acquisition of our Yakima county properties. By 1942, however, the rosy promises of 1940 had worn thin, and the two commissioners who came up for re-election were voted out of office and two economy-minded men were elected in their places. At the 1944 general election, the third of the original commissioners came up for re-election, and despite the vigorous support of the public power advocates he, too, was retired and another conservative elected to the board. . . . The Yakima PUD has not entered into the Interstate scheme. . . .

"In Clatsop county, Oregon, we serve 8,786 electric customers, all but a few of whom live within an area which voted down one PUD proposal in 1938 and another in 1941.

"In Hood River county, Oregon, we serve 3,122 customers. The City of Hood River, representing about half of these customers, voted not to join a PUD at an election in 1939. The rural PUD which was formed at that time has indicated it is not interested in the Interstate proposition.

"In Wallowa county, Oregon, we serve 1,690 customers, and no public ownership elections have been held there.

"In addition, we serve a total of about 2,500 customers in various scattered Oregon communities which either have voted against public ownership, or in which no elections have been held.

"To sum up, out of our total of 79,763 electric customers in Washington and Oregon, *approximately 62,000, or 78%, live in areas which have plainly indicated their refusal to go along on even the usual 'public power' program, to say nothing of Interstate's private—but professedly public—hybrid scheme.*

"In the face of these *facts,* there is a very hollow ring to Dr. Raver's assertion before the committee that: 'I conceive it to be my duty to cooperate with those public bodies in bringing about such an acquisition if they decide, as the result of the regular democratic process of voting in their districts, or organizing under the law in their districts to do it.'

"No one, anywhere, has ever had a chance to vote on the question of whether or not the Interstate program is what is wanted by the people.

"On the contrary, the whole scheme is set up to force a type of

167

public ownership on nearly 80,000 users of electricity *without giving them a chance to vote.*

"Dr. Raver also made the statement to the committee that: 'We are interested in selling a new purchaser power in accordance with the principles of the Bonneville Act.'

"The plain fact is that Interstate would not be a *new purchaser.* It would simply be a case of changing the sign over the door. Pacific Power & Light Company has bought and is buying Bonneville power. Our Company has endeavored from time to time to make a fair and businesslike contract to buy much more power from Bonneville, on a basis that will allow us to make long-range plans for even wider development of the market. We, like other companies, have been met consistently with one excuse or another for not being given such a contract. . . .

"You may be interested to learn that the Company's 1945 taxes totaled $1,608,435, of which $900,604 went to the federal government. These federal tax payments are equal to the annual revenue received by the United States government from the sale of 57,000 kilowatts of Bonneville power! In other words, Dr. Raver would have to sell Interstate Electric, or rather its subsidiaries, 57,000 kilowatts in *addition to the present power load in the territory involved* in order to enable the government as a whole to break even, because all our present taxes would be lost to the government if the Interstate scheme should be put over. . . .

"I wish to call attention to the fact that in the last four months of 1945, following our most recent rate reduction, we received an average of only 1.78 *cents per kilowatt-hour* for electricity sold to residential customers. This is less than the 1.85-cent average reported most recently for public distributors of TVA power. And 20% of our revenue goes for taxes! . . .

"Also for the record, I wish to state that Pacific Power & Light Company has been building rural lines ever since it was organized in 1910. The Company now serves 14,000 farms over nearly 2,500 miles of rural distribution lines, at rates substantially lower for most users than are charged for Bonneville power by neighboring REA projects. . . .

"It should seem apparent to any reasonable man that a tax-paying power system that can point to this kind of a record should

168

Giant butterfly valve went into a penstock at the Merwin project.
Its purpose is to shut off the flow of water to the turbine when the unit
is to be inspected or repaired. No 2 generator at Merwin went into service
in December, 1949, and No. 3 was completed in November, 1958.

be entitled to some measure of cooperation from a government agency its taxes help to support. . . .

"In closing, I do wish to make one or two other points. On page 1123 of the unrevised transcript, Dr. Raver suggests that the way to stop Guy Myers and other 'public' power financial promoters would be for Congress to create a Columbia Valley Authority having the power to take over the private companies of the region, or to 'pass the bill we presented to Congress about four years ago known as the Bone Bill'. . . .

"The quick and easy way to stop the Guy Myers type of promotion would be for Dr. Raver to remove from the federal payroll a varied assortment of political power agitators, and get down to the serious business of selling presently surplus Columbia River power to all legitimate purchasers, without regard to the way they vote or part their hair. . . .

"I have a firm conviction that the continued existence of business-managed, publicly-regulated electric companies means a great deal to the development of this region. . . . Nothing would give me deeper personal satisfaction than to see us all pulling on the

169

same rope to develop the untold resources of this wonderful Pacific Northwest country. There is plenty of room here for us all, and one of the reasons I have expressed myself so bluntly at times in this letter is that I believe it is time we got down to cases.

"For my part," McKee concluded, "I am willing to meet Dr. Raver more than halfway in working out our mutual problems on a wholly constructive basis, to the end that we may all go forward together."

While Interstate Electric was going through the preliminaries with its assorted constituents, the Walla Walla Electric Co-op marked time during county franchise litigation. The Hood River Electric Co-op, however, picked up some surplus power distribution materials from a wartime housing project and early in 1946 began building lines on private rights-of-way to serve member-customers who had been served by PP&L. The construction was financed by member funds advanced on the co-op's notes.

Bonneville built a Hood River substation on its Dalles transmission line to serve the co-op, and additionally built a section of so-called "transmission" from the substation to a point east of the Hood River. This took advantage of an easement BPA had obtained to cross PP&L-owned property with its line to The Dalles. Once across the Company's property, the line blended into a co-op circuit, which, at the same voltage, was a "distribution feeder." This solved a problem for the co-op, because it, as a private membership agency, had no right of condemnation.

At The Dalles, the Northern Wasco PUD was actively seeking a city franchise for a competing system to be financed out of a $475,000 bond issue that had been authorized by the voters in November, 1940, on representations that this would be enough to buy the distribution properties of PP&L in the district if Bonneville took over the transmission investment. City voters, in a close election on May 17, 1946, franchised the duplication proposal.

Soon thereafter, Interstate Electric's president went to New York to offer American Power & Light $34,440,000 for its subsidiary, Pacific.

Although Baker was quoted as saying on his return to Walla Walla that he had been given "an extremely courteous reception by Mr. Jack, the secretary-treasurer," he went on to say: "I gath-

170

ered very clearly that the concern would not willingly sell the Pacific Power & Light properties to our organization."

The *Wall Street Journal* of June 10, 1946, commented that Interstate's offer "was regarded in utility circles at the week-end as a probably hurried public ownership effort to get in ahead of possibly obstructive political eventualities in the Pacific Northwest.

"While it was 'taken under consideration' by American officials, prospects were that no sale could be executed under it at any time soon, if ever, for several reasons. One was that the amount that would remain after American retired Pacific's bonds and preferred stocks and met taxes and other costs probably would be deemed inadequate. Another was question of Interstate's ability to finance the arrangement. Still another was question of legal power of public utility districts and electric cooperatives whose officers organized Interstate last November to carry out what is promised.

"The latter issue seems bound up with whatever the Supreme Court of Washington may decide in the $135 million Puget Sound Power & Light purchase offer case, although the two matters are otherwise unrelated. Promoters of the Puget plan are trying to gain legal clearance for their bonding plans needed before investment bankers will take a hand.

"Haste in both the Puget case and in the instant offer apparently has been dictated by the threat of Initiative 166, in Washington state, expected to qualify for the November ballot. That initiative would require public district officers to submit all acquisition and bonding plans to voters, a thing they do not now have to do.

"In view of the trends against public ownership in all recent Northwestern elections, the public ownership forces obviously are anxious."

The financial publication also said: "The $34,440,000 price, Mr. Baker disclosed, was figured for Interstate by engineers for Bonneville Power Administration."

The Benton County, Washington, PUD did not wait to see what the outcome of Interstate's efforts might be and pushed ahead with a condemnation suit that was tried in June, 1946. Award of the jury for the Company's distribution lines in the county was $1,265,000, an amount substantially in excess of the original cost of the properties. The district paid the award and took possession on September 13, 1946. The property taken had produced annual revenues of approximately $300,000.

The condemnation case brought by the Cowlitz County PUD came to trial in August, 1946, resulting in an award of $493,125 for the Company's distribution facilities in Woodland, Kalama and vicinities. Amount of the award was nearly five times the annual revenues of $101,000.

A third condemnation action coming to trial during the year was that of the Klickitat County PUD, heard in November. Here the jury awarded the Company $670,000 for properties producing annual revenues of approximately $168,000. It was April 4, 1947, before the district paid the award and took possession.

In none of these districts was the question of whether or not the people favored the take-over submitted to popular vote by the PUD commission, even though periods of from eight to 12 years had elapsed since the formation of the district. Nor was any way provided by law for bringing a referendum on such action by the district commissioners.

It was to remedy this deficiency in the Washington PUD law that Initiative 166 had been placed on the 1946 general election ballot by popular petition. Strongly supported by electric companies serving outside of the Puget Sound area, the initiative became the object of much voter confusion in the populous Seattle section of the state by reason of the fact that the then head of Puget Sound Power & Light, for which a Guy Myers' purchase deal was pending, chose actively to oppose the bill. This opposition resulted in many supporters of private power receiving an impression that the initiative, in some manner, was a public power measure. Public ownership zealots, on the other hand, pictured the bill as a Machiavellian power trust scheme to throttle the PUDs. In consequence, even though opinion surveys showed a great majority of the people of the state favored the principle of public votes on PUD acquisition proposals, the bill was defeated in a cloud of confusion at the November election.

As a sidelight, Myers' ambition to consummate a system-wide purchase of PSP&L was never realized. The deal ran into various legal snags and prolonged litigation. Separate portions of the company's properties later were taken over by PUDs, and years of side-by-side competition with Seattle City Light was ultimately

Unusual line extension job was done by Northwestern Electric in March, 1937, when a pole line was built out to the Italian ship "Feltre," which sank in the Columbia River after colliding with another vessel. A Northwestern crew tapped the line between Prescott and Rainier and strung a circuit half a mile out from shore to serve two 200-horsepower pumps used in the salvage operation. The ship was refloated.

resolved by municipal acquisition of Puget's distribution lines in Seattle. But the company remained a going concern in rapidly growing service areas. In 1969 its revenues were approaching $80,000,000 compared with about $20,000,000 in 1944.

Two proposed public power matters were defeated in Pacific Power territory in 1946. One was the proposed authorization of $2,000,000 of revenue bonds to allow the city of Astoria to engage in the electric business. This was defeated nearly 3-to-1 at the May 17 election.

At the November 6, 1946, election the proposed formation of a PUD in Clatsop County, Oregon, including the cities of Astoria and Seaside was defeated nearly 2-to-1 by the voters. This was the third time that residents of the area had rejected the PUD idea.

In other sections of Oregon, nine PUD and two municipal power proposals were defeated during 1946. In three counties, the same PUD propositions were on the ballot both at the May and November elections, with the result that the 1947 Oregon legislature amended the PUD law to permit the submission of PUD formation issues only at a regular biennial general election.

Chapter 27

Northwestern Electric Merged Into PP&L

A PLAN for merger of Northwestern Electric into Pacific Power & Light came under consideration early in 1946, and by mid-year a proposal was ready for presentation to state and federal regulatory authorities. Public hearing on the plan was held before the Securities and Exchange Commission in Philadelphia in August, 1946, and a month later concurrent hearings were held in Portland before the Federal Power Commission and the state regulatory bodies of Oregon and Washington.

Orders approving the merger were issued by FPC and the state commissions shortly before the year-end and, with some modifications, the plan was cleared by the SEC on April 24, 1947. Stockholders and directors of the companies acted on May 23, 1947, to make the merger effective as of that date.

Included in the program was a refinancing of the bonds and other long-term debt of the companies at a lower interest rate (3¼ %) and the replacement of the old 7% and 6% preferred stocks with a new 5% preferred stock. A cash contribution of $2,200,000 to Pacific by American Power & Light facilitated the disposal, by charging off to surplus, of amounts remaining in the electric plant adjustment account, set up when the FPC and other regulatory bodies adopted original cost plant accounting.

Balance sheet changes were reflected in the $8,000,000 stated value of the 500,000 shares of new common stock issued to replace 1,000,000 shares of Pacific and the 45,700 shares of Northwestern common stock owned by American Power & Light.

"The result of all these transactions," it was reported to stockholders, "is to give the merged Company a streamlined balance sheet, and to improve greatly its ability to finance on favorable terms the large additions to its service facilities which will be required in the next several years."

L. T. Merwin, president of Northwestern from 1936 until its merger into Pacific and general manager for a much longer period, was named a vice president of Pacific, a post he held until his retirement in 1949.

Walter S. Babson, Arthur L. Fields and E. C. Sammons, the three directors of Northwestern not otherwise associated with the Company, were named to the Board of Directors of Pacific.

T. E. Roach, vice president and general manager of Northwestern from 1942 to 1947, was named a vice president of the continuing Company, but shortly thereafter accepted an invitation to become executive vice president and general manager of Idaho Power Company. Subsequently he became president of the Idaho company, a post he filled with distinction for many years.

Operating revenues of Pacific in 1946 were $8,758,000, derived from 90,273 electric customers, 1,580 water and 131 steam heat users. The merged operation had 1947 revenues of $15,645,-000. It had 142,864 electric customers, 1,758 water and 998 steam heat users. The number of electric customers showed a net increase of 1,262 over the previous year in spite of the loss of 5,498 accounts as a result of the condemnation actions.

The Franklin County PUD condemnation case was tried in May, 1947, and the district took over the properties on November 7, 1947, upon payment of a jury award of $1,200,000. Annual revenues from the property involved were approximately $294,000.

In Clark County, Washington, the PUD condemnation suit that was filed there in 1945 came to trial in November, 1947. The jury awarded $4,837,500 for the properties sought to be taken. Annual revenues from the area at the time the property was taken on February 28, 1948, were about $1,400,000.

The Clark County PUD had gone forward with its suit in spite of the fact that 86% of the customers of Northwestern Electric in the area said in response to a 1945 postcard opinion poll that they favored continuation of the company's service.

In the period from September, 1946, to the end of February, 1948, the Company had taken from it by condemnation properties producing more than $2,250,000 in annual revenue, and suffered the loss of approximately 25,000 electric customers. Yet growth of its remaining territory resulted in two-thirds of the customer loss being offset by the end of 1948, and increased use of electricity more than cancelled out the revenue loss.

Proceeds from the condemnation awards were used to finance the construction of similar facilities in expanding areas elsewhere.

Soon after the Pacific-Northwestern merger had been com-

Memorable spring freshet of 1948 almost made an island of Company's
steam plant on the Willamette River at the foot of S.W. Lincoln Street.
A large stock of hog fuel is mounded up to the left of the plant.
Critical areas were sand-bagged to keep the plant on the line to serve steam
customers in downtown Portland and be ready to provide standby power.

pleted, American Power & Light Company proposed the contribution of Pacific's common stock to The Washington Water Power Company as a step toward compliance with the Public Utility Holding Company Act of 1935. It then was expected that American would subsequently dispose of its common stock holdings in Washington Water Power, which would have made Washington and Pacific an independent integrated system.

Applications for approval of the plan were filed by the American and Washington companies with the SEC and the state on July 23, 1947. A public hearing on the proposal was held by the Washington Department of Public Utilities at Spokane the following November, at which various objections were raised by so-called "public power" groups. All these objections were disposed of by the department in an order issued March 11, 1948, but approval of the stock transfer was denied on the ground that the applications did not furnish a complete plan for the ultimate sale or distribution of American's common stock interest in the Washington company. The door was left open for the filing of a new application when a complete plan might be presented to the SEC, but the American company's management subsequently turned to other ideas for the disposition of its Pacific stock.

176

Chapter 28

World War II Drastically Changed
Power Situation

REAT changes came about in the Pacific Northwest power situation during the 1940's because of the impact of World War II and a huge expansion of aluminum production.

New aluminum potlines were hooked up to the BPA system almost as fast as new generators could be built and placed in the Bonneville and Grand Coulee power houses. So great was the pressure on manufacturers' facilities that two of the generators built for Shasta Dam were diverted to Grand Coulee and installed temporarily in positions awaiting much larger permanent units.

Magnesium, carbide and other types of electro-industry, together with hundreds of welding machines in shipyards, contributed to the regional power load. However, the fact that the entire economy was geared to war production effort helped enable utility systems carry most of their wartime load through existing facilities.

Diversification of demand was aided by such things as assistance given to operators of small town machine shops to help them get sub-contracts for aircraft components and other items. This was part of a national effort to make maximum use of available machine tools and production skills.

There were problems, of course, to be met by the Northwest Power Pool during the war years, and each member system had its difficulties while operating under stringent rationing of critical materials and equipment. On the whole, however, the regional pool functioned smoothly and effectively.

The Company's 1943 annual report quoted in part an article in *Electrical West* describing the pool as follows:

"This vast reservoir of electric power, that has harnessed together more than 4½ million horsepower, intrigues even the imagination of the engineers who created it. Its potentialities are so great and it portends such a promising future for the power industry of the Northwest that its full possibilities have not yet been fully explored. Yet the power companies of this region, who pioneered

177

in interconnecting their systems for mutual benefit, had themselves for years been designing the pattern for this great interconnection of systems . . . in a five-state area."

The article went on to describe early system connections such as that occurring in 1918 when Washington Water Power and Puget Sound Power & Light were tied together through the Milwaukee railroad's 110,000-volt transmission line, and the later tie made between the Seattle and Tacoma municipal systems in 1923 for mutual aid. It also spoke of the interconnections made by PP&L, Northwestern Electric, Utah and Idaho and continued:

"When, in 1941, a 161,000-volt line was built to tie in Montana Power and Utah Power, there was formed a six-company pool of the Electric Bond & Share Company system in Oregon, Washington, Montana, Idaho and Utah. This pool operated for more than a year before the larger pool was formed. Operating technique that had been worked out and the resource data that had been compiled in this operation assured success of the larger pool from the start. . . .

"In July of 1942, the radiating transmission lines from the Bonneville and Grand Coulee power projects, operated as the Bonneville Power Administration, were tied into the existing web of transmission lines to form the present eleven-member super pool. One hundred and fifty power plants, 130 privately-owned and 20 publicly-owned, make up this great power reservoir with generator rating of 3,353,500 kilowatts, or 4,500,000 horespower. Approximately 2,933,500 kilowatts of this is in hydro and the balance, 420,000 kilowatts, is in steam generating capacity. . . .

"This interconnected system . . . extends from Portland and Seattle on the west to Fort Peck, Montana, nearly over to the North Dakota border."

The pool was credited with having added 135,000 horsepower to the available electrical generating capacity of the region, simply by taking advantage of the diversity of power demand and operating conditions between the cooperating systems.

Then, as now, the Power Pool was a voluntary association of systems having a common objective. A small staff of professional engineers in Portland gathered and analyzed data from the participating utilities. A load dispatching center in Spokane supervised day-to-day and hour-to-hour operations. Proposed operating pro-

*Starting from scratch on February 4, 1941, Oregon Shipbuilding Corp.
launched 455 ships for the U. S. Maritime Commission between October
19, 1941, and October 24, 1945. Total tonnage of the World War II
output of the Portland yard was 4,755,000. General manager of this Kaiser
enterprise was Albert Bauer, who later joined the PP&L organization
and served as vice president and general manager from 1961 to 1966.*

grams were reviewed by a committee composed of representatives
of each of the pool members.

A basic principle guiding the operating committee was to start
with an assumption that all the plants in the pool were under
one ownership. "In such case," they asked themselves, "how would
we operate the system in order to get the most favorable results?"

The significant fact is that, even though the programs so outlined were not binding, the operation produced such important
benefits for all concerned that none would exercise the privilege
of saying: "Good-by, we'll go it alone!"

Settlements for credits and debits in the power interchange
transactions followed the provisions of contracts existing between
the various systems, with the power pool acting as a clearing house
for kilowatt-hours moving in and out.

Use and planning of transmission facilities was another area
in which coordination was receiving attention.

In 1940, for example, the Pacific Company was weighing alternate plans for increasing its power capacity in Clatsop county.

179

One method would have been to add generation at the Astoria steam plant. The other plan, more favorably considered, was to build a transmission line between Astoria and the Company's section of the line from Ariel to Longview.

Bonneville Power Administration at the same time was looking toward construction of a transmission line to Astoria from its St. Johns substation adjacent to Portland.

Conferences between BPA and the Company brought agreement that Bonneville would go ahead with its plan and would supply the Company with 1,500 kilowatts of power at Astoria. The agreement included an arrangement whereby the Company would wheel power on Bonneville's account to two REA systems.

Delivery of Bonneville power to the Company at Astoria began June 30, 1941. The initial one-year term of the contract later was extended to run until one year after the end of the war.

Another contract arrangement was described in the Company's May 1, 1942, letter to preferred stockholders, in which President McKee noted: "Comment has been made in these letters from time to time recognizing the Company's belief that the private and public power resources of the Pacific Northwest should be pooled to make the maximum use of existing facilities in the war effort. The Company's engineers have been working with the staff of the Bonneville Administration for a number of months on system interconnections and power interchange studies, and I am glad to report that on April 24 an interconnection contract was entered into by the government, your Company and The Washington Water Power Company.

"This contract, which will be in effect for the duration of the war, provides for interconnections between the Company's main transmission system and the Bonneville system at Hanford, Washington and between Washington Water Power and Bonneville at Spokane. Other interconnections may be established by mutual agreement. The contract also provides . . . for the delivery of energy by the companies on Bonneville's account to certain REA projects, and for vital war projects as occasion may arise."

There was no elaboration about the Hanford interconnection, and the only indirect reference to it during the war years was a paragraph in the 1943 annual report under the heading "Customer Statistics." It said: "Gains in number of customers in many areas were partly offset by the loss of customers formerly served in the Hanford-White Bluffs area in Washington, which has been evacuated of civilian residents to accommodate a large war project."

Nature of the "large war project" was a well-kept secret until after the first atomic bombs were dropped in August, 1945.

One function of the Hanford interconnection with BPA was to provide a by-pass around the AEC reservation as a substitute for part of the Company's line between Taunton and Pasco.

The Company's 1943 annual report also included the following: "On December 15, 1943, the Company jointly with Northwestern Electric Company and The Washington Water Power Company, signed a 16-month contract with the Bonneville Power Administration for the purchase of 20,000 kilowatts of prime power . . . which will be apportioned among them according to their respective operating requirements. While the companies have adequate generating capacity to meet their peak demands during the contract period . . . this arrangement provides insurance to protect loads in the event low water conditions should reduce their existing hydro resources."

The Company's 1944 annual report told of the extension of the three-company contract from April 15 to June 30, 1945, "in anticipation of the negotiation of a contract for an extended period beyond that date."

In the 1945 report, however, the story was that the contract had ultimately expired on August 31, 1945, and it said: "A number of discussions have since been held with the Bonneville Power Administration regarding the possible negotiation of a satisfactory firm power contract to provide for future growth of the Company's load, but to date no decision has been reached."

World War II was then over, but the public ownership wars had flared up again with the 1946 rash of PUD formation attempts, referred to earlier. Also, on the Congressional front, the elements behind a Columbia Power Administration push in 1942 began a new campaign that was to last several years, this time under the banner of a Columbia Valley Authority. Details of the CVA proposals varied, but all were directed toward creation of an autonomous or semi-autonomous federal authority that would dominate Pacific Northwest resource development and hold the power of life or death over the private electric companies of the region. The CVA threat was a serious one, but the bills threatened to encroach on so many different aspects of economic and political life that the opposition ultimately was sufficient to shelve the idea after nearly five years of controversy. None of the proposals put forward gained enough support to move out of committee.

The pro-public ownership attitude of individuals in key posts within the Department of the Interior undoubtedly slowed the progress of post-war contract negotiations with BPA.

The fact that a generally anticipated post-war recession did not occur in the United States seemed to give an edge for the time being to those in a position to tighten the screws. Pent up demands for consumer goods of all kinds soon had producers of metals going full blast, and the aluminum industry was quick to penetrate a civilian market that had grown hungry for all kinds of metal. The aluminum plants built by the government in the Northwest were negotiated for by private operators and went back into full production within a period of a few months.

As a result, the sharp drop in regional power demand that had occurred during 1945, particularly in the latter months of the year, proved to be of short duration.

This was a welcome surprise to all who had been concerned about possible unemployment and economic problems in the post-war period, and upset a good many power forecasts.

The annual report of Bonneville Power Administration for fiscal year 1945 said, for example: "As of June 30, 1945, 164,000 kilowatts had already been cut back. During the last six months of the calendar year 1945, an additional 416,000 kilowatts were cut back. During this reconversion and temporary power surplus period, the two Shasta generators are being removed from the Grand Coulee project and are being returned to the Shasta dam. . . . There is a current temporary surplus of power to be marketed in the amount of approximately 500,000 kilowatts. . . .

"While revenues are expected to dip to $13,800,000 by fiscal year 1948, full recovery is anticipated by 1950." Revenues in 1945 had been $22,990,000, it should be noted.

A subcommittee of utility technicians called together late in 1945 by a Natural Resources Development group appointed by

Washington's Governor Mon C. Wallgren also was guarded in its estimate of the rate of recovery. Its members, including representatives of both public and private systems, felt themselves bravely optimistic when they assumed in their forecast that as much as half of the wartime bulge in power requirements might stay on the line with the resumption of peacetime activities.

Material appraised by the subcommittee in its study included data submitted by Bonneville Power Administration as of October 29, 1945. While optimistic with respect to the long-term outlook, the agency estimated that it might be 1953 before BPA's war-time industrial loads would be fully reinstated. More rapid growth in the loads of distribution agencies was forecast, and this was expected to compensate for the loss in their war loads by 1948.

The BPA comment also noted: "A cessation of activities in the aluminum reduction plants at Spokane and Troutdale has occurred and will shortly take place in the Tacoma plant, but other aluminum plants are still operating. The operations of the rolling mill at Spokane have declined and will soon cease altogether. The difficulties in the continuing operation of this plant with aluminum rolling capacity equivalent to the entire capacity of the industry in pre-war days have been recognized. Negotiations with the war agencies to distribute its large capacity among several locations in the Northwest were unsuccessful."

But the regional power load bounced back dramatically as 1946 progressed. The boom was not only in the field of aluminum. Other phases of the economy were on the march. Workers who had come to the Pacific Northwest to build ships and airplanes liked the country and decided to stay. The region showed a 44% growth in population from 1940 to 1949.

The race to expand electric distribution systems put line materials in short supply and nearly as difficult to obtain as they had been under war-time controls.

The Pacific Company's 1947 annual report said: "The problem of obtaining sufficient power to carry the Pacific Northwest utility systems through the peak-load season late in 1947 was greatly relieved by heavy fall rains throughout much of the region. As a result of the increased output of hydroelectric energy, relatively little high-cost oil had to be burned."

183

Until well after the days of World War II, the Public Service Building was a landmark on the Portland skyline. In this picture, taken from the Ross Island bridge about 1946, the PP&L structure stands out a little to the left of center background. Hog fuel barges at the Lincoln steam plant are at the far left on the opposite shore.

The report also noted that in August, 1947, "five of the major private utility companies of the region executed one-year contracts with the Bonneville Power Administration for a total of 335,000 kilowatts of power, representing the amount available over and above the federal agency's other commitments. Of the total, this Company and The Washington Water Power Company jointly contracted for 97,000 kilowatts. The contracts run for one year . . . and may be extended for an additional year."

The short term of these contracts put them in the class of stop-gap arrangements. But the reality of the power pinch in the region already was beginning to exercise a significant influence on the course of events.

Chapter 29

Tacoma Meet Expands Group Effort

E NGINEERING representatives of the public and private systems
who worked together in Northwest Power Pool operations
had early come to know their colleagues on a first-name basis.
This in no way inhibited the sturdy arguments that went on as
operating programs were being hammered out, but it did much to
facilitate communication.

The impending power shortage brought public and private
top managements face to face in Tacoma in January, 1947, to
form another working committee that made its own special contribution toward better understanding between two groups that
had certain basic differences in viewpoint but found a broad area
within which they might work to common purpose.

The national election in November, 1946, had changed majority control of the House of Representatives in a swing which,
among other things, reflected sentiment for reduced government
spending and a balanced budget.

There was also grumbling on the part of many Congressmen
about the magnitude of federal appropriations that had gone into
river development in the Pacific Northwest in contrast to the much
smaller sums they found difficult to get for river, harbor or flood
control projects in their home districts.

Federal investment in the Columbia River power systems as of
June 30, 1946, for example, had reached a total of $332,000,000.

Bonneville Power Administration, with its revived industrial
power loads and the growth in requirements of distributors, was
concerned about the fate of budget requests for strengthening its
own transmission grid and to keep the installation of six more
120,000-kilowatt generators at Grand Coulee on schedule and get
construction started on other authorized river projects.

Public power systems, particularly those with substantial loads,
even though preference customers for federal power, could not
feel complacent about the general situation. It was recognized
that in a pinch the available energy supply would have to be

shared by all concerned. In no other way could either voluntary or compulsory power rationing be made to work, and the power pool protected against over-loads that would break the systems apart electrically and put everyone in deep trouble.

It was against this background that the City of Tacoma and its long-established municipal power system extended an invitation to utility executives in the western group of the power pool to meet there for a conference on their common problem. Acting as spokesman for Tacoma was Commissioner C. A. Erdahl, in charge of its Department of Public Utilities.

As the public and private system representatives eyed their opposite numbers across the conference table at the opening session there was noticeable tension in the air. This was quickly dispelled by the chairman and host.

"I know we took on quite a risk when we invited all you big, bad private utility tycoons to get together here with us public power renegades," Erdahl observed, "but as I look around the table I think maybe there's a chance we can get along.

"Sitting over there," he said, pointing, "is Kinsey Robinson, who, I've always been told, is Public Power Enemy No. 1, or something. When he first came in and took off his hat I expected to see horns sprouting out of his head, but, you know what, he seems to be a normal human being and didn't scare me a bit.

"Paul McKee's another fellow I was a little skittish about, on the basis of what I'd heard about him. I looked for him to have not only horns, but a forked tail. But you can see for yourself that he's no scarier than Kinsey.

"So let's all relax and get down to business. We've got a lot to discuss today and not too much time to do it."

That broke the ice into chunks small enough so that by lunch time they were just the right size to fit in a tall glass, and the Pacific Northwest Utilities Conference Committee was off to a flying start!

Based on their combined load studies, the committee estimated that new generating capacity in the amount of 318,000 kilowatts over and above the 745,000 kilowatts of generating units then on order would be required by November 1, 1949, and that 1,565,000 kilowatts would be required by November 1, 1953.

"To meet these requirements," said the committee's policy

186

statement of January 22, 1947, "it is urged that the necessary appropriations be made available as rapidly as possible to the Corps of Engineers and to the Bureau of Reclamation."

The committee also noted that "present transmission facilities of the Bonneville Power Administration are already approaching conditions of full load and it is agreed as essential that appropriations for backbone transmission facilities be made available to the Bonneville Power Administration on an annual and continuing basis adequate to provide a means for the delivery of power to load centers."

The policy statement was signed by PP&L, Northwestern Electric, Portland General Electric, Washington Water Power and Puget Sound Power & Light companies and by the Seattle Department of Lighting and Tacoma City Light.

In addition to presenting the joint statement to the appropriations committees of the House and Senate, the members of the group agreed that each would submit a supplementary statement on behalf of its own system, affirming general support of the program and adding such comments about detailed items in the budget as might be deemed necessary.

The statement presented by Paul McKee on behalf of the Pacific and Northwestern companies, for example, reviewed the development of the federal hydro projects in the region and recalled that from 1933 to 1940 the challenge was to find constructive uses for these great blocks of power.

"Then the onset of war quickly changed the problem from one of marketing to one of supply," it noted, "and the phenomenal upsurge in power demands following the end of the war has continued to keep the emphasis on the problem of supply."

Speaking of the Tacoma deliberations, the Company's statement said: "Our effort was to look at the over-all problem as objectively as possible against the background of our own particular situations. Each participant in the Tacoma meetings has, of course, his own views regarding the detail of the general program.

"My own considered opinion is that the total amount allocated to the Bonneville Power Administration in the President's budget probably is insufficient to cover all the needs. At the same time, I wish to make clear that I disagree with some of the allocations, and believe certain items should be eliminated or de-

187

ferred and the funds transferred to purposes for which immediate need can be shown."

Three lines proposed in the Bonneville budget were questioned by McKee as to need or timeliness, while full support was given to backbone facilities in the program.

The Company's statement also spoke of the situation existing in the Central Oregon area served by Pacific, "where the power load was increasing rapidly and an additional source of power would be required at an early date. For this reason the Company is considering construction of a transmission line from Tygh Valley to Madras, as shown on the attached system map.

"Now BPA has in its five-year system development program a Goldendale-Madras-Detroit line, a section of which traverses the route of the line we are considering. Here is duplication in the planning state. . . .

"The 230-kv BPA line, when completed, will have much greater transmission capacity than would a line built by the Company for its own needs. It will also play an important part in augmenting the existing BPA transmission capacity to the Willamette Valley, which, in turn, will serve to relieve the Portland-Vancouver facilities of some of the load which otherwise they would have to carry. So as between the Company's proposed line and the BPA line, the latter is the more logical."

The McKee statement ended: "It is my conviction that the West is a proper and fertile field for the investment of capital, both public and private. Prudent investments in the facilities necessary to utilize its great natural resources will pay out!"

The joint appearance of representatives of public and private power systems demonstrated unified support of basic needs of the Pacific Northwest and their candid comments about items which individual members could not support was something new and refreshing for Congressmen struggling through the budget maze. It gave new perspective to the needs of the region.

For a decade the Conference Committee was an important force in the progress of regional development, and provided an effective vehicle through which voluntary power conservation programs were set up to cope with the emergencies that continued to threaten until a greatly enlarged construction program brought generating capacity into balance with demands.

188

Chapter 30

Power Pinches in 1947-49 Period

TWO ISOLATED parts of the Pacific system where acute power supply problems arose in 1947 and 1948 were the Wallowa valley and Central Oregon, neither then interconnected with outside sources of power.

As power demand began to tax capacity of the Company's small hydro plants at Wallowa Falls and Joseph, it was decided to provide temporary relief by installing a 1,000-kilowatt diesel unit at Enterprise. Appropriately, the engine selected was an Enterprise. Work on the installation began in August, 1947, and the generator went on the line in December, much to the relief of everyone concerned with the district's operating problems.

Until the new unit came on the line, generous customer cooperation kept the system from being seriously overloaded at peak hours during the cold, dark days of early winter. Mills in the area helped greatly by shifting their working hours so as to be off the line from 4 to 7 p.m. Householders scheduled their washing and baking away from the evening peak.

The Enterprise situation had been remedied only a short time when a February, 1948, cold wave dropped temperatures in Central Oregon to as low as 16 below zero and drastically reduced the output of both hydro and steam generating facilities in the area. Flows in the Deschutes and Crooked rivers were restricted and the hogged fuel supply for boilers in the two big mills at Bend became loaded with ice and snow and burned so poorly that only a fraction of the normal steam power capacity was available.

Arrangements had been made earlier for hauling surplus fuel from mills in Redmond and Prineville to make up a deficiency in Bend, and with the sub-zero weather a dozen trucks were thrown into the supply line. These conveyances ranged from big truck and trailer rigs hauling hogged fuel to farmer-owned trucks loaded with slab and cordwood.

One generator was threatened with idleness when the dry planer shavings normally fueling it had to be diverted to mix with ice-heavy hogged fuel to get a better burning rate. District Power Superintendent Bill Childers and "Pat" Morphey, assistant superintendent of power for the system, experimented with the fire box and found that the boiler could be coal-fired. They also rounded up a coal supply and kept the unit on the line. Emergency fuel costs in the district for the critical period totaled $394,000.

In the pinches, industrial plants had to be dropped and various feeder lines killed until boiler pressures could be built up.

When the weather relented, industrial plants were returned to the lines, first on a half-day basis and then back to full time. On the first day the industrials resumed full-time operation, the energy output on the Central Oregon system hit an all-time high, even though the peak demand was below the previous record.

The problems created by the abnormal cold spell accelerated negotiations with the Bonneville Power Administration to develop a transmission line construction plan compatible with the needs of all concerned.

The way was cleared within a month for the Company to build to the government's 230,000-volt specifications a 42-mile section of the needed line. Lying between Maupin and Madras, this portion of the line represented a major segment of the 60-mile, $1,-400,000 project required to link the Deschutes area with the Company's main power system at Tygh Valley.

Under the plan, the government obtained an option to purchase at cost the 42-mile section when it was needed in the federal transmission program.

Two other construction jobs were related to the program. One was a $250,000 substation and interconnection with Bonneville at The Dalles. Another, scheduled for the following year, was a $175,000 rebuild of the transmission line between The Dalles and Tygh Valley to strengthen that circuit.

The line into Central Oregon was energized October 20, 1948, ending the dependence of that district upon local power sources. Four years later, BPA exercised its option on the section from Maupin to Madras and made it part of the new circuit that had been authorized.

Expansion of PP&L generating capacity was provided for in the Company's $8,311,000 construction budget for 1948. It included funds to begin installation of a second 45,000-kilowatt gen-

This large Company construction crew headed by A. O. Snyder, together with a contractor's force, built 60 miles of transmission line between May 11 and October 22, 1948, to relieve a tight power situation in Central Oregon. Cost of the project was $1,050,000. The line connected the Bend-Redmond-Prineville-Madras area with the Company's main power system at The Dalles.

erator at the Ariel project on the Lewis River. Like the first unit, this had a peaking capability of 50,000 kilowatts. It went into service in December, 1949.

The plant at Ariel was renamed the Merwin Project on May 1, 1948, in honor of L. T. Merwin, who had played an important part in early studies of the Lewis River. The lake formed by the dam had long carried his name. The name-changing ceremony was attended by many of Merwin's friends and associates. E. C. Sammons, president of the United States National Bank and a director of Pacific, delivered the principal address.

The Company's quarterly letter to preferred stockholders dated August 2, 1948, noted that it had been "fortunate to escape major damage during the recent Columbia River flood, and service difficulties resulting from the high water were limited in their extent. It is estimated that the total cost of repairing distribution facilities in flooded areas and of protective measures taken to safeguard plants and stations will approximate $42,000. Revenue losses . . . are estimated at about $70,000.

"During the peak of the flood, the output of the Bonneville plant was sharply curtailed as a result of water backing up below the dam, and the capacity of Grand Coulee was also reduced. This resulted in a temporary shortage of hydroelectric power in the region, and consumers of all systems were asked to conserve electricity until the emergency had passed."

The letter also reported that the voters of Portland on May 21 had given a 4-to-1 approval of a new 20-year electric and steam heat franchise for the Company.

The annual report for 1948 included this comment: "The Company is happy to report that a Retirement Plan covering the men and women of its organization received stockholders' approval on October 19 and has since been put into operation with an effective date of April 1, 1948. It is designed to fit in with social security benefits. The plan not only rewards employees for loyal service to the Company by providing them with retirement income without cost, but also provides an incentive to the younger members of the organization because of job advancement opportunities made available through the system of age retirements. As of December 31, three members of the organization had qualified under the age and length of service provisions for retirement under the plan. Fifty-eight other former members of the organization at year's end were on retired status outside the scope of the Retirement Plan. . . . It is fitting that among the first to benefit under this new Company program is one who has had a vital part in guiding and shaping Pacific Power & Light Company —Lewis A. 'Tam' McArthur. His service dates from the formation of the Company, which, during the intervening 38 years, he has served as general manager, vice president, and director."

The 1948 report noted that D. R. McClung, later to become the third president of the Company, had been named a vice president at the November 11 meeting of the Board of Directors. He was then the Company's general superintendent.

The power situation of the period was reflected in a decision reached early in 1949 by the Company and two of its neighbors, Portland General Electric and Washington Water Power, to undertake jointly the proposed construction of a 75,000-kilowatt hydroelectric project on the Deschutes River near Madras, Oregon. In reporting this to stockholders, the Company said in its February 1, 1949, letter: "This $12,000,000 project would be built by a new and separate company, Northwest Power Supply Company, with the output of the plant contracted to the three utilities. If the necessary license authorizations can be obtained promptly, the plant can be completed by the winter of 1950-51 to help relieve the area shortage."

Even as this plan was being formed, the Pacific Northwest was hit by the severest cold spell in many years. A Company report, under date of March 31, 1949, spoke of the power shortage thus created as being "of serious proportion on the interconnected systems serving the Washington-Northern Oregon area. At first the problem was merely one of keeping the evening peak demand within the generating limit of the network. Later the protracted cold created a shortage of hydroelectric energy throughout the entire day. Through concerted action, the public and private agencies allied in the Power Pool obtained voluntary curtailment on the part of customers which successfully met both problems with little adverse effect on employment or industrial output.

"The steam-electric generating plants of the area were a vital factor in carrying the region through this trying period. Operation of the Company's plants on an emergency basis during the months of January and February, 1949, is not reflected in 1948 earnings, but costs of the emergency condition will be noted next year."

A story told to illustrate the critical nature of the power situation concerns the group on duty at the Power Pool dispatching center in Spokane during the peak hour on a bitterly cold evening. Demand was overlapping the available capacity. Frequency had sagged to the danger point.

The chief dispatcher was reaching for the telephone to order fast load-shedding to avoid a break-up of the pool when, suddenly, the tense situation eased. Frequency began to creep up, instead of down. The day was saved!

Following a hunch and checking railroad records, the pool engineers are said to have found that a heavy freight train on an electrified section of the Milwaukee line had been pulling up a long grade at the time of the evening peak. When it reached the divide and began rolling down the next canyon its drain on the power supply suddenly stopped and the regenerative motors in the locomotives began feeding energy back into the system as the braking function took over. That pulled the pool through its crisis!

Chapter 31

"D-Day" for PP&L: January 4, 1950

U NDER THE ICE and snow that gripped the region in the winter of 1949 a public ownership fire was being stoked by Guy C. Myers and his cohorts, who worked day and night in the closing hours of the 1949 Washington legislature to squeeze through an amendment to the state's PUD law intended to facilitate power company take-overs.

One long-suffering target was Puget Sound Power & Light Company, but the fast-moving fiscal agent also was busy with schemes whereby control of the Pacific and Washington companies might in time be bargained away from American Power & Light Company, and their properties parceled out to PUDs in a series of transactions profitable to the middlemen. Their hope that this might be accomplished was strengthened by the fact that time was running out on American's dissolution order stemming from the Holding Company Act of 1935.

Gossip about Myers' activities in New York and Chicago financial circles was being relayed west by the grapevine almost every day. The stories were disquieting to private utility men who had seen American sell one subsidiary, Nebraska Power Company, into public ownership through a Myers deal shortly after the end of World War II.

The uncertainty of Pacific's situation was accented when the American company, which early in 1949 had indicated "probable willingness under appropriate conditions" to invest $2,500,000 in additional shares of PP&L common stock, put off any action on its tentative plan. This made it necessary for Pacific to change plans for obtaining the $9,500,000 of new capital required by the Company for the year's construction program.

McKee's November 1, 1949, letter to stockholders told how the Company "had planned that prior to November 15 it would arrange for a financing program enabling it to retire the then outstanding $6,500,000 principal amount of its 2⅜% notes held by Mellon National Bank and Trust Company of Pittsburgh, Pa., and to raise additional capital funds to finance construction requirements through 1949 and part of 1950. The tentative financing plans contemplated the sale of a new series of mortgage bonds, and obtaining, if practicable, the investment by American Power & Light of an additional $2,500,000 in Pacific's common stock.

"It developed that American considered it impracticable to make such additional investment in the Company's common stock by November 15, but that American might be in a position to do so prior to May 1, 1950. Therefore, it appeared advantageous to the Company to defer the sale of additional bonds until March or April, 1950, and to finance its construction requirements in the meantime by a new short-term bank loan of sufficient amount to retire the $6,500,000 of notes maturing on November 15 and to provide an additional $2,500,000 of cash."

Three weeks later, on November 21, a likely reason why American was holding back on any investment was disclosed in a *New York Times* story under the by-line of the newspaper's public utility specialist, John P. Callahan.

"Guy C. Myers, fiscal agent for a group of public utility districts in the State of Washington, was reported yesterday to have completed a comprehensive plan for early sale of three privately owned utility systems to public power groups in that state.

"The 'package' price for the three companies was said to be $200,000,000—$120,000,000 for the Puget Sound Power and Light Company and $80,000,000 for the Washington Water Power Company and the Pacific Power and Light Company. The latter two companies are owned by the American Power and Light Company, an intermediate holding company in the Electric Bond and Share Company.

"Involved in consideration of the proposed deal, which would be the largest of its kind in the sixty-six-year history of the electric industry, are the investments of several thousand stockholders, directly in the case of Puget Sound, and indirectly in the case of the two American Power and Light subsidiaries."

The story said: "Both Paul B. McKee and K. M. Robinson, presidents of Pacific Power and Washington Water Power, respectively, have vigorously opposed sale of their properties to public power. In this opposition, however, they have been fre-

195

quently confronted by counter attitudes of their companies' parent, American Power and Light.

"The president of American Power, Howard L. Aller, said on Thursday that he had received no definite proposal 'in the past three weeks,' adding that negotiators for sale of the two subsidiaries have been 'busy and fussing' for several years. When asked about his reaction to the reported $80,000,000 offer for the two American Power subsidiaries, Mr. Aller remarked that the offer might be considered."

For the next three or four weeks most of the information obtained by Pacific and Washington came from friends in the financial community who were sympathetic to the problem facing the company managements.

On the day before Christmas, a story broke in the Walla Walla *Union-Bulletin* saying that a deal was in negotiation for the sale of Pacific's common stock to an investment syndicate, "for resale to public and private agencies in the Pacific Northwest. . . .

"Reports reaching Walla Walla indicated that top officials of American Power and Light Company . . . have reached agreement with the investment syndicate as to sale terms but that the deal has not been completed. . . . Reports also differed as to whether Guy C. Myers, the noted utility sale promoter, was involved in the proposed transaction."

Ten days elapsed before any official word about the hotly rumored deal was conveyed to Pacific by the holding company.

The tip-off that an announcement was imminent came late in the afternoon of Wednesday, January 4, 1950, when Aller telephoned to Paul McKee to say briefly that he would be calling again after six o'clock Portland time "and please have a stenographer at hand."

There could be only one interpretation of the request for a stenographer to be standing by at that hour. An announcement was to be dictated over the telephone, and there was no question in the minds of McKee and his associates that the news would concern the sale of Pacific.

It was well past six o'clock before the second call came through, and there had been opportunity to consider strategy.

Aller first offered some pleasantries about just getting back to

New York after a few days in Guatemala, where he had a vacation residence. Then the news began to come out.

He had just closed an agreement to sell Pacific's common stock to an investment group, he said, "and I wanted you (McKee) to be the first to know it."

An announcement had been prepared, Aller went on, and he would dictate it to a stenographer if she would get on the line. The news release he dictated began as follows:

"Mr. H. L. Aller, President of American Power & Light Company, stated tonight to Mr. P. B. McKee, President of Pacific Power & Light Company, that the American Company has this evening contracted to sell the common stock of Pacific Power & Light Company to B. J. Van Ingen and Company of New York acting for themselves and others. Application for approval of the sale will be made to the Securities & Exchange Commission on January 5, 1950. Mr. Aller advised Mr. McKee that the purchasers have informed American that it is their intention to evolve a plan in cooperation with the City of Portland and the Portland General Electric Company to the end that there will be a consolidation of the operations of Portland General Electric Company and Pacific Power & Light Company."

There followed two paragraphs regarding the virtues of consolidating the two companies, an idea apparently pulled out of the blue to divert attention from the hotly rumored Guy Myers position in the deal as agent for a group of PUDs. No mention was made of Myers, or of his dual role as negotiator for the stock and PUD fiscal agent.

"The sale price of the stock," the release then stated, "is to be not more than $19,500,000. A base price of $10,000,000 is to be paid in cash, and the amount in excess of the base price is to be contingent upon the sale of certain properties of the Pacific Company."

Some additional figures were given about the stated value of the common stock and surplus of Pacific, and that was it.

"I assume you will want to be the one to release the story out there," Aller then said to McKee, "and I'll appreciate it if you will arrange to get it in your papers."

McKee was boiling inwardly but his response was icy.

"It is your story, Howard," he said. "You can release it your-

197

John A. Laing (left) came to Portland from New York as a young lawyer in 1910 to help with legal details in connection with the incorporation of PP&L, and returned later in the year to devote his life to the affairs of the Company. Allan A. Smith (right) became associated with Laing in 1940 and, following the latter's death in 1953, served as counsel for a decade until his retirement from active practice.

self in your own way. I have had nothing to do with the deal, and I want my name taken out of the statement, completely out!"

Aller was taken aback. "But, Paul," he expostulated, "you're the president of the company, and I would think you would feel it appropriate that the news should come from you locally."

McKee was unmoved. He brusquely reaffirmed his stand.

"What will I do?" Aller asked. *"The Oregonian* has been after me for a month for a statement."

"Call them up, send them a telegram, do as you please," McKee replied, "and keep me out of it!"

What occurred subsequently was that Aller first telephoned *The Oregonian* and told the night city editor he had a statement to make and was going to send it by telegram. The editor urged him to give it over the telephone, right then. Aller demurred. "You're likely to get it wrong," he was quoted as saying. "You can wait for the telegram."

The Oregonian headline in the morning said: "PP&L Sale Pact Signed, Merger Eyed."

198

The story quoted in full the statement Aller had first read to McKee, but with McKee's name omitted and with one change.

The first draft, in referring to the indicated intent of the purchasers to negotiate with PGE, said without qualification: "to the end that there will be a consolidation of the operations of Portland General Electric Company and Pacific Power & Light."

Apparently this language, on reconsideration, was felt to be too specific and limited in its meaning. So there was added to the "consolidation of operations" sentence a saving clause: "in as much of the territory served by the Pacific Company as Portland General Electric Company may wish to acquire."

It was a fine line of distinction, too fine to be significant to more than a few. What it said to the people striving to save Pacific was that Myers merely looked to PGE as the most logical buyer for the Company's Portland property after he had peddled the bulk of the system to one or another of his current or prospective PUD clients.

As a practical matter, it appeared that the emphasis placed on the merger idea in the release was to mask the unpleasant fact that the American Company was proposing to sell Pacific and its rugged organization down the river.

So far as officials of PGE were concerned, there was prompt public denial of any part in the proposal.

Myers, in Seattle, "said he had no comment on Aller's announcement but added that 'it seems to speak for itself.'"

PP&L officials, when queried as they were by newspapers and interested friends, emphasized that the Company was not a party to the deal and pointed out that any contract for the sale by American of the Company's common stock would have to be on a provisional basis, subject to approval by the SEC. They also noted that transfer of the Company's properties in Portland would require approval by the city. Another point stressed was that in the normal course of events, public hearings probably would be held by the regulatory agencies having jurisdiction.

The Wall Street Journal of January 9, 1950, reported from Washington, D. C., that the Securities & Exchange Commission had set January 23 as the date for hearing on the American Company's plan.

"SEC told the holding company it wants more details about the sale proposal," the story said.

Thirteen corporations and individuals were listed in the stock purchasing group, which "is expected to sell Pacific's properties on a piecemeal basis."

It also said: "Guy C. Myers has an option to become a purchaser to the extent of 12,500 shares, or 2½%. The SEC said in its hearing order that this option must be taken up before the hearings open. If it is exercised, the number of shares to be sold to other purchasers will be reduced proportionately. . . .

"Under an agreement between the purchasing group and Mr. Myers, he will be employed to sell Pacific's properties and stock, with his compensation contingent on the amounts realized from such sales. Myers is to be paid 10% of any amounts above $10 million (excluding $300,000 in regular annual dividends on Pacific's common stock) until American receives from the purchasing group the maximum amount to be paid to it. If the purchasing group receives any additional proceeds after this final payment, Myers is to receive 19% of the next $3,000,000 and 10% of any amounts over this."

Among matters listed for consideration in the SEC hearing were questions of whether the stock sale should be exempted from competitive bidding requirements, whether the proposed sale complied with the SEC's integration order against American, whether the accounting treatment of the proposed transactions was "in accordance with sound accounting principles," and whether the purchasing group should be exempted from the Holding Company Act.

Following announcement of the hearing, many different groups interested in preserving the Company began to urge critical examination of the Myers deal.

In New York there emerged a rival investment syndicate which made American a cash offer of $15,000,000 for Pacific's common stock.

The Seattle *Post-Intelligencer* of January 18 said: "The new offer—which was revealed by Herbert Allen, New York investment banker—received the prompt endorsement of Paul B. Mc-Kee, PP&L president."

The story quoted a McKee statement: "It is my understanding that this group, if permitted to purchase the common stock of our company, intends to keep Pacific in business as a forward-looking private enterprise."

With this cash offer interjected, American was reported to have filed an amendment to its SEC application including the Allen proposal as a matter for consideration.

The Seattle *P-I* further reported that Governor Arthur B. Langlie had asked Raymond Clifford, of the Washington public service commission, to represent the state at the SEC hearing.

"Langlie said Clifford would inquire into all aspects of the Van Ingen offer particularly as they may affect rates to the Washington consuming public.

"The governor asserted he wanted Clifford at the SEC hearing because he has received information of an arrangement under which Guy C. Myers, New York and Seattle broker, might make $950,000 if the sale to the Van Ingen group is completed. . . .

"In New York Myers readily admitted he was 'in' the Van Ingen transaction on a commission basis, but added that his commission might not run over $400,000. . . .

"Meanwhile, officials of the Washington PUD Commissioners' Association, now holding their annual convention in Seattle, said they were 'tremendously interested' in the PP&L negotiations."

Writing in his "It Seems To Me" column in the Salem *Statesman* on January 19, Charles A. Sprague, publisher and former governor of Oregon, noted:

"When the SEC holds its hearing next Monday on the application of American Power & Light Co. to sell the common stock of Pacific Power & Light it will find considerable opposition to the proposal. The cities of Portland, Bend, Prineville have moved to have their opposition recorded. Utility departments for Washington and Oregon will be represented, and while no announcement has been made as to the stand each will take the inference is that they will be skeptical of the deal. SEC attorneys themselves will probably have some pointed questions to ask with reference to the apparent plan to break up the system and peddle the pieces to sundry public or private buyers, with liberal commissions to the broker, Guy C. Myers. . . ."

In a January 20 editorial the Yakima *Republic* outlined the two purchase offers that would be before the SEC. It suggested that Myers might have his problems in selling Pacific's properties in Portland to PGE, and then queried:

"What about Mr. Myers' chances of selling Pacific's second biggest chunk of properties, those in Yakima county? The people have voted 2 to 1 as recently as 1948 for continued operation of PP&L. The issue was spelled out clearly and the people knew what they were voting on, too. Mr. Myers certainly cannot claim to represent the Yakima county PUD in any negotiations to buy Pacific's common stock, much less to distribute its properties, if and when the stock is acquired.

"That leaves a scattering of Pacific's properties in smaller communities in only one of which, Wasco county, Oregon, is there an active PUD. Yet we were astonished to read recently that Mr. Myers, by implication, is representing the 'public power interests' in this deal. Mr. Myers represents Mr. Myers; and we hope the securities and exchange commission understands that even though his colleagues in the transaction may not. . . .

"If the Pacific Northwest is going to become, literally, a public power empire; if the private companies are going to be eliminated entirely from the field, then such a change should be allowed to come about in a manner and at such a pace as the people themselves indicate. The record indicates that the past notwithstanding, the Pacific company today enjoys the support of the people in the areas it serves. . . ."

The Walla Walla *Union-Bulletin* of January 21 reported that the city commission had addressed a telegram to the SEC stating: "City of Walla Walla requests preference be given sale of PP&L to group that will operate as privately owned utility over sale to syndicate that will re-sell to PUD agencies."

In a similar vein, the Walla Walla Chamber of Commerce pointed out to the SEC that voters of the area had twice turned down proposals for establishing a PUD and urged favorable consideration of plans that would keep PP&L in business. Many others made similar expressions.

On the other side of the fence, the Washington Grange News of January 21 fulminated about "Power Trust on the March" and declared the contest over PP&L to be the "battle of the century of private versus public power."

When the SEC hearing opened on January 23 there were present representatives of the principal parties, their respective attorneys and the state regulatory staff members.

With Paul McKee on the Pacific team were John A. Laing, general counsel, and Allan A. Smith, his associate.

To their great disappointment, Guy Myers was nowhere in sight, nor was he there later when a request for his appearance was voiced by the presiding examiner. The architect of the scheme for picking apart the Pacific Company had quitely vanished from public view.

Information developed in the hearing did, however, make clear the nature of the Myers plan and raised serious question about validity of the assumptions on which it was predicated.

The fact that another willing buyer was ready to bet on Pacific's future as a private enterprise, together with an impressive showing of public support for the Company from its service areas, also had an enlightening effect on sharp listeners.

Sale of Pacific's stock to purchasers who would liquidate the Company was opposed vigorously by American's parent, Electric Bond & Share Company, whose board chairman, Curtis Calder, testified during the proceedings.

The third day of the hearing was devoted to oral arguments before the full Securities & Exchange Commission.

In a three to one decision, the commission decided that the usual competitive bidding requirements need not apply to the sale of the stock but said in its opinion that the agency "will not grant the requested exemption for the sale to either the Van Ingen or Allen groups unless and until American negotiates freely under competitive conditions with any interested person, including the Van Ingen and Allen groups, for the sale of such stock."

Another hearing was set for January 31 to deal with "any amendments which may be filed reflecting the results of further negotiations for the sale of Pacific stock" undertaken "with any prospective purchasers."

As reported in the *Wall Street Journal* of January 30, the order also said: "It appears that American assumed that only purchasers interested in disposing of some of Pacific's properties to public utility districts would pay American an adequate price. . . .

"Subsequent developments indicated beyond doubt, however, that at least one other group was interested . . . and that a more favorable contract to American would probably have been secured if competitive conditions had been maintained."

When the SEC hearing reconvened on January 31, the most significant development to be revealed was a drastic reorganization of the group making the original offer to American, and the complete exclusion of Guy Myers from any association with it.

Moving into the management position of the group were A. C. Allyn & Co., Inc., and Bear, Stearns & Co. The revised offer they presented to American was $16,125,000 cash for Pacific's stock.

The rival bid was $15,525,000 from Herbert Allen & Co.

On February 3 the SEC approved the sale of Pacific's stock to the higher bidder.

The headline of a story about this decision in the Seattle *Post-Intelligencer* of February 4 said: "Pacific Power Sale O.K. Hailed by PUD Group." It quoted Frank A. Stewart, managing director of the Washington PUD Commissioners Association, as being "very pleased with the SEC decision."

Whatever pleasure the PUD leader enjoyed was considerably lessened three days later when the following statement was released by spokesmen for A. C. Allyn and Bear, Stearns:

"As representatives of the group which today purchased all the common stock of Pacific Power & Light Company from the former owner, American Power & Light Company, and after meeting with Mr. Paul B. McKee, president, and with other officers of the company, we feel that a statement should be made to the people of the Pacific Northwest now served by the company.

"First of all, the company will continue under the present management to render the best possible service to its customers at the lowest possible cost. This is, and will continue to be, the primary purpose of the company. All other considerations are secondary. We have purchased the common stock of the company because we believe in its future—we are thoroughly convinced of the future of the Pacific Northwest . . .

"We have at the moment no plans for the disposition of this stock. . . . It is our hope that ownership . . . will eventually be held to a large extent by residents of the Pacific Northwest."

Back in circulation again in Seattle after his disappearance from Washington, D. C., Guy Myers had only two words for the Seattle *Times* to quote: "No comment."

Chapter 32

Last Gasp Thrusts Fail Purpose

Two weeks after the transfer of Pacific's common stock to its new owners, leaders of the purchasing group came to Portland to confer with the Company's staff members and directors and tour the system to view the properties and get acquainted with the service areas.

J. Douglas Casey, president of A. C. Allyn & Co., Inc., and Donald C. Lillis, a partner in Bear, Stearns & Co., held a press conference at breakfast in the Arlington Club before starting out from Portland on their tour.

The *Oregon Journal* of February 20 told of Casey's comment that the group planned to offer the stock for sale to the investing public in six or nine months unless market conditions became adverse. He went on to say that under the SEC rules the group "can't own it forever" but must sell within two years.

"We're as anxious as anyone to complete this job as fast as possible," Lillis told the reporters. He also said that the new owners planned to leave the system "exactly the way it is." This was prompted by an inquiry regarding an earlier quotation ascribed to him to the effect that some of Pacific's properties might be sold before the stock was offered on the market.

The interviewers termed Lillis' denial as categorical.

"I don't think there's any chance of that at the present time," he said. "We feel this lends itself to a public distribution of stock."

The position of the managers of the investment group was frequently reiterated as they traveled over the system in company with Paul McKee, George Bragg and Don McClung.

One statement on the subject came as the aftermath of a meeting in Pendleton of representatives of 14 public power and co-op power organizations on February 20. Their announced purpose was to work toward purchase of Pacific's transmission and distribution lines "in a wide area of Eastern Oregon and Washington."

The public record does not reveal whether this meeting was designed as a publicity gesture to make it appear to investors that the Company faced an uncertain future, or had been scheduled before the public ownership forces realized that the Guy Myers program had been derailed.

The Walla Walla *Union-Bulletin* of February 25, in reporting the visit of Messrs. Casey, Lillis and associates to that city, said that Joseph P. Crosby, of the Bear, Stearns staff, had been asked about the public power meeting in Pendleton.

"We have had no conversations with any representatives of the group and we have no intention of having any conversation with them on the subject of selling any of this utility's properties," Crosby replied.

Such unequivocal statements did not, however, quench the ardor of Guy Myers, who at that very time was working desperately behind the scenes to throw a monkey wrench into any plan to make Pacific a free and independent company through the resale of its common stock to the investment public.

Three months elapsed before his machinations became public knowledge. The curtain was lifted on May 25 when the Chelan County, Washington, PUD filed a surprise condemnation suit in the U. S. District Court at Tacoma for the stated purpose of acquiring the Merwin hydroelectric plant on the Lewis River.

In its May 26, 1950, story telling of the suit, the Seattle *Times* said: "The Chelan PUD suit is looked upon as another chapter in the long fight between public and private power groups for Pacific Power & Light properties."

L. J. Richardson, president of the PUD, was quoted by the Associated Press to the effect that "The action was taken to assure an adequate supply of power to meet the district's steadily increasing demands. Merwin and Chelan dams would fit together most economically."

The Chelan dam north of Wenatchee, to which Richardson referred, was owned by Washington Water Power and the PUD had a slow-motion condemnation suit hanging over the plant, located at the outlet of Lake Chelan.

Paul McKee promptly called the PUD suit against Merwin "ridiculous" and declared: "You would think that if the Chelan PUD has the money to pay for a power plant it should go out and build one, and thus add to the region's available power supply instead of attempting to invade the existing resources of other areas."

206

He pointed out that the Merwin plant was 150 miles across a rugged stretch of mountains from the condemning district, "which already has another suit pending in court on a 40,000-kilowatt plant right in its own backyard.

"According to our information, the Chelan PUD is now get-ing all the power it needs from the Bonneville Power Administration and has a supplemental contract with the Puget Sound Power & Light Company.

"The entire output of the Merwin plant is required to meet the needs of the public served by Pacific Power & Light. If the Chelan suit is pressed, we shall defend the interests of that public with the utmost vigor, and are confident that the equity of our position will be recognized."

But the most significant and revealing information about the Chelan district's step came in a story published May 26 by the Longview *Daily News*. It said:

"Guy Myers, the former Wall St. bond dealer who promoted numerous PUDs in the Northwest and Nebraska, gave the Cowlitz PUD the first chance to acquire Merwin dam on the Lewis River by condemnation.

"Cowlitz PUD officials today said Myers approached them last February and attempted to induce them to file the same kind of a suit which was filed by the Chelan PUD yesterday. Efforts to convince the Cowlitz group that such a move would be wise were continued by Myers and his representatives through the spring, they said, but for several reasons they were not 'sold.'

"The Clark PUD and the Klickitat PUD also were approached, the Cowlitz officials were told, and they, too, turned the deal down."

Decision of the Cowlitz PUD commissioners, the Longview paper said, was based on several factors, including lack of need for additional power at the time, uncertainty about what the plant would cost in a condemnation action and the fact that Myers "would have to be paid a huge fee if the transaction went through —probably more than $100,000."

The story also noted that the cost of condemnation would be around $20,000, adding: "Then if, as Myers said might happen, the company agreed to sell out after the suit was started, this money could not be recovered."

In other words, what Myers was saying was that a condemnation against the Merwin project hopefully would "soften up" Pacific's interim stockholders and let the ubiquitous fiscal agent get back into the picture.

An editorial in the Longview *Daily News* the following day commended the Cowlitz PUD commissioners for refusing to become a party to the thrust against Merwin and went on to say:

"Myers had an obviously ulterior motive in getting a PUD to condemn the dam, which, incidentally, lies half in Cowlitz County and pays real and personal property taxes amounting to $67,470 to the county each year. (That amount may be lost to us if Chelan wins its suit.) Myers is in the money making business for Myers. He is a wealthy man and has made his money by acting as 'fiscal agent' for PUDs as they take over private utilities. He works on a percentage basis. Cowlitz County, for example, paid him $33,000 in 1940 for handling the Washington Gas & Electric Co. acquisition. The more it costs to acquire a new facility the more he gets. On the Merwin dam deal he ought to collect at least $150,000.

"But Myers is after much bigger stakes than that. His objective is the whole Pacific Power & Light Co. . . . He has not been successful heretofore in efforts to cause that whole utility to change hands in such a way that he could collect his usual fee, so he is after it piecemeal. With Merwin dam lopped off, the PP&L would be seriously weakened and therefore would be much more vulnerable for some future effort, instigated by Myers, to bring about its acquisition by some public body. . . ."

Opinion of the Company's counsel was that "said petition in eminent domain is without merit, in fact and in law." This unexcited characterization of the Chelan action seemed to be generally accepted. There was some curiosity about the Myers' maneuver, but no evident concern.

Chapter 33

Stock Offered in October, 1950

A<small>N UNEXPECTED</small> development that did set back temporarily the timing of a public stock offering by the investment group was the outbreak of war in Korea on June 25, 1950. This unsettled the market for several weeks. Meanwhile, preparations for the sale went ahead.

One step not immediately connected with a stock offering but important to the Company's construction capital requirements was the sale on June 1 of the Public Service Building to New England Mutual Life Insurance Company for $3,000,000, and the concurrent lease-back of the structure for 30 years, with two successive 10-year renewal options.

The sale of this non-utility property netted the Company a profit over book cost, and the net proceeds of the sale became available for construction. In reporting the transaction to stockholders, the Company said the estimated effect would be to increase annual net income by approximately $100,000.

The Company in April had sold $9,000,000 of 30-year bonds at the very favorable effective interest rate of 2.91% to retire a like amount of short-term loans incurred in 1948 and 1949 and the building sale put it in a good cash position.

Looking forward to the distribution of its common stock, the Company on July 18, 1950, obtained approval at a special stockholders' meeting of a 3½-to-1 split of the common shares. This proposal had received prior approval of the Federal Power Commission and the Oregon and Washington regulatory bodies. Purpose of the split was to put the stock on a lower unit price basis and enable the smaller investor to purchase "round" lots rather than "odd" lots, and thus facilitate a wider distribution of the shares, particularly in the areas served by the Company.

Restive public power adherents made two more thrusts against the Company before the summer was over. The Wasco county PUD, which had been operating a duplicate, competing electric system in The Dalles since mid-1949, announced on August 11 it

(Top) Yale site on the Lewis River, developed by the Company in 1951-52, looked like this in 1925. Picture was taken by O. L. LeFever, Northwestern Electric Company engineer. In many respects it resembles one taken by him on the same day at the Ariel site downstream. (Bottom) The 12-mile reservoir created by Merwin dam at the Ariel site reaches to the toe of Yale dam. Water stored as ice and snow on the slopes of Mt. St. Helens (left) and Mt. Adams (right) contributes importantly to the annual flow of the Lewis.

was making an offer of $1,065,000 for Pacific's properties in that area. The Dalles *Chronicle* said the PUD wanted an answer to its letter within 30 days and "if the properties could not be obtained by negotiation the PUD 'might finally' embark on condemnation proceedings."

Queried by the newspaper, Paul McKee's comment was: "I don't see how the PUD directors can expect anyone to take seriously an offer that is not backed up by actual cash or legal ability to perform."

This remark was based on the fact that the PUD had used up much of a meager 1940 bond authorization to build its duplicate lines and faced the necessity of getting voter approval of a major bond issue before it could back up talk with money.

In his formal reply, McKee said the $1,065,000 offer "is actually less than the new investment made by the Company in additions and improvements to these properties since January 1, 1948," adding that he "was forced to conclude that the offer was not made seriously or in good faith."

At almost the same time the small Hood River PUD, quiescent since the defeat in January, 1944, of Guy Myers' $175,000,000 bond scheme, called for a special election on the question of authorizing a $1,000,000 revenue bond issue. Stated purpose of the bond proposal was to purchase the properties of the Hood River Electric Cooperative and to purchase or construct additional electric distribution facilities in the area, already fully served by the Company. Citizens of the rural area comprising the district again refused to authorize a bond issue. The proposition was defeated September 19 by a vote of 1,014 to 729.

The investment market settled down after the initial uncertainties created by the fighting in Korea, and the common stockholder group decided to put the first block of their shares on the market in October.

Although the Company was not the seller, SEC regulations required it to file a registration statement and prospectus covering the transaction exactly as though these were new shares being issued and sold by the corporation itself. These documents presented detailed information about the Company's balance sheet and income statements for a five-year period and included a comprehensive description of the Company's properties and business.

211

When the registration statement was filed with the SEC at the end of August there was an immediate outcry by die-hards in the Myers' public power camp, who knew that once the stock became widely owned by the investing public the chance of a "big deal" was gone. One of their assertions was that since the holders of the stock proposed to sell it for more than its cost to them this would be "injurious to investors and rate-payers alike."

As a matter of fact, what one owner might get for outstanding shares in an arm's length sale to a willing buyer could in no way be reflected in the Company's capital structure or in the property accounts that enter into the establishment of a rate base.

An examination of factors entering into an investment analyst's appraisal of a utility stock's value might well be included in the narrative at this point, as much as a matter of general information as to shed light on the immediate transaction.

The October 11, 1950, offering included 1,078,744 of the 1,750,000 common shares outstanding after the 3½-for-one stock split. Sale of the stock was handled by a group of underwriters separate and apart from the selling group. The price was fixed at $14.00 per share, of which $13.00 went to the selling stockholders and $1.00 represented the underwriting discount or commission to the brokerage firms handling the public offering.

The shares marketed at that time represented the entire holdings of nine of the 16 members of the group that had purchased them from American, and part of the holdings of four others.

One judgment decision made jointly by the selling stockholders and the underwriters had to do with the question of how many shares of a common stock completely new in the market might be absorbed by investors at a given time.

The offering price also involved a judgment decision, and the fact that the figure was well above the amount for which American Power & Light sold the stock reflected nothing more or less than a difference in judgment about its value.

The $16,125,000 received by the American Company, in a sale it had brought upon itself, was equivalent to $9.28 a share on the stock-split basis. Under the original Myers' deal, American might have realized a maximum of approximately $11.00 a share but, on the other hand, could have ended up with as little as $6.00.

212

An examination of several tests of the value of Pacific's common shares at the time reveals some interesting things.

For example, the head of the American Company had expressed pessimism about the future of private power in the Pacific Northwest, where the possibility of losing properties through condemnation by public power agencies admittedly was present.

But suppose all of PP&L should be taken over a result of condemnation actions. What would be left for the common stockholders, or equity owners?

A rule of thumb, developed through study of actual condemnation awards in that period, was that such a suit might be expected to bring a price of four and a half or five times the annual revenues derived from the property. Pacific in 1949 had revenues of $17,464,000. Four and a half times that amount is $78,588,000.

To retire bonds, notes, preferred stock, current liabilities, etc., as of December 31, 1949, would have taken $54,142,000. The balance left for the equity owner would have been $24,446,000, or the equivalent of $13.96 per share.

Another test is on an earnings basis. Many utility common stocks have sold at a market price approximately 14 times a company's net income per share available for common.

Pacific's net for common in the 1949 calendar year was $1,-776,000, or $1.02 per share. If this is multiplied by 14, the result is $14.28, within a few cents of the calculated liquidation value.

With growth in business and favorable operating conditions, the Company had made good progress in the first six months of 1950. For the 12 months ended July 31, 1950, net earnings available for common (shown in the prospectus filed with the SEC) amounted to $1.35 per share. On this basis, the offering price of $14.00 was equivalent to no more than 10½ times earnings.

On the basis of dividend returns, dividends declared in 1950 through September and the stated intention of the management regarding subsequent payments in the year indicated a payout of 83.6 cents a share, or a return to the investor of 6% on common shares purchased at $14.00.

From all of this, it seems apparent that if the transactions as they developed were to the disadvantage of anyone it was the stockholders of American Power & Light, who had accrued to their benefit a lesser amount than subsequently was proved to be the real value of Pacific's common stock.

There were 671,256 common shares remaining in the hands of members of the original syndicate after the October, 1950, offering and of these 318,464 were sold in July, 1951. At the same time the Company sold 250,000 new shares on a 1-for-7 pro-rata rights offering basis. These shares were offered at $14.25 and the proceeds to the Company from the new issue were equivalent to $13.46 a share.

On January 22, 1952, the Company sold 200,000 additional new shares of common. The offering price of $15.875 a share yielded $15.475 net to the Company. At the same time, the 352,-464 shares remaining from the original lot also were sold to complete the disposition of that stock within the two-year period allowed by the SEC. By agreement with the underwriters, 287,792 of these previously outstanding shares were purchased as an investment at the offering price by members of the selling group in their individual capacities.

"With the completion of this transaction," it was noted in the Company's 1951 annual report, "the Company's presently outstanding 2,200,000 shares of Common Stock are owned by more than 13,300 stockholders, no one of whom owns as much as 5% of the total shares."

How the number of stockholders increased in subsequent years and the extent to which stock ownership has moved toward the West are evident from the Company's 1967 annual report:

"There were 76,793 stockholders at the end of 1967, of whom 68,954 were holders of the Company's common shares and 7,839 held preferred shares.

"More than half of the stockholders reside in the six western states where the Company operates, and 65% in states west of the Mississippi River. Approximately 15% reside in East Central States, 5% in South Atlantic states, 8% in the Middle Atlantic states and 7% in New England.

"Among individual ownerships, 30,193 are women and 18,-835 are men. The joint accounts, many of which represent husband and wife ownershiip, number 21,218. Approximately 77% of the outstanding shares are held by individuals or in joint accounts of individuals."

214

Chapter 34

New Status Stimulates Action

A NEW ERA of development began for Pacific Power & Light when it emerged from the shadow of the holding company to become an independent utility with thousands of stockholders, representing a cross-section of the investing public.

These were investors interested in the future. Prominent among them were men whose knowledge of the problems Pacific had survived served to buttress their confidence in its people.

The testimony of good friends who had rallied to the Company's support at critical moments also had helped establish the name and reputation of this newcomer in the investment market.

Favorable reception of the first offering of the Company's common stock indicated that equity capital would be availabe to help finance expansion and, as eventful 1950 drew to a close, plans for construction of a second large hydro project on the Lewis River were nearing completion.

Power requirements had pushed up so rapidly in the region that the idea advanced early in 1949 of a joint venture by Pacific, Portland General Electric and Washington Water Power on the Deschutes River was soon outgrown. Instead, each of the companies undertook its own project—PGE on the Deschutes at Pelton, Pacific at the Yale site on the Lewis and Washington Water Power at Cabinet Gorge on the Clark Fork River.

Although combined capacity of the three projects approached 400,000 kilowatts—five times the earlier objective—there was no question the power would be needed as quickly as developed.

Use of electricity by the Company's customers was increasing 9% a year, as was typical of the area. The number of customers was growing. Average residential use on the system had increased from 3,730 kwh in 1947 to 4,765 in 1950.

Installation of the second generator at the Merwin project had reduced the Company's 1950 power purchase requirements from 56% of its total load to 45%, but load growth immediately started the purchase percentage edging up again.

Supply of federal power available to the private companies of the Northwest was limited. Every distributor in the region, whether public agency or private utility, was deeply concerned about the need for decisive action on programs to expand generation.

Pacific's decision to move ahead with a project at the Yale site on the Lewis River was logical. The site was quite similar to Merwin in terrain and power potential. Much information about it was available. Geologic investigation had indicated that a fill-type dam would be best suited to the site, and the most economical.

The Company already owned the greater part of the necessary reservoir lands. The project was one on which an early construction start could be made.

The Company on January 23, 1951, filed formal application with the Federal Power Commission for license to construct the Yale project, with an initial installation of two 54,000-kilowatt generators. Operated in tandem with the Merwin plant, it was estimated that the project would generate 550,000,000 kwh annually, or a little more than two-thirds of the amount of power purchased by the Company in 1950.

License to build the project was granted by the FPC on April 25, 1951. Access roads were ready and it was possible to get a full-scale construction program in progress quickly.

The National Production Authority gave the project a defense order rating and the Defense Production Administration formally certified the project as being necessary in the national defense. The certificate of necessity made 75% of the project costs, excluding lands, subject to accelerated amortization for federal income tax purposes. This made it practicable to finance approximately one-half of the initially estimated cost by short-term obligations that would be largely retired during the five-year amortization period following completion of the plant. Remainder of the financing was done by selling bonds and more common stock.

From the defense standpoint, with the Korean war making heavy demands for military equipment, one important consideration was that the Yale plant was scheduled to be in service by November, 1952, to help relieve the tight power situation. Another point was that much of its output would come during the winter months when the flow of the Columbia was at a minimum.

The Lewis River watershed lies on the rainy west slope of the

216

Cascade Mountains, and flow of the stream is normally high during the peak power load season. Thus plants like Merwin and Yale help supplement projects on the Columbia, the flow of which is restricted during winter months when freezing weather blankets its upper tributaries in the Rocky Mountain country.

Design of the Yale project and supervision of construction was handled by Ebasco Services, Incorporated, and the principal contractor on the job was Morrison-Knudsen Company.

As the owner's representative on the job, the Company obtained the services of E. Robert de Luccia, formerly chief of the bureau of power of the Federal Power Commission, who assumed his duties in June, 1951, as manager and chief engineer of Lewis River development. He subsequently was elected a vice president of the Company and named chief engineer for the system.

The original plan was to build a conventional rock-fill dam. This was modified when it was determined that adjacent deposits of easily handled glacial conglomerate could provide a more economical and equally satisfactory structure. The deposits included a supply of ideally-sized impervious core material of a type which could be compacted most effectively when wet, thus making it possible to place core throughout the winter months.

The main dam required approximately 4,200,000 cubic yards of fill. It is 1,500 feet long at the crest, 1,300 feet wide at the base and rises 320 feet above the low point of the foundation and 264 feet above the normal level of the Merwin pool downstream.

A secondary dam, or dike, 1,600 feet long and about 45 feet high traverses a saddle between two hills adjacent to the main dam. It was built with material excavated while clearing the main dam area to bedrock.

The river diversion tunnel was completed September 16, 1951, and work started on placement of the main dam structure. The Company's September 28, 1951, letter to common stockholders reported that more than 1,700 men were then on the job "and work goes on around the clock, seven days a week."

The same letter spoke of the tight power supply situation in the region and noted the possibility that the Company would have to generate and purchase large amounts of steam-produced energy to carry its load. Then existing steam plants in the area were normally used only to carry short duration peak loads and for

217

Yale project on the Lewis River was just getting well started when PP&L's Board of Directors met at construction headquarters September 14, 1951. Pictured from left are Walter S. Babson, Portland; Josiah Richards, Spokane; Arthur L. Fields, Portland; Clarence Penland, Pendleton; W. M. Marshall, Spokane; Lyman J. Bunting, Yakima; A. W. Peters, Hood River; Sherman Lovell, Astoria; J. R. Roberts, Redmond; Henry G. Lambert, New York; E. C. Sammons, Portland; Paul B. McKee, Company president; and John A. Laing, general counsel.

emergency standby, it was pointed out, and their continuous use would increase operating costs substantially.

"Since the Company's rates are based upon the normal availability of low-cost hydroelectric power," the letter said, "application has been made to the Oregon and Washington regulatory authorities for temporary surcharges to cover the actual excess costs resulting from abnormal use of steam generating plants."

It was noted that other electric companies of the area had made similar applications for relief.

The November 1, 1951, letter to preferred stockholders (whose quarterly dividend payment dates then differed from the common) reported that timely rains had removed the immediate threat of a serious power shortage in the region.

But the letter included a note of caution. "Power loads of the region are so heavy in relation to the available generating capacity, however, that if cold, dry weather occurs at any time during the winter season ahead, it may become necessary for the Defense

218

Electric Power Administration to put a curtailment program into effect. An order setting up steps to be taken to meet varying degrees of power shortage was issued by DEPA on September 20, and the electric systems of the region are prepared to cooperate in the general effort to meet whatever conditions might develop with the least possible hardship to users of electricity."

Referring to the Company's applications for relief from possible steam power costs, the letter said the Oregon Public Utilities Commissioner had issued an order providing that if excess costs were incurred the Company could then apply for compensating surcharges and, upon verification of the need, put such charges into effect. Action by the Washington Public Service Commission was held in abeyance, pending developments in the situation.

As part of its power supply planning program, the Company had for a number of months been negotiating with the Bonneville Power Administration for new contract arrangements, and in October, 1951, an agreement was reached with BPA.

The Company said in its 1951 annual report: "While these contracts are subject to the then current commitments to industries and the preference provisions of the Bonneville Act, they are nevertheless an important step in the development of businesslike relations between the federal government as a power wholesaler and the five major electric companies operating within the Bonneville Power Administration transmission area."

Effective October 1, 1951, the contracts were for an initial and minimum period of five years and were described as assuring the companies' customers a reasonable share of the additional firm power made available for sale from federal projects "now under construction or to be built." They provided for yearly extensions made at least three years in advance of the expiration date of the current contract, "so that there will always be a minimum period of three years in which to carry on further negotiations for an extension or to provide a new source of supply."

The 1951 annual report also noted "the loss during the past year of two distinguished members of the organization, both of whom had been prominently identified with the Company since its establishment in 1910.

"Lewis A. 'Tam' McArthur, retired vice president of the Company and for 20 years its general manager, died November 8,

1951, after a long illness. He was 68 years old. McArthur joined the organization March 1, 1910, prior to the Company's formal incorporation, and became general manager in 1917, a post which he held until 1937. He was a vice president of the Company from 1922 until his retirement in 1948, and a member of the Board of Directors from 1922 to 1947. In addition to his great contributions to the development of the Company, McArthur earned wide recognition as a geographer, map authority and historian. His 'Oregon Geographic Names' is a standard reference work. His vigorous and colorful personality was projected into many other useful fields, including long and active participation in the advancement of reclamation.

"Josiah Richards, whose continuous service on the Company's Board of Directors since 1910 made him its senior member, died in Spokane, Washington, on December 10, 1951, at the age of 70. Throughout the 41 years he was a director of the Company, he took an unflagging interest in its affairs, and his buoyant spirit and wise counsel gained him affection and respect."

The Company *Bulletin* of September, 1951, carried a feature story about another pioneer staff member. It said:

"The longest career made under the banner of Pacific Power & Light Company was attained September 1 when George L. Myers, assistant secretary and assistant treasurer, exercised an option to take early retirement under the Company's retirement plan. He had been with the Company for more than 41 years."

Recital of 1951 events would be incomplete without mention of the climactic battle in Guy C. Myers' campaign to make a public ownership deal with American Power & Light Company for its remaining electric subsidiary in the Pacific Northwest, Washington Water Power.

The scheme was to use three Washington PUDs, representing less than 7% of the Spokane firm's customers, as the vehicle to acquire its entire system in Washington and Idaho.

While legislation to bar such a PUD maneuver was locked up in bitter conflict in the 1951 session of the Washington legislature, the Idaho legislature passed a law prohibiting out-of-state power districts from owning property in that state.

*One of 70,000-horsepower water wheels, with wicket gate assembly, being
lowered into place at the Yale project in 1952. Complete with shaft
and rotor, each generator assembly weighed 325 tons.*

An attempt subsequently was made to get around this obstacle
through an alleged "non-profit corporation."

The PP&L *Bulletin* of April, 1952, in reviewing the background of the Washington Company's escape, said: "A storm of
public protest followed disclosure of the scheme in December,
1951, and the SEC ordered a hearing. This was halted briefly by a
temporary injunction from the ninth U. S. circuit court of appeals.

"Subsequent decision by the court that the proposed hearing
was within the powers of the SEC was followed by capitulation
of the AP&L directorate."

The American company then filed with the SEC a proposal to
distribute WWP's common stock to American's individual stockholders, and it was via this route that Washington Water Power
reached the independent status earlier attained by Pacific.

In the case of Portland Gas & Coke, which had no officers in
common with PP&L after 1949, American in 1953 distributed its
stock holdings in that company to American's shareholders.

221

Chapter 35

Dam On Schedule, But Not Fall Rains

PACE OF CONSTRUCTION on the Yale project in 1952 reflected the urgency of the region's power situation. Work on the dam itself proceeded at top speed throughout the winter months and early in July the last of 4,200,000 cubic yards of fill topped out the structure.

Gates of the diversion tunnel were closed August 1 and the reservoir was expected to reach operating level by November 1, "assuming median water conditions."

But water conditions proved to be most unfavorable as the Power Pool approached the reservoir drawdown period. From April 1 to August 31, precipitation at the Portland weather station, for example, was only 52% of normal.

September brought only three-tenths of an inch of rain, and in the entire month of October there was only slightly more than seven-tenths of an inch recorded at Portland.

At the end of November, precipitation for the three-month period amounted to only 25% of normal and stream flows in the pool area had dropped steadily to duplicate almost exactly the pattern of the same period in the critical 1936-37 water year.

Steam plants began operating on an energy basis about September 1. A total of 395,000 kilowatts in interruptible loads, largely at aluminum plants, was dropped by September 8.

As reported in the Northwest Power Pool Operations Review for 1952-53: "The West Group Operating Committee on October 27 recommended to the executives that firm load be reduced by 100 to 150 mw starting on November 17, to improve the prospects of carrying the remaining firm load through the balance of the storage season. As a result, DEPA curtailment Order EO-4A and Directive No. 2 was issued on October 29 calling for a 10% cut in firm loads of customers in the West Group who would normally use in excess of 8,000 kwh per week, the curtailment to become effective on November 17. In addition, it called for voluntary load curtailment by other West Group customers."

On the curtailment date, natural flow at the pool's hydro installations was approximately 1,000,000 kilowatts below median, and had dropped 500,000 kilowatts more by the time early December rains finally brought a slight measure of relief.

Excess costs to Pacific as a result of generating and purchasing extraordinary amounts of steam power had then passed $1,-100,000 and continued to accumulate through December.

With the Lewis River seriously affected by the long drouth, filling of the Yale reservoir was slow. By November 1, however, target date for testing the first generator, the reservoir level was sufficient to give the unit a trial run. This event came only 17 months after the beginning of full scale construction.

After 45 days of operation, the unit was shut down for inspection and it was discovered that cracks had developed in the penstock tunnel. Subsequent investigation determined this to be the result of small and unpredictable subsidence of the surrounding rock structure, and a decision was made to line the entire length of both penstocks with steel.

Meanwhile, the December rains that had checked the drastic decline in stream flows were followed by a deluge which, in the first two weeks of January, added 2,000,000 kilowatts of flow to the rivers of the area and created flood conditions in many places.

Mandatory curtailment of power loads was suspended on January 13. The sudden transformation of the power outlook for the remainder of the storage season made it possible for the steam power plants to be returned to their normal function of carrying short-time peak loads and providing emergency standby.

The Company's excess steam power costs at that point amounted to $1,470,000. With regulatory approval, surcharges to recover this amount over a period of months had been instituted with December billings. These charges were ended May 28, 1953. The fact that surcharge authorization could not be obtained until after much of the excess expense had been incurred meant that it took several months after the end of the power shortage to recoup.

The task of lining the Yale penstock tunnels was pushed throughout the spring and summer of 1953, and the No. 1 unit went on the line September 5. Two months later the No. 2 unit went into service.

With a full reservoir, the two generators proved to be capable of producing 133,000 kilowatts continuously, or 25% more than their nameplate rating of 54,000 kilowatts each.

With the Merwin plant, this gave the Company a peak capability of 235,000 kilowatts from the Lewis River.

As a sidelight on the Yale penstock problem and the ensuant loss of power production, the Company had in effect a use and occupancy insurance policy on the project and claims aggregating $1,050,000 were filed with the insurers on December 8, 1953. Payment was resisted by the five insurance companies involved, whereupon the Company went to court. A settlement in the amount of $650,000 ultimately was arrived at in June, 1956.

The Company's 1953 annual report noted: "New power installations put into service during the past year have eased the power supply situation in the Pacific Northwest, and it is estimated that projects now under construction will carry the region's steadily growing energy requirements through the next five years. These include three large multiple-purpose dams on the Columbia River being constructed by the U. S. Corps of Engineers, which will have a total installed generating capacity of approximately 3,000,000 kilowatts. One, the 980,000-kilowatt McNary Project, began producing power late in 1953 and additional generators will be placed in operation during 1954.

"The power load of the region has increased to such magnitude, however, that the maintenance of normal growth requires the addition of approximately 400,000 kilowatts annually to generating capacity. For this reason, all the principal utilities are looking actively to plans to initiate new projects that would be ready . . . when plants now under construction will have had their output absorbed. . . .

"Your Company and four other electric utilities of the region have joined in the filing of a preliminary permit with the Federal Power Commission to investigate the feasibility of developing 536,000 kilowatts of power at the Bruces Eddy and Penny Cliffs sites on branches of the Clearwater River. . . . These projects would provide substantial flood control benefits as well as power generation, and are proposed to be developed in harmony with the announced 'partnership' policy of the national administration.

"Participating with your Company in the joint venture are Mountain States Power, Portland General Electric, The Washing-

224

ton Water Power and The Montana Power companies. Served by the group are approximately 800,000 electric customers, representing nearly 50% of all power users in Oregon, Washington, northern Idaho and Montana. They . . . estimate a joint need for between 150,000 and 200,000 kilowatts of new capacity annually."

The "partnership" policy referred to had been enunciated by the Eisenhower administration when it took office in 1953. In essence, it proposed that the federal government join hands with non-federal utilities in the construction of desirable river developments where this might be feasible and appropriate.

For example, a private company or a local public power system might finance and construct power generating facilities at a federal flood control dam. The formula proposed that all of the reimbursable costs that would be assigned to power if the entire project were built with government money would be borne by the local partner. Only that portion of the total project cost assigned to such non-reimbursable public benefits as flood control and navigation improvement would need to come from federal appropriations. The hope was that this division of capital costs would make possible the acceleration of river development.

The "partnership" idea, however, bogged down in Congress. The proposal was attacked by anti-utility elements as a "giveaway" and explanations of its equity were shouted down. Interestingly, the idea of joint endeavors on the part of non-federal agencies was to be responsible later for large developments on the Columbia River.

With respect to the Bruces Eddy and Penny Cliffs sites, the latter was shelved because of opposition by conservationists and questions about relative costs and benefits. A dam at the Bruces Eddy site was authorized later for construction by the U. S. Engineers as a flood control and power project, and was named "Dworshak" in recognition of a former senator from Idaho.

The Company's 1953 report also spoke of a new 20-year contract with Bonneville Power Administration, which was characterized as "a constructive step toward the development of a more equitable power sales policy on the part of the federal government." This was one of several similar contracts entered into by BPA with the electric companies of the area in that year.

A construction project important to Wallowa Valley electric

users was completed by the Company in August, 1953. This was a 39-mile section of 66,000-volt transmission between Elgin and Enterprise to end that area's primary dependence upon the two small hydro plants and the diesel installation, with total capability of about 3,000 kilowatts.

The new line was able to deliver up to 5,000 kilowatts from outside sources. It connected at Elgin with California-Pacific Utilities Company, whose ties with Idaho Power to the east gave access to the resources of the eastern group utilities in the Northwest Power Pool. When the project was announced, the Company *Bulletin* noted that completion of the Bonneville Power Administration's transmission line to La Grande "will provide an additional source of supply for the northeastern Oregon area when the present tight power situation in the western section of the pool is solved by construction of additional generating plants."

Initiated in the spring of 1953 was an employee common stock purchase plan, giving employees the opportunity to buy from 10 to 200 shares of the Company's common stock at 95% of the average bid and ask price for the preceding 30-day period. Payment could be made over 36 months, using payroll deductions.

Taking advantage of the initial offering were 297, or about 25%, of the Company's regular employees, who subscribed for 13,076 shares at a price of $19.30 per share. A subsequent 2-for-1 stock split made this equivalent to 26,000 shares. Dollar amount involved was $246,000.

Seventeen years later, succeeding offerings had pushed the total of shares subscribed to 526,145 and the total employee capital investment in the Company to $9,883,381.

In 1953, as in every year, there were sad notes, too. The April-May, 1953, issue of *The Bulletin* reported: "John A. Laing, the man who was always at hand during the stormiest periods in Pacific Power & Light Company history, died May 12 at his summer home at Weddeburn on the Oregon coast. . . .

"A public-spirited citizen, his activities in community welfare were enormous. From 1937 to 1941, he was president of the Portland Symphony Society; in 1930, president of the Portland Rose Festival; secretary of the Multnomah Civic Stadium Association; member of the Oregon advisory commission on liquor control in 1933; a member of the state highway advisory commis-

Yale project on Lewis River was first of series of new plants undertaken by Company after gaining independent status in 1950. Mt. St. Helens overlooks the nine-mile reservoir. Peak capability is 133,000 kw.

sion on promotion of tourist travel; president of the Portland planning commission from 1931 to 1935; and a trustee and chairman of the board of regents of Reed College.

"Well-known nationally as a utility lawyer, Laing had served as general counsel for Pacific Power & Light for the past 42 years. He was also general counsel for Portland Gas & Coke Company and the former Northwestern Electric Company. During Pacific Power's fight in 1950 to gain independent status, Laing distinguished himself for his handling of the legal matters at hearings in Washington, D. C.

"Laing came to Portland in 1910 as a young attorney on a special legal assignment in connection with the formation of Pacific Power & Light. In December of the same year he returned to Portland permanently to become counsel for the Company.

"In February, 1911, he was named to the Company's board of directors and then in 1918 became vice president, too. When Northwestern Electric Company became affiliated with Pacific in 1925, Laing assumed similar duties of general counsel, vice president and director of that organization. He also was associated with Portland Gas & Coke Company in the same capacities.

227

"Under terms of the public utility holding company act of 1935 prohibiting interlocking directorates of operating utilities, Laing in 1936 resigned the Pacific directorate and vice presidency although continuing as general counsel. . . .

"Friends who knew him intimately found his knowledge on a great variety of subjects to be somewhat amazing. He required little sleep, and frequently did the equivalent of a second day's work after dinner. . . .

"A native of Albany, New York, he was born on November 14, 1883. After completing work at Dartmouth College, he entered Columbia University, where he received his law degree in 1908. He was only two years out of Columbia when he was sent to Portland in 1910. . . ."

To these words might well be added a further note from the Company's 1953 annual report: "Mr. Laing played a great part in the development of the Company to its present status as a respected public service organization. His keen mind, steady judgment and his resolute courage and integrity made him a tower of strength in the Company and in the community. We shall miss greatly his reassuring presence as a trusted advisor on all matters relating to the Company and its organization, and will always hold him in affectionate memory as a true and kindly friend."

Chapter 36

Mountain States Power Merged

"**M**OST OUTSTANDING event in the Company's record of progress during 1954 was the merger of Mountain States Power Company with and into Pacific Power & Light Company," were the opening words of Pacific's annual report for that year.

"Addition of the Mountain States properties and service areas to your Company's system greatly broadened its operating base and gave it greater diversity and expanded opportunity for business development throughout a prosperous and rapidly-growing territory. The merger combined two vigorous organizations to increase their ability to meet well a large public service responsibility and facilitate the system developments required to keep pace with the area growth."

This comment about the merger proved to be well founded, and conservative.

Negotiations looking toward a possible consolidation of the Albany, Oregon, based company with Pacific had begun during 1953. The companies jointly had employed Stone & Webster Service Corporation and Ford Bacon & Davis, Inc., engineering and business consulting organizations, to study the business and operations of the two companies and independently and separately arrive at and report their conclusions with respect to a proper ratio of exchange of the common stocks in the event of a merger.

In consideration of these studies and other pertinent factors, an "Agreement and Act of Merger" was entered into by the boards of directors on January 8, 1954, subject to necessary approvals.

The agreement provided that one share of Mountain States common would be exchanged for nine-tenths of a share of Pacific's. The $50 par value preferred of Mountain States was to be exchanged on a two-for-one basis with the $100 par value preferred of Pacific.

Adoption of the merger agreement required a two-thirds favorable vote of stockholders of Mountain States and a majority vote of all of Pacific's shares, including a majority of the total number of shares of Pacific's 5% preferred stock voting as a class.

The proposal received almost unanimous endorsement by the stockholders of both companies and, with state and federal regulatory approval, the merger was consummated on May 21, 1954.

Z. E. Merrill, chairman of the Mountain States board and long head of that utility, became chairman of the Pacific board. A. W. Trimble, president, was named a vice president of PP&L.

The merger papers included a by-law amendment increasing the number of directors of Pacific from 15 to 21 and provided for the election of the following members of the former Mountain States board to that of Pacific:

H. R. Baxter, Philadelphia, Pennsylvania; Harry H. Campbell, Kalispell, Montana; John Ferguson, Coos Bay, Oregon; J. H. Irvine, Lebanon, Oregon; W. D. Johnston, Casper, Wyoming; Z. E. Merrill, Albany, Oregon; David S. Soliday, Philadelphia, Pennsylvania; and A. W. Trimble, Albany, Oregon.

Mountain States Power was organized by Standard Gas & Electric Company December 13, 1917, and began operations on January 1, 1918, when properties formerly operated by Northern Idaho & Montana Power Company and its subsidiary, Oregon Power Company, were put into the new corporation. Predecessor companies in this grouping included Flathead Valley Water Power Co., Northern Electric Co., Pend d'Oreille Electric Co., Coos Bay Gas & Electric Co., Big Bend Light & Power Co. and Willamette Valley Co.

From 1918 to 1945, acquisitions made by Mountain States in Oregon included Coast Power Company, Beaver Improvement & Power Co., Jefferson municipal system, Aumsville Electric Co., Lebanon Electric Light & Water Co., Cloverdale Electric Co., Cottage Grove Electric Co., Creswell Power Co., Sublimity Light & Power Co., Scio municipal, Foster Electric Co., Stayton Light & Power Co., and Mill City Light & Power Co. In Montana the company acquired the Columbia Falls Telephone Co. and Libby Electric Light & Water Co.

Systems acquired in Wyoming in that period included Natrona Power Co., Midwest Public Service Co., Thermopolis Northwest Electric Co., Northwest Transmission Co., Cowley Gas Co., Glenrock municipal, Buffalo Northwest Electric Co., Shoshoni

230

A good natured crowd posed for the photographer who took this picture on First Street in Albany, Oregon, in 1910. Now in PP&L service territory, the city got its first electric service in 1892 from a combined steam and hydro plant. The hydro unit was supplied with water from a canal dug in the 1870's from the South Santiam River at Lebanon across the valley floor to Albany 10 miles away. It still serves as a domestic water source. Photo is from the files of the Oregon Historical Society.

Light & Power Co., Wyoming Hydro Electric Co., Douglas Light & Power Co. and Oil Fields Power Co.

Common stock of Mountain States Power was owned for many years by its parent company, Standard Gas & Electric. Problems growing out of the depression years necessitated the presentation of a reorganization plan to the Securities and Exchange Commission. This plan, as amended, was approved by the SEC on January 25, 1940. About 42.5% of the new common stock then issued went to holders of Mountain States preferred along with shares of a new preferred, and Standard Gas & Electric received 56.4% of the new common, which it disposed of in 1947 through a public offering. The holding company in the same year liquidated its common stock interest in The California Oregon Power Company, acquired about 20 years earlier.

Oregon communities supplied with electricity by Mountain States at the time of merger included Albany, Coos Bay, Coquille, Corvallis, Cottage Grove, Dallas, Independence, Junction City, Lebanon, Lincoln City, Mill City, Myrtle Point, North Bend,

231

Philomath, Powers, Springfield, Stayton, Sweet Home and Tilla-mook.

In Idaho the company served in the Sandpoint area, and in Montana it operated in Kalispell, Whitefish, Columbia Falls and Libby. Wyoming cities served included Casper, Worland, River-ton, Lander, Thermopolis, Buffalo, Douglas, Greybull, Lovell and Glenrock.

It had water systems in Albany, Independence, Lebanon, Mill City and Springfield, Oregon, and Libby and Bigfork, Montana.

Mountain States had grown rapidly from 1941 to 1953, with revenues increasing from $4,718,000 to $15,577,000. Number of customers had increased from 75,404 in 1941 to 131,685 in 1953. Utility plant expanded from $20,008,000 to $52,300,000.

A great part of the added plant investment went into distribu-tion facilities following the end of World War II. Growth in power load had been met by increased power purchases. Total gen-erating capacity in company plants was only 44,394 kilowatts, divided among 12 steam installation, 14 hydro plants and seven internal combustion units. These provided about one-eighth of the system's power requirements. Seven-eighths of its supply was ob-tained by purchases from The California Oregon Power Company, Bonneville Power Administration, the U. S. Bureau of Reclama-tion, the U. S. Flathead Irrigation Project, electric companies in the Northwest Power Pool and from a number of sawmills.

Pacific Power, with the Yale project in full service, had 285,230 kilowatts of generating capacity and was producing half of its total requirements. More importantly, from the standpoint of the merger, the peaking capability of Pacific's installations made possible more efficient utilization of power purchases.

Mountain States derived about 60% of its $15,577,000 annual revenues from operations in 71 communities in the Willamette Valley and on the Oregon Coast. About 25% of its business came from 23 communities in Wyoming, chiefly in the Casper and the Wind River and Big Horn Basin areas, and the remainder from the Flathead Valley in western Montana and from electric distri-bution properties in the Sandpoint, Idaho, district.

In addition to 112,000 electric customers, the Mountain States merger brought 11,000 water customers and 8,500 telephone

Oregon Agricultural College (now Oregon State University) had been enjoying electric service nearly 20 years when this 1910 picture was taken of the campus. First electric lights in Corvallis dated back to 1889. A transmission line from Albany was built in 1906 to boost the community's power supply. OSU engineering students began getting practical training in the field of electricity in 1891 and over the years the institution has produced many eminent electrical engineers. (Photo courtesy Oregon Historical Society)

accounts, the latter in the Kalispell district. Also acquired in the transaction was Linn County Telephone Company, a Mountain States subsidiary, which was serving 6,620 telephone customers in parts of the utility's electric service area in Linn County, Oregon.

Pacific at the time of the merger had annual revenues of approximately $21,772,000 and 153,000 electric customers.

Utility plant investment of Mountain States was $54,115,000. The consolidation brought Pacific's total plant figure at the end of 1954 to $191,106,000.

Consolidated revenues in 1954 amounted to $39,952,000, 8.2% more than the previous year.

Number of active employees in the Company increased from 1,259 at the end of 1953 to 2,317 at the end of 1954. All employee benefits, such as group life insurance and retirement plans, were extended in full to the men and women who came into the Company as a result of the Mountain States merger.

At the end of the merger year, the Company had a total of 284,716 utility customers compared with 154,022 in 1953.

233

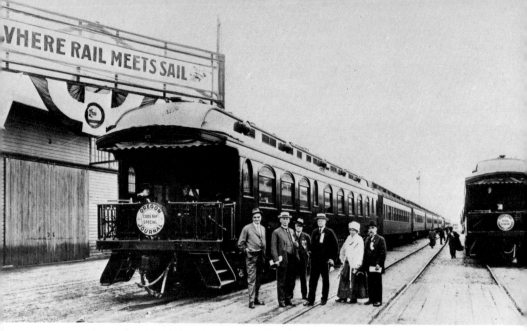

*Inauguration of rail service to Coos Bay in August, 1916, brought
two special trains from Portland. The rail trip took 12 hours. Citizens of
North Bend and Coos Bay, then known as Marshfield, staged a three-day
jubilee. Electric service in the coast community was then supplied
by the Oregon Power Company, succeeded in 1918 by Mountain
States Power and in 1954 by PP&L. (Photo courtesy
Oregon Historical Society.)*

The annual report noted that at the November, 1954, general
election, voters in two Oregon areas served by the Company had
rejected public ownership proposals "and in another area voted to
dissolve a People's Utility District organized in 1940."

Residents of the North Lincoln County communities served
by the Company on the Oregon coast voted nearly four to one
against the proposed annexation of that territory to a neighboring
PUD. This was the fifth time that PUD proposals had been rejected in the area.

Also on the Oregon coast a proposed $2,700,000 PUD bond
issue was defeated in Tillamook County by a vote of 3,694 to
2,535. A major issue in the campaign was the possible use of the
bond issue to condemn the Company's properties in the district.

In Union County, Oregon, adjacent to two of the Company's
operating districts, the voters balloted nearly two to one to dissolve an existing PUD, which earlier in the year had twice sought
unsuccessfully to obtain approval of a $5,500,000 bond issue for
the purpose of establishing itself in business.

234

Chapter 37

Glenrock Gets New Payroll It Needed

EXPANSION of the Company's service area with the Mountain States merger added greatly to Pacific's power supply responsibilities. Happily, it also opened up a new field of power development—coal-fired steam generation—that was to play an important role in the Company's future progress.

In Wyoming, Mountain States had long been a good customer of the U. S. Bureau of Reclamation. Revenues from the sale of power produced at irrigation reservoirs on the North Platte River played a major role in making these projects feasible. As long as such power was available, it was in the common interest to put it to productive use.

But by 1954 the amount of USBR power available in Wyoming for sale to private electric companies had shrunk to the point where new sources of supply soon had to be found, and Pacific assigned a high priority rating to the studies Mountain States had under way.

Sections of Wyoming are underlaid with vast deposits of coal, and construction of a coal-fired steam generating plant was clearly indicated. Location of the most favorable site for such a plant, however, was not as simple as the decision to build one.

To hold down fuel transportation costs, the plant had to be close to the coal supply. Further, the coal deposit should lend itself to economical strip mining, and a supply of cooling water had to be available for the plant.

To top it off, this combination of siting requirements should be at a point from which power could be transmitted economically to system load centers.

The Company's decision to build a steam plant in Wyoming, to be ready for service in 1958, was made known early in 1955, before a site had been determined. Later in the year, plans were announced for construction of a 40-mile, 161,000-volt transmission line between Billings, Montana, and the site of the USBR's proposed Yellowtail dam on the Big Horn River north of the

235

Wyoming-Montana border. At Billings the line was to connect with facilities of The Montana Power Company and at Yellowtail with a Bureau of Reclamation line under construction between that point and Lovell, Wyoming. Through these connections, power from the Montana Power system could be brought into the Wyoming area to tide over its requirements. Power wheeling arrangements with the USBR were part of the program.

A survey of the more promising steam plant sites was still under way in the fall of 1955 when a request for consideration came from the town of Glenrock, about 30 miles east of Casper.

Glenrock grew up beside a coal mine astride the Old Oregon Trail. Coal from Glenrock in the early days went to fuel the stoves of Nebraska settlers. More went to railroad customers. But shortly after 1900 water problems in the shaft mine combined with market problems to close down the mining operation.

Then came the development of an oil field in the area and the establishment of a refinery, which for many years provided an important local payroll. But by 1955 the refinery had become obsolete. Oil production of the area began moving to more modern and efficient refineries elsewhere, and Glenrock was facing the loss of a payroll that meant much to a town of 1,200 population.

Citizens moved to meet the challenge by forming a small committee and raising several hundred dollars to go out and seek a new industry. Pacific Power was at the head of their list.

To urge consideration of the Glenrock area as a power plant site, a trip to PP&L headquarters in Portland was planned and, through R. H. Sallee, the Company's local representative, an appointment was sought with Paul McKee.

McKee sent back word that their trip wasn't necessary. Instead, he would come to Glenrock to see them.

On a Sunday morning in October, 1955, McKee and several of the Company's Wyoming staff met with the local committee in the Glenrock city hall. The editor of the weekly paper was there as one of the local group. So was a garage proprietor whose father had once worked in the old coal mine. Another committee member ran a lumber yard. And so on.

They spoke warmly of the community's known qualifications as a power plant site—ample land, adequate cooling water from the North Platte River, good rail and highway transportation and

W. D. "Dave" Johnston, long a leader in the Wyoming power industry, turned the first shovel of earth at the June 30, 1956, groundbreaking for the coal-fired plant bearing his name. Paul B. McKee, PP&L president, cheered the effort. A fourth unit at the plant near Glenrock will increase capacity to 750,000 kw in 1972.

proximity to power load centers. But to one key question no definitive answer could be given: "How about a fuel supply?"

The citizens could only express their personal confidence that there was a lot of coal under the grazing lands north of Glenrock.

"We've seen outcroppings," they said. "It's never really been investigated but we think it would be worth a look."

The sincerity and enthusiasm of the group was not to be denied. "Well," McKee said, "if you have so much confidence in the area and are so willing to work for your community, the least we can do is send a geologist into the field to make a reconnaissance, and we'll do that promptly."

Within a short time, the geologist put on the job reported the area did look promising. He recommended exploration by core drilling, so drill crews were lined up to probe the formations.

The drill cores revealed extensive coal seams 25 to 40 feet thick, lying close enough to the surface to be worked easily by the open pit method. Within a few months enough coal had been proved out to supply as much as 1,000,000 kilowatts of power generating capacity for a 50-year period.

237

*Explorations started by the Company in 1955 at the behest of
hopeful citizens of Glenrock proved up more than 200,000,000 tons of coal
in a field only a few miles north of the Wyoming community.
Coal seams range up to 40 feet in thickness. Another comparable
field has since been located in the same section of the state.*

In April, 1956, only six months after that Sunday morning conference in the Glenrock city hall, PP&L's decision to locate a 100,000-kilowatt plant on a site near Glenrock was announced. Ground was broken June 30, 1956, and the plant was named in honor of Dave Johnston, Company vice president and director and a long-time leader in the Wyoming power industry.

At the dedication of this unit on December 20, 1958, the Company announced its plan to go forward with construction of a second unit of the same size.

In 1962 construction was started on a 220,000-kilowatt third unit. It was dedicated September 11, 1964, to bring capacity of the station to 420,000 kilowatts and annual payroll associated with the development to more than $1,000,000.

In 1968 plans were announced for a 330,000-kw fourth unit, which in 1972 will increase plant capacity to 750,000 kilowatts and total capital investment to more than $146,000,000.

Unit fuel costs at Glenrock are among the lowest in the country, and the Company has never ceased to be grateful that citizens of the community had the initiative to get out and do something for their home town.

238

Chapter 38

Swift Hydro Project Begun in 1956

DEVELOPMENT of more hydroelectric capacity on the Lewis River at the Swift Creek site, above the head of the Yale reservoir, was under intensive study throughout 1955 and, in December, application was filed with the Federal Power Commission for license to construct a 250,500-kilowatt project at an estimated cost of $58,700,000. Capacity was later increased to 274,000.

The plan called for a fill-type dam made of glacial material such as was used at Yale. Height of the structure is 512 feet, making it one of the highest of its type in the world. Two thousand feet long at the crest and 2,100 feet thick at the base, the dam required 16,000,000 cubic yards of fill. The reservoir, 12 miles long, provides approximately 450,000 acre feet of useful storage. Rated capacity of the three generators is 204,000 kilowatts and peak capability is 268,000.

To utilize the fall of the river between the dam site and the Yale reservoir, a 3½ mile canal was designed to carry tailwater from the Swift generators along a contour line to a point where it could be dropped 128 feet through a second power house to produce 70,000 kilowatts.

It was estimated that the project would produce about 928,-000,000 kilowatt-hours annually, including energy output added at the Merwin and Yale plants downstream.

The Company's 1955 annual report, dated March 14, 1956, said: "Early approval of the license application would make it possible for construction to be started in the spring of 1956, and the plant would be in service by the end of 1958. The Office of Defense Mobilization has issued a certificate designating Swift as a defense project, making the project eligible for rapid amortization of 65% of its depreciable costs for tax purposes."

A restrained further comment was: "Public Utility District No. 1 of Cowlitz County, Washington, which adjoins part of the Lewis River, has indicated by protest to the Federal Power Commiission that it wishes opportunity to share in the output of the

Swift project, and discussions of possible plans of participation are in progress between the Company and the district."

An early start of construction was imperative if the plant was to be completed within the tight time schedule dictated by the area's power needs as well as by requirements of the defense certificate. The district was not unaware of this and, in what its officials termed a move "to protect their position," a condemnation suit (later withdrawn) against both the Merwin and Yale projects was filed by the PUD on March 28, 1956.

Speaking for PP&L, Paul McKee characterized the suit as being without merit and emphasized the urgency of prompt construction of the project.

Among proposals put forward by the PUD in early conferences was that it take over Merwin and Yale and build Swift itself, selling the combined output to the Company on a long-term basis. This idea received no consideration, but vigorous discussions were pressed looking to a resolution of the potential problem of construction delay.

Before the end of April sufficient progress had been made toward an understanding to have the parties join in a request that the FPC issue a pre-license construction permit, which was granted.

On May 1 heavy equipment and workers from the Guy F. Atkinson Company moved into the dam site and began prelimiinary work. The timetable called for completion of a 32-foot-diameter river diversion tunnel before the start of heavy fall rains.

One of the alternative proposals made by the Company to the PUD was that it might undertake to build and own the No. 2 powerhouse, selling the power to Pacific until such time as the district might have need of it. The Company also indicated its willingness, on an interim basis, to use and pay for an allocation of 25,000 kilowatts from the Priest Rapids and Wanapum projects that the district had obtained from the Grant County PUD.

The idea of owning the 70,000-kilowatt No. 2 plant gained acceptance by the district. An agreement was worked out for participation in an integrated development plan, with the Company to pay 74% of the total cost of the entire project and the district to pay 26%, with the power output similarly proportioned. The contract also provided that the Company would purchase at cost

Started in 1956, Swift dam had a base nearly 1,400 feet wide in October, 1957. A fleet of huge haul trucks looked like toys as they scurried about conveying 16,000,000 cubic yards of glacial fill material from nearby borrow pits. The finished dam rises 512 feet from its foundations.

all the district's allocation of power from the project until such time as required by the district, with three years notice of any withdrawal of power. A basis for joint participation in possible up-river developments was also outlined.

The agreement was signed July 16, and the Company and the district joined in requesting the FPC to license Swift No. 1 to Pacific and No. 2 to Cowlitz. This plan received approval.

To provide additional peaking capability at the Merwin plant, plans were made in 1956 for the installation of a third 45,000-kilowatt generator at that project, to be ready in 1958 when the Swift development went into service. This unit brought Merwin's effective capability at full head to 150,000 kilowatts.

The Company also was looking at possible hydro developments upstream from Swift, one at the Muddy site, where preliminary investigations indicated a 100,000-kilowatt plant might be built, and another named Meadows. The latter would involve small dams in a high mountain meadow to gather the flow of several tributaries of the Lewis and drop the water through penstocks to the valley floor to produce about 75,000 kilowatts in a high-head plant. Cost of power from these sources, compared with alternatives subsequently available, deferred action on the projects.

241

Another interesting power possibility then under investigation by the Company was at the Eden Ridge site on the South Fork of the Coquille River, in Coos County, Oregon. Here a dam and a penstock tunnel piercing a sharp ridge might produce a peak of 67,500 kilowatts in a power house located below a series of falls at a point where the river doubled back on itself. In the same ridge are horizontal veins of coal, which tests showed to be adequate in quality and quantity to fuel a 100,000-kilowatt steam-electric generating plant. Again, economic feasibility of the possible developments had to be studied critically.

To accelerate construction of multi-purpose federal projects in the Pacific Northwest, electric companies of the region, and several non-federal public agencies, early offered to join the government in partnership developments consistent with policies enunciated by the Eisenhower administration in 1953.

PP&L, for example, in 1954 expressed its willingness to construct under FPC license the power facilities at the Green Peter flood control and water conservation dam planned by the Army Engineers to regulate the South Santiam River in the Willamette valley The Eugene municipal power system made a similar offer in connection with the authorized Cougar project on the Mackenzie River's south fork. In each case, the non-federal partner would have financed in full the reimbursable costs assigned to power under the established formula for federal developments.

Willingness of the Company and Montana Power to join the financing of the power installation at the USBR's Yellowtail project on the Big Horn River just north of the Wyoming-Montana border was also voiced.

Another project in which PP&L, Portland General Electric and Washington Water Power offered to participate was the John Day dam on the Columbia River between The Dalles and McNary. In this instance, the proposal was that the several companies would advance to the government the total estimated cost of the power facilities and pay the annual operating and maintenance costs, receiving in return the project's power output under a 50-year prepaid contract.

Each of these proposals was dependent upon authorization by Congress, but the required legislation was politically stymied.

A type of partnership arrangement that did evolve and meet with success grew out of a proposal by the Grant County, Washington, PUD that Congress make the authorized Priest Rapids project on the Columbia, upstream from Hanford, available for licensing by the FPC for non-federal construction, With the combined support of the utilities of the region, a bill to permit this was passed and, after further studies had been made, the FPC licensed a two-dam development instead of the single higher structure initially planned. Proximity of the Priest Rapids site to the Hanford AEC project was a factor in modification of the plan.

Financing of the project was made possible by long term power purchase contracts worked out between the Grant County district and private and public systems desiring to share in the output. The Pacific Company in 1956 initially contracted for 13.9% of the Priest Rapids output, or 87,681 kilowatts, and took an option on a similar percentage of power from the upstream Wanapum dam, construction of which was to follow. These agreements provided for use by the Company over a term of years of approximately 151,000 kilowatts of Priest Rapids and Wanapum power. In addition, the Company arranged to purchase on a withdrawable basis 95,000 kilowatts of Priest Rapids and Wanapum power contracted for by several small public agencies but not expected to be required by them for a considerable period of time.

The subsequent development of the 711,000-kilowatt Rocky Reach project by the Chelan County PUD on a similar basis was also participated in by the Company through contract, and by 1960 PP&L had signed up a total of 590,000 kilowatts from the three developments for periods ranging up to 50 years.

Chapter 39

4-Company Studies Turn to Snake River

JOINT EFFORTS of the Company, Portland General Electric, Washington Water Power and Montana Power to develop a major hydroelectric project or projects, which began in 1954 with the organization of Pacific Northwest Power Company and a study of the Clearwater River, next turned to the middle reach of the Snake River below Idaho Power Company's Hells Canyon site.

Under a preliminary permit from the Federal Power Commission, the companies in 1955 carried on extensive engineering investigation of a 54-mile stretch of the Snake, above the mouth of the Salmon River. Two dams were envisaged, one a gravity-type concrete dam 255 feet high at the "low" Mountain Sheep site and the other a 534-foot arch dam at Pleasant Valley 20 miles up the river. This would form a reservoir 34 miles long, reaching to Hells Canyon. Cost of the entire development, including transmission lines, was then estimated at $213,000,000 for a project having an initial installation of 1,183,000 kilowatts.

License to build the two-dam project, with its 500,000 acre feet of useful storage for power generation and flood control, was applied for in September, 1955. It was then hoped that the timely issuance of a license would make possible the start of construction a year later, with a completion target date of January 1, 1960.

On July 23, 1957, the presiding examiner submitted his report finding that a license should be granted. Exceptions to the examiner's findings were subsequently filed by intervenors and on November 26, 1957, the matter was argued before the Commission. On January 20, 1958, the Commission acted to deny the application on the basis that a dam at the Nez Perce site, located below the mouth of the Salmon River, would constitute a more comprehensive development, even though the weight of testimony in the hearings was to the effect that was no proved method of downstream fish passage over a high dam such as Nez Perce.

Because construction of Nez Perce could jeopardize the annual migration of spawning salmon into the Salmon River and its tributaries, PNP chose to file on March 31, 1958, for license to build a high dam at an alternate Mountain Sheep site subsequently recommended for development in a report by the Army Engineers. As modified to parallel the Engineers' recommendations, the plan called for a dam 690 feet high, providing 2,250,000 acre feet of usable storage with an ultimate capacity of 1,750,000 kw.

The High Mountain Sheep site is above the mouth of the Salmon River but below the Imnaha, and to protect the fish run in the latter stream extensive by-pass facilities were planned.

A hearing on the High Mountain Sheep project application was set for March 21, 1960, by the Federal Power Commission. Less than a week before the hearing was to open, the Washington Public Power Supply System, an instrument of a group of Washington PUDs, filed with the FPC for license to construct the Nez Perce project. The proceedings were then consolidated by FPC and requests for delay by WPPSS were granted in May and August of that year. Hearings began in November, 1960.

In March, 1961, Secretary of Interior Stewart L. Udall recommended that the FPC stop the hearings pending results of a five-year "crash" fisheries research program. In April, WPPSS filed a motion to amend its Nez Perce license application to include the High Mountain Sheep site, and hearings were recessed until June. The FPC meanwhile denied the motion to amend.

It was April, 1962, when the "final" briefs in the case were filed with the FPC presiding examiner. On June 28 the Secretary of the Interior asked the FPC to recommend that High Mountain Sheep be built by the government. The commission opened the record to admit "as statement of position only" the Secretary's letter.

On October 8, 1962, the FPC presiding examiner issued an opinion and order, subject to review by the Commission, recommending that PNP be licensed to build High Mountain Sheep, saying the plan "emerges from this record as the comprehensive plan of development for the common reach which provides for prompt and optimum multipurpose development of the water resource under the standards of the Federal Power Act." The rival applications of WPPSS were rejected and the request of the Secretary of Interior for recommendation of federal construction was refused.

245

On December 3, 1962, the Secretary of the Interior belatedly asked to intervene in the case in favor of federal construction of the project. All parties opposed the move, which came 15 months after the official record closed and two months after the examiner's opinion had been issued. The FPC did, however, permit Interior "limited participation" in the case, including filing of exceptions to the examiner's decision and participation in oral argument.

On February 4, 1964, the Commission announced its decision granting Pacific Northwest Power Company license to buildt its long-sought project at the High Mountain Sheep site.

Applications for rehearing made by WPPSS and the Secretary of the Interior were denied by the FPC on April 30, 1964, and late in June the protestants petitioned the United States District Court of Appeals for the District of Columbia to set aside the license that had been issued to and accepted by Pacific Northwest Power Company. WPPSS asked the court to remand the case to the FPC with direction to give the public power group a preference for a license. Interior wanted the case reopened for further consideration of the question of federal construction.

Briefs were filed and oral argument was heard by the Court of Appeals on April 15, 1965. The court on its own motion subsequently ordered reargument, held November 16, 1965. On March 24, 1966, the Court of Appeals unanimously affirmed the FPC licensing order in favor of Pacific Northwest Power.

The Supreme Court of the United States, on petition of WPPSS and the Secretary of the Interior, agreed in November, 1966, to review the lower court decision. Arguments were held before the court on April 11, 1967, and on June 5 a majority opinion delivered by Mr. Justice Douglas remanded the case to the FPC "for further proceedings consistent with this opinion."

As a consequence of the ruling, WPPSS and Pacific Northwest Power Company subsequently agreed to a joint development plan providing for an equal division of costs and benefits, and, on January 4, 1968, they filed new applications with the FPC, proposing a project with an initial capacity of 1,470,000 kilowatts and an ultimate installation of 3,430,000 kilowatts. The modified proposal and possible alternates were presented to the Commission in hearings that began early in 1970.

Chapter 40

Wyoming Service Areas Expand

THE COMPANY'S service area in Wyoming underwent considerable expansion in the period following the merger with Mountain States Power in 1954.

On November 1, 1955, The Western Public Service Company, serving Laramie, was merged with and into Pacific after stockholder and regulatory approval had been obtained. The merger added 5,485 electric customers and $702,000 of annual revenue to the Company's Wyoming system.

The Laramie distribution system was interconnected with other principal operations of the Company in Wyoming through lines of the U. S. Bureau of Reclamation. A small coal-fired steam plant supplied part of the community's power requirements.

Located on transcontinental Interstate Highway 80 and the main line of the Union Pacific, Laramie is the seat of the University of Wyoming. Population at the time was about 17,500.

On June 1, 1959, Rawlins Electric Company was merged into Pacific, again with an exchange of stock. This company served 3,300 electric customers in the city of Rawlins and adjoining territory and had annual revenues of $580,000. The community, like Laramie, is on Interstate 80 and the main line of the Union Pacific.

On March 10, 1961, the Company acquired by purchase from Union Pacific Railroad Company the properties of Southern Wyoming Utilities Company and the 20,000-kilowatt steam generating plant of Union Pacific Coal Company, serving the Rock Springs and Green River areas, in the southwestern part of the state. Lines serving the community of Hanna, about 40 miles east of Rawlins, were included in the purchase. These properties served approximately 5,900 electric customers and 4,200 water customers. Annual revenues were $1,200,000.

The three acquisitions added nearly 15,000 electric customers to the Company's system in Wyoming and increased revenues of the division by about $2,500,000 a year.

(Left) D. R. McClung, president of Pacific Power & Light Company, from 1958 to 1966. (Right) Z. E. Merrill, Chairman of the PP&L Board, 1954-56, and previously chairman of Mountain States Power.

Two other small properties were acquired later. In 1963, the residents of Elmo, Wyoming, near Hanna, voted almost unanimously to sell their municipally-owned electric system to Pacific Power for $10,000. It served 40 customers. In 1966, Farmers Light & Power Cooperative, serving 22 rural customers in an area southwest of Lovell, Wyoming, elected to sell its lines to Pacific. The cooperative was organized in 1933 and had long been a wholesale customer of the Company.

However, growth in the Company's business in Wyoming in the 1954-69 period came not as much from property acquisitions as from industrial expansion and increased use of electricity throughout the state. Annual operating revenues of the Wyoming division increased from $4,150,000 in 1954 to more than $23,-000,000 a decade and a half later, and the customers total went from approximately 27,000 to more than 52,000.

Growth in power loads during the period were met by expansion of the Dave Johnston steam plant at Glenrock. Corresponding additions to the Company's transmission system in the state were made to carry the power supply to load centers.

First of the big transmission line projects was the 251-mile,

248

161,000-volt circuit completed in 1957 between Casper and Billings. Along the way, this line provided a high-line power source for the Company's distribution system at Buffalo, previously served only by local hydro and diesel installations of limited capacity. It also made possible an arrangement to supply power at wholesale to the Sheridan properties of Montana-Dakota Utilities Company to supplement its other resources.

Lines from the Dave Johnston plant to Casper were strengthened as needed, and in 1961 another big transmission project was completed to augment power supply in the Wind River basin and meet the needs of a large taconite mining and beneficiation development that was being carried forward by U. S. Steel Corporation atop the continental divide at Atlantic City. The 230,000-volt circuit was 161 miles long. The following year the line was extended south to Rock Springs and west to Kemmerer, where Utah Power & Light was building a 150,000-kilowatt coal-fired steam plant.

At the north end of the Big Horn basin a 230,000-volt line was built in 1962 from Frannie to the Yellowtail dam site to interconnect there with the Company's Casper-Billings line. Construction of other 230,000-volt links from Frannie south to Thermopolis in the next two years completed a high-voltage loop around the Big Horn Mountains and further strengthened the systems.

Further coordination of power facilities in the Rocky Mountain region was aided in 1963 by the Company's construction of a 230,000-volt extension from Rock Springs to the Flaming Gorge project of the U. S. Bureau of Reclamation, on the Green River not far south of the Wyoming-Utah border. There the line interconnected with the federal transmission system of the Upper Colorado Storage Project, under arrangements following the pattern of power wheeling and interchange agreements in effect between the Company and the USBR in Wyoming.

The lines built by the Company in southwest Wyoming also provided a new tie to the west through the systems of Utah Power & Light and Idaho Power Company.

249

Chapter 41

Much Accomplished in 1955-60 Period

THE YEARS from 1955 to 1960 were among the busiest in the Company's history. Gross construction expenditures of $217,-000,000 nearly doubled the Company's utility plant account and more than doubled its generating capacity.

In fact, new generators that went into service in one year alone, 1958, added 349,000 kilowatts to the system's resources. Three units at the Swift hydro project added 204,000 kilowatts and Unit No. 3 at Merwin added 45,000 kilowatts. The first 100,-000-kw steam generator at the Dave Johnston plant in Wyoming rounded out the year's record. Construction expenditures in 1958 amounted to $62,715,000, a new high.

In 1955, the system had 338,106 kw in generating capacity. At the end of 1960 the figure was 778,444 kw.

Most extensive transmission line construction was in Wyoming, but significant new links were built elsewhere.

In 1955 the Company's distribution system at Libby, Montana, was connected with the Northwest Power Pool through a $500,-000 transmission link extending 18 miles to the west, tying in at Troy with a circuit of Bonneville Power Administration.

Work was nearly completed in that year on a 115,000-volt line from Astoria to Seaside, which in 1956 was extended to Tillamook to complete a transmission loop over which the northwest Oregon coast area could receive power from alternate sources.

Ready for service when the Swift project was completed was a 26-mile, 230,000-volt circuit down the Lewis River to a point near Woodland, where it connected with a BPA circuit. BPA, in turn, delivered by contract equivalent power into the Company's system in the Portland area.

A large transmission project completed in October, 1959, was a 39-mile, 230,000-volt circuit from the vicinity of the Priest Rapids hydro project to the Company's Union Gap substation adjoining Yakima. This line brought to an important load center a portion of the power contracted for by the Company from Priest Rapids and Wanapum.

In the Portland area the Company in 1960 added a 230,000-volt interconnection between the Troutdale substation of Bonneville Power Administration and a new Company substation at Linneman Junction, east of Portland, where 150,000 kva of transformer capacity was installed. New connections were built between this substation and the Portland grid.

The Company's 1960 annual report, which noted the 50th anniversary of the business, told that load growth in the preceding 10 years had been at the rate of 8% per year— from a peak of 489,000 kilowatts in 1950 to 1,059,000 kilowatts in 1960.

"Presently, the Company is supplying 51% of its energy load with power generated in Company-owned plants, 19% with power purchased from Bonneville Power Administration and 30% from other sources."

Newest generator then on the system was the second 100,000-kilowatt unit at the Dave Johnston Plant, completed on schedule and reported to be performing satisfactorily at the year-end.

The 1960 report also told of the resolution of a long standing problem of electric service duplication in the Tillamook area, after voters of the district had authorized a $4,400,000 PUD bond issue to finance acquisition of the Company's facilities there.

"The utility district, which was formed in 1933, originally sought unsuccessfully to purchase lines of the former Mountain States Power Company for $625,000," the report said, "and after World War II began to build a duplicate power system. Your Company repeatedly pointed out the waste and ultimate cost of discriminate competition as it had developed in the county and had urged many times that one or the other of the two systems be designated by the people as their sole serving agency. Assuming the district completes its financing and institutes condemnation proceedings, the Company has agreed to stipulate in such proceedings that $3,915,000, plus or minus additions or retirements since March 15, 1960, would be the fair value of the properties involved." The Company had about 4,700 customers and $800,-000 of annual revenue in the county. Transfer of the properties took place on May 22, 1961, for a consideration of approximately $4,000,000.

In another area a problem of duplication had been resolved in 1959 when the City of Milton-Freewater, Oregon, acquired a

Important new Wyoming power link was dedicated September 12, 1957, at Casper substation. Line extends 251 miles north to Billings, Montana, where it ties with facilities of The Montana Power Company. It constituted the state's first link with the Northwest Power Pool.

small section of the Company's electric distribution facilities in and adjacent to that community. For many years there had been two separate municipalities existing side-by-side in the area. Milton was served by a long-established municipal electric system and Freewater by the Pacific Company. Eventually the citizens voted for a consolidation of the municipal governments, resulting in an anomalous power situation. Rather than extend duplicating lines, the city chose to move toward acquisition of Company lines serving about 500 customers and providing annual revenues of $88,-000. The case was settled by a decree of condemnation.

In Springfield, Oregon, where the city had chosen to enter into competition with Mountain States Power in 1949, there developed among community leaders a gradual recognition of the long-term problems created by the uneconomic duplication of power systems. Desirability of coming to a decision as to which system should be the sole supplier of power in the community was stressed many times by the Pacific Company following its entry into the picture, and in 1958 the city put forward a realistic bond issue proposal to finance an acquisition. The voters, however, turned it down, as they did a $3,900,000 bond issue presented for the same purpose in 1961.

252

The public airing of the problems of duplication of services in these several communities did, however, have a salutary effect. An important step toward the future avoidance of uneconomic duplication of electric distribution lines was taken by the 1961 Oregon legislature. It enacted a law under which suppliers of electric energy were authorized to execute contracts providing for the elimination of duplicate facilities by agreeing upon the territory to be served and providing for the transfer of facilities within the agreed upon territories. Such contracts are subject to approval by the Public Utility Commissioner of Oregon after hearings. The act also authorizes voluntary proceedings for allocation of territory where there is no duplication. Contracts made under authority of the act and approved by the commissioner are subject to court enforcement.

A project started in 1956 under a program worked out with New England Mutual Life Insurance Company was a 43,000-square-foot expansion of floor space in the Public Service Building by the addition of seven floors to the wings of the structure. Completed in 1957, this brought the wings to a height of 12 stories. Extensive remodeling of Company space within the building was carried on to provide better facilities and more effective grouping of departments. The elevator installation was refurbished and converted to electronic control as part of the improvement program.

The Company's 1957 annual report noted that "present day construction costs and increases in wage rates and other costs of doing business sooner or later would make adjustments necessary in retail rate structures, which have been maintained at or below pre-war levels through diligent efforts on the part of all concerned." The 1958 report said that detailed studies of the rate situation had been started early in the year, recognizing the large amount of new plant that soon would be coming into service.

"It is evident," the report said, "that in the Oregon and Washington service areas rate relief must be obtained in 1959 in order to maintain a reasonable level of earnings on electric plant now devoted to the service of customers . . . and to enable the Company to meet its steadily expanding public service responsibilities.

"Accordingly, on December 22, 1958, the Company filed application with the Washington Public Service Commission and the Public Utility Commissioner of Oregon for the first general rate increase in its 48-year history. The adjustments requested would produce an estimated $4,931,000 of additional annual electric revenue and amount to an average increase of about 10% in the Washington areas served and about 15% in Oregon."

The 1959 report stated that hearings on the rate requests had been substantially completed during the year and that decisions of the regulatory authorities were pending.

The April 11, 1960, quarterly letter to stockholders reported that findings had been made by the two regulatory bodies, "with the over-all result that the Company obtained about 60% of the total annual increase requested. . . .

"The decision of the Oregon Public Utility Commissioner was that a return of 6.1% on an original cost base was appropriate, and that the Company's existing rate schedules did not furnish revenues sufficient to provide a fair and reasonable return on its investment in that state. He accordingly granted a rate increase which, after necessary adjustments, is estimated to amount to approximately $3,000,000. The Washington Public Service Commission reached a similar conclusion regarding the type of rate base and rate of return, but held that the Company was now earning 6% on its Washington properties and denied any rate increase."

Revised rate schedules conforming with the several requirements of the Oregon order were filed promptly by the Company.

Another matter of interest to stockholders in the area was a reminder in the letter that the annual meeting of the Company would be held in Portland on April 19, 1960. Although informal meetings had been held from time to time to afford stockholders opportunity to meet members of the management and hear a review of the Company's affairs, this marked the first opportunity for the official annual meeting to be held outside of Maine, the state in which the firm was incorporated in 1910. The change in meeting place was made possible when the 1959 Maine legislature amended the corporation law to permit certain companies incorporated in the state, like Pacific, to hold stockholders' meetings where the directors might determine.

Public use of Company reservoirs for recreation has grown tremendously since the projects were built. A swimming and picnic area on Lake Merwin and a Thistle class sailboat race on the Yale reservoir are illustrative of activities now being enjoyed by more than 250,000 persons visiting the Lewis River hydro developments annually.

Chapter 42

Research Pushed in the '50's

THE DECADE that began in 1950 was marked by the Company's research activities as well as by burgeoning construction programs. Studies of nuclear energy applications for production of electricity, for example, began early in 1954, when the industry was first invited by the Atomic Energy Commission to consider participation in reactor design and ownership. In March of that year representatives of the Company and three neighboring utilities organized the Pacific Northwest Study Group, which centered its work at AEC's Hanford facility while also studying the activities of equipment manufacturers. Following this indoctrination, the Company in 1956 associated itself with the Rocky Mountain Nuclear Power Study Group to participate in further studies at Idaho Falls, where the Arco AEC facility is located.

In 1958, with national policy encouraging industry to proceed with specific experimental reactor development, the Company and others formed the Rocky Mountain-Pacific Nuclear Research Group, which entered into an arrangement with General Atomic Division of General Dynamics to develop a conceptual design for a high-temperature, graphite-moderated, gas-cooled unit.

Congress soon thereafter authorized AEC to proceed with development of a gas-cooled reactor, and Pacific was one of 53 utilities to join in forming High Temperature Reactor Development Associates, Inc. Out of this joint effort developed a 40,000-kilowatt prototype plant at Peach Bottom, Pennsylvania, on the system of Philadelphia Electric Company.

Again, in the fall of 1963, the Company joined with 10 other western utilities in formation of an advanced reactor development group to study feasibility of a 300,000-kilowatt nuclear plant on a typical western system, a plant such as Public Service Company of Colorado subsequently undertook to construct.

The very favorable situation of the Company with respect to availabilities of low-cost coal at strategic locations made it possible to defer active consideration of nuclear plant construction.

The story of the Company's good fortune in finding the Glenrock coal field has already been told. Subsequent investigations and negotiations vastly expanded its Wyoming coal reserves.

Long-range planning for power supplies elsewhere on the system stimulated the Company in 1957 to begin an investigation of Washington coal resources, jointly with Washington Water Power. These studies centered in an area near Centralia, about 100 miles north of Portland, in the Cascade foothills.

Considerable coal had been mined in the area in earlier years, but changes in the fuel market had brought activity practically to a standstill. Sub-bituminous in type, the coal made good boiler fuel although not high enough in BTUs to be competitive in any market where transportation costs became a significant factor.

The Pacific and Washington companies obtained rights and options enabling them to proceed with a core-drilling program on an extensive acreage. By the end of 1958 they had blocked out approximately 70,000,000 tons of coal that might be mined by the open-pit method, or enough to supply a 300,000-kilowatt steam plant for a period of 50 years. The 1960 report noted that the joint venture had by then "obtained and proved a coal reserve in western Washington of at least 150,000,000 tons under favorable stripping ratios."

This anticipation of the region's forthcoming need for thermal power later proved to be most timely, putting the two co-operating companies in an advanced position to develop a major steam generating resource for the Pacific Northwest.

There was another investigation started in the '50s and carried through to a successful conclusion which stands high among examples of the way Pacific's development philosophy has returned dividends. This was the program that resulted in obtaining a new supply of industrial water for the Coos Bay area from coast sand dunes that superficially resemble the Sahara desert.

The U. S. Chamber of Commerce cited this development at its 1961 annual meeting as being "more than an example of initiative and enterprise—it demonstrates dramatically what cooperation at all levels of citizenship can achieve for community growth—when everyone works together in common purpose."

The citation was bestowed shortly after Menasha Corporation had completed a multi-million-dollar pulp and paper complex at the tidewater edge of Coos Bay, utilizing fresh water pumped by Pacific Power from a system of wells established in the extensive dune area bordering the ocean north of the bay.

In addition to providing an important new plant payroll, the Menasha mill opened a new market for alder and other pulp wood to expand the economy of the community.

Pacific Power's quest for water to make such developments possible was launched in 1954 after the Mountain States merger brought the Company into the area. In an early meeting with community leaders, it was learned that a principal deterrent to expansion of the pulp and paper sector of the forest products industry was insufficient fresh water for such uses.

This was a challenge. Coos Bay is the leading lumber shipping port of the Pacific, backed by the most extensive commercial forest lands of the nation. Surveys indicated that fiber residue from then existing lumber and plywood mills was ample to support 1,000 tons per day of paper production.

The potential was so great that Paul McKee promptly directed Company engineers to start looking for possible water sources that would be economically feasible.

A reconnaissance soon confirmed that, while the area benefits from annual rainfall of 65 inches or more, the terrain of the back country offered an economic obstacle to conventional impoundments on streams tributary to the bay.

The investigators next tried drilling deep wells at points on the perimeter of the bay, hoping to intercept an outflow from the hills. This met with disappointments.

Studies of available literature turned up some interesting data from the U. S. Geological Survey relative to fresh water lakes in the sand dunes north of the bay. Year-around, the lakes hold their level, some cupped in dunes 40 feet above sea level, even during summer months when there is little rainfall.

The possibility of getting large amounts of water from the dunes was deemed to be worth a try. No one expected quick answers, but neither was it anticipated that the work would continue five years to accumulate convincing proof of the long-term adequacy of a water supply on which to base large industrial plant investments. Community understanding and the patience of cooperating officials and community leaders encouraged the Company to pursue the work. Also, as each step of the project unfolded, there was greater promise of success.

The engineers on the job got an early shot of confidence when in 1955 they tried unsuccessfully to pump dry a small lake at the edge of the dunes near the bay. This was evidence of an underground water source of replenishment. Probes of the area traced fresh water to depths of 125 feet below sea level. Tracer elements revealed a continuous movement of water from the dunes toward the ocean. As the tide ebbed, fresh water was seeping to the sea. On the 13,000 acres of sand which the study ultimately included, the annual rainfall was equivalent to 63-million gallons a day.

The dunes were proved to be like a giant sponge, an underground reservoir holding billions of gallons of fresh water.

To test dependability of the source, PP&L buried a horizontal gallery-type collector system and again began pumping. Around the clock, for 30 months, the water kept flowing. The Company's engineering and consulting staffs next looked to the problem of economic production. New techniques for extracting the water without collecting sand in the system had to be devised.

Included among the consultants on the dunes water project was an internationally-known specialist from Amsterdam, where the Dutch for more than a century have relied on a water system based on a somewhat comparable situation.

As the research work neared the end of the fifth year, and production data was established for wells located in a one-square-mile area, the interest of major forest products manufacturing companies was increasingly attracted to the potential for expansion of pulp and paper production.

In July of 1959, officials of Menasha and Pacific Power gathered in Coos Bay to announce plans for the first new paper mill to be established in the area in more than a quarter century. In April, 1961, giant rolls of paper were moving to market.

Menasha was using approximately 2,000,000 gallons of wa- daily. The area where Pacific Power's research centered had been proved capable of providing as much as 30,000,000 gallons daily.

The Company operated this water development until 1967, when the extraction facilities were sold to the Coos Bay-North Bend Water Board, which required an additional supply and had

*In 1956 George Mackenzie, Company treasurer, was pictured describing
to President Paul B. McKee a model of the computer installation that had
been selected to do customer billing and other tasks. The change-over
to the new equipment began in 1957 and was completed in 1958.*

determined that the sand dunes offered the most economic source.
The established wells, pumps and water lines were made available
to the Water Board at the Company's cost, and the research effort and engineering studies that went into the program were
offered as a contribution to the community. Water continued to
be supplied to Menasha by the Water Board on mutually agree-
able terms worked out in advance of the transfer.

Expansion of the original paper mill facilities has increased its
daily capacity. The community has an economical water supply for
growth, and the Company's electric business has enjoyed its share
of the general benefits that have accrued.

260

Chapter 43

Fish and Computers Were on Study List

A COMPANY PROGRAM related to another facet of the region's economy is fish research, or the effort to resolve or minimize conflicts of interest between far-ranging anadromous fish runs and power dams. This has absorbed the attention of many persons and agencies for a long period of time.

Company activities in this field were enlarged with the construction of the Yale and Swift projects on the Lewis River, and the need for extensive fish studies in connection with the plans of Pacific Northwest Power for major hydroelectric developments on the Snake River.

Early hydro installations were small and often were located where a natural waterfall itself formed a barrier to fish passage. Others had low diversion dams, where a simple fish ladder could provide passage for migrants and screens could be devised to keep them out of canals and penstocks leading to the turbines.

When the Company's Merwin project, first on the Lewis River, was in the planning stage in 1928 it was necessary to work out a method of handling salmon when they encountered the 200-foot barrier. A conventional fish ladder was out of the question.

Working with state fisheries staff personnel, the engineers devised a plan to attract upstream migrant salmon into a trap-tank at the base of the dam and then haul them by truck to a holding pond operated in conjunction with a hatchery and rearing pools. Fish trapped in excess of hatchery capacity were released in the reservoir above the dam to spawn naturally, and an undetermined number of fingerlings would escape over the spillways during high flow periods.

Expanded interest in development of Lewis River fisheries came with construction of the Yale hydroelectric project, which added more storage control to the river. This, together with installation of a second generator at Merwin, reduced the amount of seasonal spill. When the Swift project was completed in 1958

261

Depth and water content of the snow pack in the Cascade Mountain watershed of the North Umpqua River are measured by Company observers traveling by "Sno-Cat". Findings help estimate hydro potential of the river in the season ahead.

and a third generator was installed at Merwin, the Lewis River was under nearly complete control.

Meanwhile, the Company's fish biologists, working with state and federal agencies, in 1959 undertook a comprehensive research program devoted to the idea of utilizing the Merwin reservoir as a rearing lake for salmon hatched at a new incubation station. They also carried on an intensive investigation of ways to collect young salmon in the lake at the proper time for transport into the river below Merwin dam to begin their instinctive migration to the sea.

The "incubation-type" hatchery built for the studies produced millions of young Coho salmon, which were released in the reservoir and into tributaries of the reservoir in a series of controlled experiments. Some of the fingerlings were collected by an experimental "skimmer" installed in the lake by the U. S. Bureau of Commercial Fisheries. Others were taken in various types of trap nets, which also are used in studies of fish movement in the lake and fish count by species. Extent of the trash fish problem and how to control these voracious predators were also investigated.

The cooperating biologists carried on extensive limnological and ecological studies of the Merwin reservoir, which contains

262

422,000 acre feet of water and has a maximum depth of 200 feet. Scuba diving gear was used frequently by the researchers as they pressed to expand their knowledge. They also worked with tests to determine if Sockeye salmon from Canadian waters could be established in the Lewis River.

The complexities of the life cycle of anadromous fish make such studies time consuming but the Company has continued its efforts, turning more recently to further experiments with a conventional fish hatchery and fully controlled rearing ponds at the incubation-type hatchery adjacent to Lake Merwin.

While this work progresses, the Company's fish biologists give substantial time and effort toward the maintenance of fish production on streams in Oregon and northern California that are famed for their sports fishing.

In an allied field, the Company has established numerous recreation facilities for the public at suitable locations on its hydroelectric reservoirs. Some of these developments were started 40 years ago. They now include picnic parks, boat launching ramps, camp grounds and scenic view points. More than 500,000 persons enjoyed use of these facilities in a recent 12-month period.

The rapid advances made in the computer field following World War II prompted the Company in 1952 to become one of the first utilities in the nation to start looking into the feasibility of using electronic data processing equipment for customer accounting and billing and other routine accounting procedures.

This was a project in which President Paul B. McKee had an intense interest. He anticipated the use of computers for many Company purposes, including the handling of complex engineering problems concerned with generation, transmission and distribution of power as well as a huge volume of routine accounting work.

George Mackenzie, Company treasurer, set up a special task force to work on the project with staff members of Stanford Research Institute and the electronics industry. The goal was to develop a practical program that would fit the particular needs of the business. Leader of the task force was Don C. Frisbee, later to succeed Mackenzie in the treasurer's post and ultimately become president of the Company.

It took nearly three years of concentrated effort to work out a program that met the Company's requirements and to determine what equipment to obtain. The 1955 annual report told of progress that had been made and said the system decided upon would be ready for installation in 1957. Cost of the equipment and the training of employees in new procedures was estimated at approximately $1,000,000, "from which investment substantial economies will be gained."

The 1956 report said: "An outstanding group of younger men, recruited from within the organization, have been devoting their entire time to programming the change-over, now scheduled to commence in May, 1957. Employees whose present work is to be performed by the electronic equipment will be trained for other more productive tasks within the Company."

The installation was completed on schedule and put to work. By the end of 1957, about 50% of the Company's customers were being billed electronically and the change-over was virtually completed during 1958.

"Experience with the electronic equipment has been very satisfactory," the 1958 annual report said, "and its supplemental uses for engineering problems and data analysis have proved invaluable."

At the end of 1958 the Company had 295,562 electric, water and steam heat customers whose monthly bills and accounting records were being handled by the computer.

Ten years later, an enlarged and improved "third generation" installation was handling nearly half a million customer accounts, getting out the payroll, issuing dividend checks to more than 77,-000 stockholders, handling stores accounting and doing a wide range of engineering tasks.

Chapter 44

Time Brought Changes in Family Roster

ADVANCEMENTS, retirements and death brought a number of changes in the roster of Company officers and directors during the 1950s.

H. W. Millay, who started work for the Company as a meter reader in 1925 and had been serving as assistant secretary, was named secretary in 1951 to succeed James G. Hawkins.

When Hawkins retired the following year, he had the longest record of continuous service of any Company employee, beginning in 1909 with Astoria Electric Company. He served as secretary and treasurer for a 10-year period. Hawkins died January 4, 1962, at the age of 75.

Duties of treasurer had been assumed in 1950 by George F. Mackenzie, who previously was assistant secretary and assistant treasurer. Mackenzie had joined the Company family in 1913 as a bookkeeper with Portland Gas & Coke Company, then an affiliate. Years later he made the comment: "In 1913 a person got a job as a bookkeeper because he could write a neat Spencerian hand," an accomplishment Mackenzie had mastered as a schoolboy in his native Scotland.

An earlier reference noted the death on November 8, 1951, of Lewis A. "Tam" McArthur.

In 1955 came the retirement of Will T. Neill, a vice president of the Company since 1936. The annual report spoke of him as having made "a notable contribution to the Company during his 34 years of service. Since 1924, Mr. Neill had been in charge of the Company's rate department and carried many major responsibilities in connection with financing and regulatory matters."

Not recognized at the time was the great historical value of a project Neill directed from 1937 to 1940, which resulted in a volume labeled "Statement 'A' — History of Origin and Development of the Company and Its Predecessors — Prepared Pursuant to Federal Power Commission Electric Plant Instruction 2D — Uniform System of Accounts — and Order of May 11, 1937."

265

The FPC order required a restatement of property accounts on the so-called "Original Cost" basis. It was a monumental research job. The task force had to dig deep into community history to find facts not covered in available records. Old newspaper files were among sources sifted to help reconstruct the cost story.

The background information so collected provided much of the basis for early chapters of this narrative. The author is most grateful to Neill and his diligent colleagues.

Death came November 27, 1956, to Z. E. Merrill, who became chairman of the board of Pacific in 1954, following the merger of Mountain States Power. As president and as chairman of the board of Mountain States, he played a particularly important part in the progress and development of that utility.

Retiring in 1956 was W. D. "Dave" Johnston, vice president and Wyoming division manager, after 36 years with the Company and its predecessors in that area. It was in recognition of his contributions to the electric industry in Wyoming that the Company's steam plant near Glenrock was named in his honor.

At the September 15, 1958, meeting of the Board of Directors, Paul McKee was named chairman of the board and D. R. Mc-Clung, executive vice president since 1952, was advanced to president. George Mackenzie, vice president and treasurer, was named vice president and controller. Don C. Frisbee, assistant treasurer, was elected treasurer and, upon Mackenzie's retirement in 1960, was named vice president and treasurer.

The Company's 1959 annual report noted that Paul McKee had been named Portland's First Citizen of the Year by the Portland Realty Board on December 12, 1959, "in recognition of his many contributions to the community, state and nation."

To follow through on a period in history, Guy W. Talbot, first president of the Company, died on December 1, 1961, at the age of 88, leaving behind many memories of his early leadership.

A little more than a month later came the passing of L. T. Merwin, also 88, on January 10, 1962. He had been president of Northwestern Electric from 1936 until 1947, when that company was merged with Pacific. His association with the firm went back to 1912. He was designer and construction supervisor of the first transmission line built through the Columbia River gorge.

266

Chapter 45

PP&L's 50th Year — Copco Merger on Way

C LIMACTIC event of 1960—the Company's 50th anniversary year—made the news on December 30, when it was announced that the Boards of Directors of Pacific Power and The California Oregon Power Company had reached general agreement of the terms of a proposed merger of Copco into Pacific.

Pacific's January 10, 1961, letter to stockholders said in part:

"Subject to approvals by stockholders and by the regulatory commissions having jurisdiction, the merger would be effected by an exchange of stock in the ratio of 1.2 shares of Pacific common stock for each share of Copco common. Details of the proposed consolidation, including provisions for the exchange of Copco's preferred stocks, are being worked out by a joint committee of officers and directors for submission to stockholders of each company. It is hoped that the proposal may be acted upon at special meetings of the stockholders tentatively scheduled for early March."

On January 30, 1961, the Company sent its stockholders a copy of the merger agreement dated January 18 and notice of a special meeting of stockholders on March 14 to act on the proposal. The letter of transmittal included the following:

"The California Oregon Power Company is an electric utility serving 93,000 electric customers in important areas of southern Oregon and adjoining portions of northern California. It has annual revenues of $25,000,000 and a gross utility plant account of $179,000,000. The company was established in 1911 and has played a progressive part in the extension of electric service and the development of hydroelectric resources in its operating territory, which has a population of 254,000. Copco's service area in Oregon adjoins that of your Company and the two systems are interconnected.

"Principal cities served by Copco are: Medford, the Company's headquarters, Klamath Falls, Roseburg and Grants Pass in Oregon, and Crescent City, Yreka and Dunsmuir in California.

"Average annual residential use of electricity on the Copco

267

system exceeds 9,700 kilowatt-hours, one of the highest in the industry. Of its total electric customers, 72,000 are in Oregon and about 80% of its revenue is derived from business in that state. Copco's operating revenues have doubled in the past 10 years, during which period the company has added 226,000 kilowatts of hydroelectric generating capacity to its system. A large hydroelectric potential, including additional storage for peaking purposes, remains to be developed to serve future power needs.

"Your Company has annual revenues of $63,000,000 and a gross utility plant account of $398,000,000. Merger of the two companies would result in a broad-based utility operation with annual revenues of $88,000,000 and a gross plant account of $577,000,000. The merged company would serve 243,000 electric customers in Oregon and have a total of approximately 411,000 utility customers. . . .

"Copco has 406,000 kilowatts of hydroelectric capability in the watersheds of the Umpqua, Klamath and Rogue rivers. The stream flow characteristics of these rivers have marked differences from those on which your Company has its 590,000 kilowatts of hydroelectric capability. The integration of these two systems through heavy duty transmission lines to take advantage of diversities in stream flow and power loads, and the consolidation of the forward-looking development programs of the two companies, will bring about beneficial operating results through increased capability and lower power costs."

Copco's management similarly addressed the stockholders of that company, recommending a favorable vote at its special meeting on March 14. Stockholders of each company voted almost unanimously in favor of the merger. More than 90% of the shares of each were represented at the meetings.

All regulatory approvals were obtained and the merger was completed on June 21, 1961. Retained in Pacific's employ were all former Copco employees who desired to remain with the merged enterprise and there was made available to them on an equitable basis benefits under Pacific's retirement, group life insurance and group medical-surgical hospital plans.

For Paul McKee the consolidation of Copco with Pacific was tinged with sentiment. He had begun his business career with Copco in 1914 after graduation from Stanford, and served as assistant to the president from 1914 to 1920 and as vice president and general manager from 1920 to 1926.

The merger agreement provided that the initial Board of Directors of the surviving Pacific Company should consist of 15 of the 21 prior members of that Board and eight of the nine prior directors of Copco.

McKee continued as chairman of the board of Pacific and Don McClung as president. Two of Copco's senior officers were named vice chairmen. One was A. S. Cummins, president of Copco since 1941. Prior to taking that post, he had been vice president and secretary of Standard Gas & Electric Company.

Glenn L. Jackson, a vice president of Copco, also was named a vice chairman. Jackson started in the utility business in 1925 upon graduation from Oregon State University. He was a salesman for Mountain States Power from 1925 to 1927, sales manager from 1927 to 1929 and vice president from 1929 to 1938. In 1933 he became director and in 1935 a vice president of Copco, then an affiliated company. His service with Copco was interrupted only by a military leave during World War II, when he became a colonel in the U. S. Air Force.

John C. Boyle, vice president and general manager and a director of Copco, became a vice president and director of Pacific. He began his utility career with Copco following graduation from the University of California in 1910, and his accomplishments over many years of service to the company included the planning and execution of major development programs.

Frank C. Bash, vice president and treasurer of Copco, became a vice president of Pacific and later was appointed manager of the Copco division.

H. P. Bosworth, Jr., Copco vice president who came to the company in 1923 as a graduate engineer from Cornell, became a vice president of Pacific and served until his retirement in 1966.

Copco directors who went on Pacific's Board were Messrs. Boyle, Cummins and Jackson, of the company's staff; Alfred S. V. Carpenter, Medford; Gregory A. Harrison, San Francisco; Henry H. Pringle, Medford; George M. Roberts, Medford; and Eugene Thorndike, Medford. E. B. Hall, Klamath Falls, was named a director emeritus of Pacific and served in that capacity until his death in 1965 at the age of 93.

Chapter 46

Copco's Life Story Colorful

E ARLY HISTORY of electric service in the Copco area parallels that of other segments of the Pacific Power system. Much credit is due to George V. "Buck" Taylor, Seth M. Bullis and H. P. Bosworth, Jr., for their contributions to the story of the company with which each was long associated.

Utilization of water power in Klamath Falls, for example, began in 1882 when a canal was constructed along Link River to operate a flour mill located near the site of the West Side hydroelectric plant. It was 1896, however, before electric service was established from a small plant built on the east side of Link River, under a franchise granted in 1895 to H. V. Gates, founder of the Klamath Falls Light and Water Company.

The franchise required Gates "to burn the street lights all night on July 4, Christmas and New Years. On other nights, upon notification of a public meeting, he was to light the street lights until thirty minutes after the meeting was dismissed."

Grants Pass got its first electric service from the Grants Pass Water, Light and Power Company in December, 1889. A wing dam located downstream from the highway bridge across the Rogue River diverted water to a low-head hydro plant. The diversion dam was later rebuilt to span the width of the river.

In 1890 a dam was built on the South Umpqua River by Roseburg Water Company to supply electric and water service to the town. In the same year, Douglas Electric and Water Company installed a dam and pumping plant at Winchester on the North Umpqua River to serve that community. The Douglas utility bought the Roseburg Company's plant in 1903.

Yreka, California, saw its first electric lights in 1891. James Quinn built a 36-kilowatt plant on the Shasta River three miles north of town. It had a Knight water wheel with rope drive to a 133-cycle, single-phase generator of German manufacture. The power was transmitted to Yreka at 6,600 volts and stepped down to 50 volts for distribution.

Old No. 7, a gear-driven Shay, hauled sightseers up Mt. Tamalpais before going to the Klamath Lake Railroad to haul in equipment for the Copco No. 1 hydro plant on the Klamath River. Here it is easing the upper half of a generator frame down the switchback spur to the plant site. The year was 1917 or 1918. The railroad was built to haul logs to a big mill at Klamathon, near Hornbrook. It was initially planned to extend the line through to Klamath Falls but a Southern Pacific branch from Weed got there first. The Klamathon mill burned and the railroad subsequently was leased to California Oregon Power and later purchased by Copco. (Photo courtesy Klamath County Museum, H. L. Ogle Collection.)

Dunsmuir received its first electric service in the same year from a plant built on the Sacramento River by Herman Scherrer.

A small wood-burning steam plant on Bear Creek gave Medford its first electric service in 1894. It was owned by R. A. Proudfoot.

In 1898 the Mt. Shasta Milling Company installed a 100-kilowatt hydro plant on Little Shasta River east of Montague and transmitted energy about nine miles to the flour mill. Some lighting service was furnished to other customers in Montague.

Scott Valley, west of Yreka, saw the Etna Development Company and the Kappler Brewing Company install generators for their own uses in Etna in 1900. A few customers were served in the immediate area.

Copco's most directly related predecessor company, Siskiyou Electric Power Company, was incorporated August 15, 1902. Its corporate successor in 1908 was Siskiyou Electric Power & Light.

Initial activity of the Siskiyou company in the fall of 1902 was to start work on a high-head hydro plant on Fall Creek, a tributary of the Klamath River flowing into that stream from the north near the head of the present Iron Gate reservoir. Still in use, the site is occupied by a hydro plant of 2,300-kilowatt capacity.

Also in 1902 work was started on a dam and powerhouse at Gold Ray on the Rogue River by the Condor Water and Power Company, which was incorporated July 31, 1902, by C. R. Ray, Col. Frank H. Ray and others. The first generator went into service in December, 1904. Two 750-kilowatt generators replaced the original unit in 1905. They had rope drive from the shafts of submerged horizontal turbines. First customers were some mines between the dam and Gold Hill. A 12-mile transmission line delivered wholesale power to Medford. The Gold Ray units probably hold some kind of a record for the long period of years they have operated.

A hydro plant on New Pine Creek south of Lakeview, Oregon, gave that community its first power in 1902.

In 1903 Siskiyou Electric Power built a transmission line from Fall Creek into Montague, with a tap line to Hornbrook, and bought the Mt. Shasta Milling Company's hydro plant in Little Shasta valley. That plant was then closed down. Siskiyou supplied power from Fall Creek to the flour mill and its other customers in Montague. The Fall Creek transmission line was extended from Montague to Yreka and the new firm competed with Yreka Electric Light and Power from 1903 until 1905, when the company, then owned by E. T. Osborn, was acquired by Siskiyou.

In 1904 the Siskiyou company built into Scott Valley and acquired the two small plants at Etna and the 45-kilowatt plant of Manuel Perreira at Fort Jones.

Also in 1904 a steam generating plant was installed in Alturas by the Alturas Light and Power Company.

The Condor Company in 1905 built a line from Gold Ray to Grants Pass and thence 18 miles north to the Greenback mine, and acquired the plant and system of the Grants Pass company.

The original steam plant in Medford was purchased by the city in 1900 and the utility began buying power from the Condor company after the Gold Ray plant went into operation. In 1907 the Condor firm leased and contracted to buy the city's system. In the same year, the Condor properties were deeded over to a subsidiary, Rogue River Electric Company.

In the Klamath Falls community, a second electric company, Klamath Light and Power, completed a hydro plant on the west side of Link River in 1908 and began competing with Klamath Falls Light and Water Company. The new company extended lines to Merrill and Bonanza. Two years later it bought out its older competitor and sold the combined properties to Siskiyou Electric.

Service in the Phoenix-Talent area was established in 1909 by the Jackson County Light & Power Company, which bought its power supply from Rogue River Electric.

In 1910 an application for water rights on the Klamath River near Keno was filed by B. E. and J. W. Kerns and a diversion dam and power plant installed a short distance downstream from the site of the present Keno regulating dam. An important purpose of this plant was to provide power for irrigation and drainage of extensive lands brought into agricultural production on the Keno flat. It also supplied power to residents of the Keno area and a line was extended to Klamath Falls. The plant went into operation in 1912. It was acquired by Copco in 1920.

The Ray interests, through Rogue River Electric Company, formed the Prospect Construction Company early in 1911 to build a plant at Prospect on the North Fork of the Rogue River and a line to Gold Ray. Later in the year, Siskiyou Electric acquired the stock of Prospect Construction and of Rogue River Electric.

On December 15, 1911, California-Oregon Power Company was incorporated by the Siskiyou group to acquire the stock and consolidate the properties of Siskiyou Electric, Rogue River Electric, Prospect Construction, Klamath Power Company and Klamath Falls Light and Water Company. This was accomplished as of January 1, 1912. However, the Siskiyou, Rogue River and Prospect companies remained active for several years in order to complete or acquire certain properties.

A project carried forward by the Siskiyou company was construction of the Copco One hydroelectric plant on the Klamath River above Fall Creek. Preliminary work on the project began in 1912 and the first 10,000-kw unit went into service in 1918. Prospect Construction completed the Prospect One plant and a transmission line to Gold Ray and placed them in operation February 20, 1912.

Control of the California-Oregon company passed to San Francisco interests during the period Copco One was under construction. When that plant came into operation the transmission line from Fall Creek to Dunsmuir and Castella was extended south to a point known as Delta where it connected with a line built northward from Kennett by Pacific Gas and Electric Company. The interconnection was made at government request to augment power supply in the San Francisco area at a time when World War I was imposing heavy load on existing facilities.

A program to regulate the water of Upper Klamath Lake for both irrigation and power was worked out with the U. S. Bureau of Reclamation just before the outbreak of World War I and a contract signed on February 24, 1917. This involved construction of a dam at the Link River outlet of the lake and arrangements for Copco to supply power for pumping and other purposes to the Klamath Basin Irrigation Project. Actual work on the dam was started in 1920, together with the erection of dikes around the lake to increase storage capacity without overflowing agricultural lands. The dam was completed in 1921.

The California-Oregon ("hyphen") company was reorganized into The California Oregon Power Company, incorporated October 16, 1920, with headquarters in San Francisco. The new corporation took over the assets of its predecessor January 1, 1921.

In December of that year the head office of the firm was moved from San Francisco to Medford. About the same time, work was started on raising the dam and installing a second unit at the Copco One plant on the Klamath River, and arrangements were made with Mountain States Power for construction of a transmission line from Prospect to Springfield to supplement the supply of power in the Willamette valley. This line was completed and went into service November 1, 1922, and the added Copco One generating unit was in operation within the month.

Properties of the Douglas County Light and Water Company in the Roseburg area were acquired July 1, 1923, and in 1924 the new East Side plant at Klamath Falls was completed to replace the one built in 1906. Work was started in 1924 on Copco Two at a site just below Copco One and a 110,000-volt line was built from that point to Delta to increase capacity of the PG&E tie.

In October, 1925, the stockholders owning all of the common stock and part of the preferred stock of California Oregon Power exchanged their stocks for securities of California Power Corporation, a subsidiary of Standard Gas & Electric Company, which in turn was controlled by H. M. Byllesby Company of Chicago. The Byllesby holdings also included Mountain States Power, with which Copco was interconnected at Springfield. A second tie between the companies was established in 1929, when a 110,000-volt line was built from Dixonville to North Bend, where Copco leased Mountain States' 5,000-kilowatt steam generating plant and in 1930 increased capacity of the station to 15,000 kw.

During the depression years and throughout World War II the company's construction activities were necessarily limited. It did, however, effect a recapitalization in 1942, made possible by a capital contribution by Standard Gas & Electric of approximately $4,500,000 worth of debentures, preferred and common stock. This enabled Copco to meet requirements of the Federal Power Commission with respect to restating plant accounts on the "original cost" basis.

Through lines constructed earlier, Copco had been supplying power to California Public Service Company serving Lakeview and Alturas, and in 1944 these properties were acquired and added to the Copco system. A year later the diesel plant and distribution system of Public Utilities California Corporation in and adjacent to Crescent City were acquired and work began on a connecting transmission line from Grants Pass to the coast.

Power demand in the Copco service area continued to grow throughout World War II and in 1945 field studies were completed on a long-envisioned hydroelectric development on the North Umpqua River east of Roseburg. Reconnaisance of the power potential of the stream had begun as early as 1922 with a study of 64 miles of the river and its tributaries from the confluence with Little River to Diamond Lake.

A preliminary permit for appropriation of water was obtained from the Oregon Hydroelectric Commission in the fall of 1945 and application for license to construct was filed with the Federal Power Commission. An FPC license was granted July 19, 1946.

275

*When the first unit at Copco No. 1 plant on the Klamath River
started up in 1918 part of its output went over a brand new interconnection
with Pacific Gas and Electric Company to serve World War I
power needs in the San Francisco area. The dam was raised and
another generator installed in 1922, increasing capacity to 27,500 kw.
The 32,000-kw Copco No. 2 plant downstream was built in 1924-25.*

Project plans called for eight separate plants located within a radius of about ten miles on the upper watershed of the North Umpqua. Construction was scheduled over a period of ten years, beginning in 1947.

The big development required an investment of $57,000,000 and resulted in the addition of 208,600 kilowatts of generating capacity to the company's system. Largest of the plants is Toketee, with 44,900 kilowatts produced by three generators. Net effective head of water on the turbines is 420 feet.

The 12,300-kilowatt Fish Creek plant has an effective head of 995 feet and the 32,000-kilowatt Clearwater No. 2 plant has a head of 742 feet. Lemolo No. 2, the second largest installation in the group, has a capability of 35,000 kilowatts. A canal and flume system carries water 13.2 miles to a forebay 705 feet above the turbine level.

Lemolo No. 1, with a head of 710 feet, has generating capability of 33,000 kilowatts and is the uppermost unit. Also a high-head plant is Clearwater No. 1 with 18,700 kilowatts of capacity and a net effective head of 627 feet.

276

The Slide Creek plant has 20,000 kilowatts of capacity and a head of 177 feet. Just downstream from it is the 12,700-kilowatt Soda Springs plant, which derives its head from a 126.5-foot concrete dam across the river. Primary function of this dam is to smooth the flow of the stream below the project area by leveling out variations in discharges of water at the upstream plants.

In conjunction with the power development, a cooperative program for construction of access roads was undertaken. This helped to open up a large area for recreation and also facilitated harvest of important timber resources. The entire project is located within the boundaries of the Umpqua National Forest.

Start of the North Umpqua development in 1947 was one of two important events occuring in that year of Copco's history. The other was the sale by Standard Gas & Electric Company of its stock holdings in Copco to an underwriting group, which in turn resold the stock to the public. This terminated 21 years of holding company control of the utility.

Looking beyond the North Umpqua program, Copco began in 1951 initial steps toward obtaining licenses to construct another hydro plant on the Klamath River at Big Bend, between Keno and the California state line. A Federal Power Commission license for the plant was granted January 28, 1954, on condition that the company secure an extension of its 1917 agreement with the Bureau of Reclamation relating to the regulation of Upper Klamath Lake and operation of Link River dam. On January 31, 1956, the company and the USBR executed the required new agreement running to the year 2006, the life of the FPC license. Construction was started in July, 1956, and the plant and related transmission facilities went into service on October 1, 1958.

Capacity of the plant is 88,000 kilowatts, making it the largest of the Klamath River developments. Name of the installation was changed from Big Bend to the John C. Boyle Hydroelectric Project in a ceremony held June 25, 1962. A plaque unveiled at that time describes Boyle as "a distinguished engineer, who designed the project and supervised its construction and whose talents since graduation from the University of California in 1910 have been devoted to the advancement of electric service throughout the system of The California Oregon Power Company and its successor company, Pacific Power & Light."

Iron Gate dam on the Klamath River in northern California was dedicated February 3, 1962. The 18,000-kw, $7,500,000 project regulates for the benefit of fish habitat the flow of the river downstream from the hydro plants lying between this site and Upper Klamath Lake. It includes holding ponds and hatchery facilities operated by the California Department of Fish and Game for the propagation of salmon and steelhead.

In 1959 Copco entered into an agreement with the California Department of Fish and Game providing that the company would construct a regulating dam on the Klamath River at the Iron Gate site about seven miles below the Copco Two plant. A fill-type dam 173 feet high was designed to create a reservoir with a capacity of 58,000 acre feet to re-regulate the flow of water released from upstream plants and eliminate controversial fluctuations in the lower river. Provision was also made in the project for comprehensive fish facilities, including holding tanks and a hatchery, built to state specifications and owned and operated by the state.

License to construct the project was issued by the Federal Power Commission in January, 1960, and the 18,000-kilowatt development was dedicated on February 3, 1962. It brought hydro installations on the Klamath River to a total of 160,000 kilowatts.

On the upper stretch of the Klamath, a new control dam was completed near Keno in December, 1966, to replace a wooden structure damaged in the 1964 flood. The new concrete dam ultimately will serve as a diversion for an additional hydro development upstream from the John C. Boyle plant. Potential of the site is 48,000 kilowatts.

278

Chapter 47

Columbus Day, 1962, Remembered

GROWTH of the Company's business in 1962 put revenues of the enlarged system over the $100,000,000 mark and brought the total number of electric customers close to 400,000.

Final links were completed in a 230,000-volt line to provide a heavy-duty interconnection between the Company's Willamette Valley system and the power production facilities in the Copco division area in southern Oregon and northern California.

In southeastern Washington the Company's portion of a 230,-000-volt line between Walla Walla and Lewiston, Idaho, was completed and work started on the extension of this circuit from Walla Walla to the Wanapum dam on the Columbia. PP&L and Washington Water Power each built half of this transmission project. Among other purposes, the line carries into the Company's system part of the 662,000 kilowatts of power under contract from non-federal projects on the mid-Columbia.

In Wyoming, work was started on a third generating unit at the Dave Johnston steam-electric plant. The new 220,000-kilowatt unit was to bring total capability of the plant to 420,000 kilowatts upon completion in 1964.

The Company in 1962 launched a system-wide program to sell an area lighting service to provide automatic dusk-to-dawn lighting for farmyards, parking lots and similar off-street areas. Under the plan, the Company installs, owns and maintains an efficient mercury-vapor lamp fixture, suitably mounted on a pole, at a price of $4.00 per month. In the first year, this program resulted in the installation of 8,143 of these units. By 1968 the total had reached 20,000, yielding $1,300,000 in annual revenue.

A two-for-one split of the Company's common stock was overwhelmingly approved by the stockholders at a special meeting held February 7, 1962, and became effective February 23.

Long to be remember by the Pacific organization was the 1962 Columbus Day storm. A special edition of *The Bulletin* described as the "big blow" as follows:

"The electric service system of Pacific Power & Light Company suffered the most devastating and disruptive damage in the 52-year record of the Company on October 12 as the worst storm in West Coast history roared off the Pacific Ocean and battered its way from California northward along the coast into Oregon's populous Willamette valley and the Portland area.

"Within six hours after the hurricane-force gusts had ripped into Crescent City, Calif., the first hard-hit PP&L area, the brute force of the storm had caused damage to Company properties estimated at approximately $5,000,000, interrupted services to more than 200,000 customers.

"Toppled, shattered and tilted were thousands of power poles and uprooted trees and these were tangled with miles of transmission and distribution conductor.

"Power supply lines from PP&L's Merwin and Yale hydroelectric plants on the Lewis River and Toketee on the North Umpqua River were severed. Major transmission lines to the coast districts and throughout the Willamette valley system were downed at many locations. Links with other utilities were broken. At Coos Bay a 200-foot-high transmission tower was a crushed maze of steel pushed into the bay. In Portland harbor, a drifting freighter had dragged an anchor through a submarine power crossing. . . .

"In the annals of all utility industry in the West, no other company has ever been confronted with as widespread and destructive damage to its system.

"The havoc had begun at 12:28 P.M. at Crescent City, and minutes later the storm slammed into Grants Pass, Medford and Klamath Falls, and northward. The Roseburg area was blacked out by 3:00 P.M. One hour later the winds were ripping apart the services to Cottage Grove, Springfield, Junction City, Corvallis, Albany and Lebanon and adjacent towns and rural areas. While the poles and lines came tumbling down in the heart of the Willamette valley, the full force of the storm began whistling into the canyons of downtown Portland. . . .

"At the nerve center of Pacific Power's operations headquarters in Portland, the big power dispatch board, the storm's progress had been logged minute by minute, mile after mile of destruction. Dispatchers had worked feverishly at the board and with men at substations in the field to reroute power, isolate troubled lines, and

280

*Largest Copco development on the Klamath River, the 88,000-kw
plant at Big Bend, was designated the "John C. Boyle Hydroelectric
Project" on June 25, 1962. Plaque was unveiled by Boyle's granddaughter,
Sue Ann Rutherford. Boyle is on platform at left. Glenn L. Jackson
and D. R. McClung are by the microphone.*

maintain the flow of energy into service districts that lay behind,
amidst and ahead of the storm front.

"While most of the system lay dead, downtown Portland, its
underground core area being supplied by the combined steam-
electric generation of PP&L's Lincoln Street Station and neighboring Portland General Electric Company's Station L, had withstood
the onslaught for three hours.

"The Pacific Power sign atop the Public Service Building kept
flashing a message of light and reassurance into the darkened sky.
Suddenly at 6:48 P.M. the downtown system became overloaded.
Now the big sign was out. For six long minutes the largest city on
the system experienced a complete power outage.

"Then 'Pacific Power' flashed bright again atop the tower.

"The Pacific Power organization, its mobilization ordered in the
first hour of the storm, was functioning in the honored tradition of
its half-century of public service. As far east as Wyoming and
Montana, PP&L crews began to assemble and to move by air and
ground transport toward western Oregon to join many other hundreds of co-workers already on the job.

281

"Servicemen, groundmen, linemen, the engineers, 'phone and office girls, salesmen, power and district superintendents, managers, the executives, all did their jobs around the clock. Together they successfully surmounted the greatest test of their skills and experience, and reaffirmed by their performance, their dedication to customer service. Nearly all customers again had power by the end of one week, but it will be many more weeks before final repairs to the physical system are completed."

A later inventory of damage caused by the storm put the loss at about $3,500,000, which was covered by catastrophe insurance to the extent that the costs exceeded $250,000.

Prompt to give aid in the emergency were utilities outside of the storm zone. Southern California Edison Company, for example, sent 26 linemen from Los Angeles via an Air Force transport. Utah Power & Light sent 27 from Salt Lake City. Contractors also rallied to the challenge, among them Line Constructors, of Kalispell, with six crews.

In a special message to members of the Pacific family, President Don R. McClung said: "The exemplary performance of everyone in this period of crisis for our system will remain a memorable one. . . . All of you share in the fine compliments that have been received from the many hundreds of customers who have expressed their appreciation for the heroic effort that was made to restore their electric services under the most difficult circumstances."

The generally good spirit in which customers endured the widespread and often prolonged service outages was indeed heartwarming to the weary repair crews.

As a postscript to the 1962 storm story, it may happily be noted that less than a month later the Company's customers in Josephine County, Oregon, voted more than 4-to-1 to reject a proposal to establish a people's utility district and put their electric service under public ownership. The Grants Pass area involved was among the first on the Company system in Oregon to be hit by the blow.

Chapter 48

Company Contracts Additional Power

UNDER LEGISLATION passed by Congress in 1962, the Company and other private utilities of the region late in the year were offered the right to contract for up to 50% of the power to be made available by the construction of generating facilities at the Hanford Works of the Atomic Energy Commission. The power plant was to be built by the Washington Public Power Supply System in connection with a new dual purpose plutonium producing reactor to be built by the AEC.

Pacific signed a contract jointly with WPPSS and Bonneville Power Administration for 10% of the output of the plant. Washington Water Power, Portland General Electric, Montana Power and Puget Sound Power & Light each took similar shares.

The Hanford installation called for two 400,000-kilowatt generators, and it was estimated that the average amount of power to be obtained by the Company would range between 60,000 and 153,000 kilowatts. The actual amount would vary in proportion to the difference in annual costs, experienced principally during periods when the reactor may be operated to produce plutonium as contrasted with periods when the reactor is operated to produce steam for power production only. Total output of the plant was scheduled to go into the BPA system.

Under the 30-year, three-party contracts, BPA agreed to deliver to each participant in the plan an amount of power valued at Bonneville rates that was equivalent to the participant's share in the annual costs of the power installation. This meant a power cost the same as if purchased directly from Bonneville.

In the following year the Company contracted to acquire for approximately 50 years 6.9% of the output of the 774,000-kilowatt Wells hydroelectric project on the Columbia River downstream from Chief Joseph Dam. The Wells project had been licensed by the Federal Power Commission for construction by the Douglas County, Washington, PUD. The Company also contracted for an additional 4.2% of the project output for a shorter period.

283

The Wells agreement gave the Company a total of 356,000 kilowatts under contract for 50-year periods from four non-federal projects on the Columbia, and an additional 306,000 kilowatts from these installations for shorter periods.

In 1964 the Company arranged to purchase 10% of the Canadian share of the power to be made available under the Canadian-United States Columbia River Treaty during the period from 1968 to 2003. The Company's portion of this power varies from a maximum of about 140,000 kilowatts in 1975 to approximately 20,000 kilowatts after the year 2000.

The treaty was negotiated by the two governments to provide a basis for development of storage reservoirs at three sites on the upper Columbia River in Canada, to be operated by British Columbia so as to provide more firm power at U. S. hydroelectric projects downstream. The resulting benefits are to be divided equally.

On September 11, 1964, the third generating unit at the Dave Johnston steam plant in Wyoming was dedicated, with members of the Company's Board of Directors and more than 1,000 state and civic leaders present for the ceremonies.

This 220,000-kilowatt expansion of the plant made it economical to install rail haul facilities in place of the heavy-duty, off-highway trucks that had been used to transport coal from the field to the plant. The truck road was designed and built with curves and grades to rail specifications, and the laying of track and conversion to a rail haul operation was substantially accomplished in the month of October, 1964.

In northern California and much of Oregon the closing days of 1964 are remembered for unusual floods that caused much loss and human distress in the affected areas.

Heavy snows accumulated at higher elevations in early December. Then, toward Christmas, warm rains swept in from the Pacific Ocean to drench the region and bring out the snow in torrents.

Although the Company's properties were not damaged to the extent that first was feared, several of its smaller hydroelectric projects suffered varying degrees of flooding. Sections of canals and flumes were washed out in some locations and removal of debris was a major task. Distribution facilities were affected only in localized areas and relatively few customers were without service for any extended period of time. In its 1964 annual report,

284

the Company estimated that damages, when fully assessed, would exceed $3,000,000, with all but the first $500,000 covered by catastrophe insurance.

On the whole, however, the Company year was a good one and the 1964 annual report was prefaced with a summary of progress since 1954.

"In this 10-year period," it said, "annual operating revenues increased 94%, crossing the $100,000,000 mark in 1962 and reaching $112,682,000 in 1964. During the same period, sales of electric energy doubled, more than 62,000 electric customers were added to the Company's lines, and peak load on the system grew from 967,000 kilowatts in 1954 to more than 2,000,000 kilowatts in December, 1964, a new record. All of these figures are on a combined basis for years prior to mergers."

There were sad notes, too, in the record of the year, among them the death of George T. Bragg on April 29, 1964, at Faulensee, Switzerland, while on a European trip. He was 67. Bragg served as vice president and general manager of the Company from 1936 to 1960 and was a member of the Board of Directors.

In its memorial resolution, the Board noted that more than 40 years of Bragg's life had been dedicated to the Company and spoke of him as "one of the stalwarts." It went on to quote from a *Bulletin* editorial tribute:

"His was a large and close family of friends — friends who held him in deep affection and respect. . . . It is easy for these friends to understand why the young lad who joined the army at Hood River in 1917 came out of the service as a sergeant major. Then and throughout his life, willing acceptance of responsibility and the faithful fulfillment of duties, pleasant or otherwise, were among notable characteristics of the man. . . . Those who worked at his side through dark and troublesome days in the Company's history . . . gained the fullest appreciation of his unbounded courage, loyalty and essential kindness of heart. . . . In spirit he still walks beside us with the long, brisk pace of the drill field, hat brim upthrust to the wind, a twinkle in his eye, and a smile ready to illuminate his face. May his soul rest in peace."

Dave Johnston steam plant as it looked upon completion of 220,000-kw third unit in 1964. Including the coal field development, Company's investment at this point totaled more than $67,000,000 and the plant payroll had become a major economic benefit in the area. (Below) With No. 3 unit in operation at Dave Johnston, the 14-mile truck haul road from the coal field was converted to rail operation.

Chapter 49

Jackson Succeeds McKee

THE COMPANY'S 1965 annual report noted that at the June meeting of the Board of Directors Glenn L. Jackson was elected chairman to succeed Paul B. McKee, who had guided the affairs of the Company through an eventful 32-year period. Jackson had been vice chairman since the Copco merger in 1961.

Of McKee, who became president in 1933, the report said: "His imaginative, courageous leadership contributed immeasurably to the maintenance and progress of the enterprise through critical years in its history. . . . He continues to be associated with the Company as a director and a member of the executive committee."

Don C. Frisbee, formerly vice president and assistant to the president, was named executive vice president at the same meeting.

Elected a vice president at the September, 1965, Board meeting was John Y. Lansing, whose representation of the Company in the field of public affairs had done much toward the achievement of a better understanding of power problems that were of common concern.

A construction project embarked upon in 1965 was a 50-mile portion of one of the extra-high-voltage regional intertie lines being built between the Pacific Northwest and the Pacific Southwest by federal and non-federal agencies in a coordinated program. Two of these lines were to be 500,000-volt alternating current and two were to be 750,000-volt direct current.

As described in the annual report: "The section of 500,000-volt line being built by your Company extends from a point near Malin, Oregon, 35 miles east of Klamath Falls, into northern California and will connect with a similar line being built by Pacific Gas and Electric Company. The northern segments of the line from Malin to the Columbia River are being built by Portland General Electric Company and Bonneville Power Administration.

"A 230,000-volt tie between Malin and the Company's 230,000-volt network at Klamath Falls was completed in 1965 and when the new tie to the south is completed early in 1966, the

(Left) Glenn L. Jackson was named Chairman of the Board of PP&L in 1965. (Right) Don C. Frisbee became president of the Company in 1966.

interconnection will be operated initially at 230,000 volts. This will give the Company a heavy-duty interconnection with Pacific Gas and Electric capable of handling greatly increased amounts of exchange power under contract arrangements made in 1962. Upon completion of the 500,000-volt circuit to the north, the interconnection will be operated at designed voltage and will be used by the Company and others for the inter-regional marketing of surplus power and energy.

"Including a large transmission substation at Malin, scheduled for completion in 1967, the Company's facilities associated with the regional intertie will cost approximately $10,000,000."

The line was energized at 230,000 volts in April, 1966, and the Company began delivering over it substantial amounts of power into the PG&E system under the companies' agreements for the mutually beneficial exchange of energy. Northern segments of the circuit were completed the following year and the line went into operation at the 500,000-volt level in September, 1967.

In the financial area, the Company's directors took action at the September, 1965, meeting to authorize the filing of applications for listing its common stock on the New York Stock Exchange and the Pacific Coast Stock Exchange. These shares had been traded over-the-counter since 1950.

288

After submission of all required information to the governors of the exchanges, the Company's applications were approved and the stock admitted to trading on January 3, 1966. It was the first new listing of the year. Ticker symbol assigned was PPW.

In New York for the informal ceremony noting the initial trading of PPW on the "Big Board" were several members of the Company's executive staff, headed by D. R. McClung, president.

It was a happy occasion for a man who had been with PP&L for nearly a half-century and was beginning to plan for his retirement years starting in the middle of 1966.

But on March 25 Don McClung was taken by death, following a brief illness and exploratory surgery that revealed a fast-moving and inoperable cancer.

The Company's 1966 annual report spoke sadly of the loss of a member of the family "who had served the Company as a director since 1953, its president since 1958, and its chief executive officer since 1963. His untimely passing at age 67, a few months before he planned to retire, closed a career of 49 years with the Company. During these years he helped build Pacific Power into one of the largest electric systems in the West.

"Pacific Power was only seven years old and served only a few communities in Washington and Oregon when he joined the firm in 1917 as a draftsman. His work was marked by a devotion to the progress of the Company that carried him to positions of increasing responsibilities in engineering, construction and operations, and then to the corporation's principal position of administrative trust.

"During the Korean war he was called to Washington, D. C., to be director of the Materials Equipment Division of the Defense Electric Power Administration. His career was also distinguished by roles of leadership in affairs of the utility industry and in Portland, where he resided. He had served as a director of the National Association of Electric Companies, the National Association of Manufacturers, Northwest Electric Light & Power Association and the Portland Chamber of Commerce, and held chairmanships in a number of community betterment programs."

Shortly thereafter, following the annual meeting of the Company's stockholders on April 19, 1966, the Board of Directors elected Don C. Frisbee to succeed McClung as president. Executive vice president since 1965, Frisbee previously had served suc-

Two muddy PP&L trucks were first vehicles ferried across Klamath River near its mouth after December, 1964, flood washed out bridge on California coast highway. U. S. Army Engineers supplied pontoon equipment to meet emergency. Restoration of electric service was high on priority list in flooded areas.

cessively as treasurer, vice president and treasurer and vice president and assistant to the president. He was 42 years old when the responsibilities of the presidency were placed on his shoulders. Some guessed he was the youngest man ever to head the Company. But this was not the case. Guy W. Talbot was only 36 when he was selected to be PP&L's first president in 1910. Paul McKee was 41 when he took over the reins in 1933.

Also at the April, 1966, Board meeting two new vice presidents were named. One was George L. Beard, assistant chief engineer, who later was appointed general manager following the retirement on June 30, 1966, of Albert Bauer, vice president and general manager since 1961. The other was Howard Arnett, Wyoming division manager. Also retiring on June 30 was John Dierdorff, vice president, after 32 years of service with the Company in the field of advertising and public relations.

290

Chapter 50

Growth Calls for Bigger Plants

THE UTILITY SYSTEM operating under the Pacific Power & Light banner in 1966 was a large enterprise, serving 462,000 electric customers.

In the five years since the Copco merger the Company had spent more than $200,000,000 for the construction of improved and expanded facilities to serve the needs of its customers.

Average annual residential use of electricity had increased more than 1,000 kilowatt-hours to put the average over the 10,000-kwh mark. Industrial customers were using a billion and a quarter more kilowatt-hours of energy per year than in 1961.

The system peak load had increased 500,000 kilowatts in five years, and this was an up-front consideration in two development decisions made by PP&L during the fall of 1966 and early 1967.

Orders were placed in September, 1966, for the major equipment components for a 250,000-kilowatt fourth unit at the Dave Johnston steam plant in Wyoming. Size of the unit was later increased to 330,000 kilowatts as a result of continuing studies of the needs of the Company and of neighboring utilities. This would boost capability of the plant to 750,000 kilowatts, when the unit came into service in June, 1972.

With reference to utilization of its coal deposits in western Washington, the Company's 1966 annual report said:

"Load and resource studies for the Pacific Northwest indicate that by the early 1970's most of the major base-load hydroelectric potential of the region's rivers will have been developed. Your Company has been actively participating in regional studies in cooperation with others regarding the timing, size and location of new steam-electric power plants that will be needed.

"In this connection, your Company and The Washington Water Power Company recently announced plans for two 500,000-kilowatt steam-electric units to be located near Centralia, Washington. The first unit is planned to be in service in the early 1970s, and the second shortly thereafter. . . . The site is adjacent to extensive coal deposits owned by the two companies since 1957, and is advantageously situated close to the principal load centers in western Oregon and Washington. The coal field could eventually support two million kilowatts of generating capacity."

Size of the Centralia installation later was increased to 1,400,000 kilowatts, as reported in the Company's 1967 annual statement:

"Planning has involved discussions with other companies and publicly-owned agencies of the Pacific Northwest on possible joint ownership, and negotiations with the United States Bureau of Reclamation and Bonneville Power Administration. On December 26, officers of the two companies (PP&L and WWP) signed an agreement with the two federal agencies whereby the first 700,000-kilowatt unit will be placed in service by January 1, 1972, to meet requirements of the Bureau's Central Valley Project in California and to supply temporary deficiencies in BPA's firm power resources. A major portion of the output will be available to your Company in 1974 and to other participants at later dates.

"Preliminary field and engineering work is in progress, and boiler and generator-turbine components have been ordered. Foundation construction will start by mid-1968. A pilot mine operation opened one coal seam late in 1967 to provide data for development of the mining plan."

The decisions to go ahead with bigger units at both Centralia and Glenrock reflected the high degree of coordination that was being attained in power development planning within the region.

The Company's 1967 report commented that the revised schedule at Glenrock had been made "in anticipation of power exchange agreements with three other companies of the Rocky Mountain region . . . which will enable the companies to take advantage of the operating economies of larger generating installations."

The plan provided for the initial output from a new generating unit of Utah Power & Light to be shared by Idaho, Montana and Pacific while the additional unit at Glenrock was constructed.

Further interest in long-range power supply planning was recounted in PP&L's 1968 report. It said:

"Significant progress was made during 1968 in planning with neighboring electric systems and federal agencies for the construction of generating plants and transmission circuits that will be required for the years ahead.

"In October an accord was reached by the 109 electric systems

292

and federal agencies in the Pacific Northwest Joint Power Planning Council on a 20-year plan for the development of new power facilities. It envisions the existing and future hydroelectric capacity being used primarily for peaking purposes and the base energy load for the Pacific Northwest ultimately being shifted to new thermal-electric capacity, of which an estimated 21-million kilowatts will be needed through the 1970s and 1980s.

"The program calls for the power companies and local publicly-owned systems to construct the steam-electric plants, and federal agencies to continue the development of the remaining hydroelectric potential of the region's major river system. In the early operating years of each new steam-electric plant, the Bonneville Power Administration will absorb capacity which is surplus to the needs of the sponsoring utilities. This will make it feasible to build larger and more economic installations, and at the same time provide sources of power for BPA to meet its system requirements.

"The continuing planning work, in which Pacific Power is an actve participant, has been widely endorsed as a realistic approach to the orderly development of future power supplies."

Note was made that completion date of the first 700,000-kilowatt unit at Centralia had been advanced to September, 1971.

"Completion of the second 700,000-kilowatt unit has been advanced to an in-service date of September, 1972, in response to the needs of the Bonneville Power Administration, which will absorb the entire output during the first year and the sponsors take it thereafter. Before the Centralia plant is fully in service, other jointly-owned projects will be under construction."

The Company's favorable position with respect to coal supplies available to it in the region's emerging thermal-power era was evident from other comments in the 1968 report, which spoke of explorations carried forward by the Company's geologists in Wyoming and southern Montana.

"The work proved up an additional 200,000,000 tons of reserves near the Company's Glenrock coal field. . . . The additional tonnage more than doubles the reserves at that field, assuring fuel for future plant expansion possibilities at that location.

"In southwestern Wyoming, a drilling program approximately 35 miles northeast of Rock Springs proved up reserves of 100,000,000 tons of low-cost coal suitable for power plant use.

Company's first 500,000-volt transmission line, built in 1965-66,
is part of a major tie between Pacific Northwest and Pacific Southwest.
It covers a 50-mile section south from Malin, Oregon, to a
northern California connection with a similar line of Pacific
Gas and Electric Company. Towers are 140 feet high.

294

"Including the reserves in the large Decker field in southern Montana, the exploration program has proved up in excess of one billion tons of sub-bituminous coal available to the Company in the two Rocky Mountain states. The deposits under federal and state lands are held through leases and prospecting permits, and those under private ownership are held through purchase options or royalty agreements."

Importance of these coal reserves in terms of power supply potential was dramatized on September 26, 1969, when Pacific Power & Light and Idaho Power Company announced plans to construct jointly a $300,000,000 coal-fired generating complex in the vicinity of Rock Springs.

"The plant will have a rated capacity of 1,500,000 kilowatts," the announcement stated, "and is being constructed to meet the needs for generation of large new quantities of electric energy for the Pacific Northwest and Rocky Mountain regions in the 1970's."

It would include three 500,000-kilowatt units and be the second largest coal-fired steam-electric plant west of the Mississippi when the full installation is completed in 1978.

The first unit was slated to come into service in 1974 and would be built for Idaho Power. The second and third units were planned for 1975 and 1978 to serve needs of Pacific Power.

Included in the power development program were three high-voltage transmission lines, planned to operate at 345,000 volts. One circuit would run from the plant to connect with the Idaho system at Pocatello. The other two would tie in at American Falls.

Power put into the Idaho system from the Wyoming plant would displace power theretofore moving east from that company's hydro plants in the western part of the state. Corresponding portions of their output would then flow to the west. Such transfers of energy would minimize transmission losses and make very effective use of facilities.

Marked diversity in seasonal peak loads between southern Idaho and the western area adds to mutual benefits from the arrangement.

Presidents Don Frisbee of Pacific and Albert Carlsen of Idaho said studies had confirmed that the Rock Springs project "will produce power at a substantially lower cost than any nuclear-fired plant that could be ready for service in the mid-1970's."

295

They also noted that the new Wyoming facility was part of the program of the Pacific Northwest Joint Power Planning Council, calling for seven major new plants to come into production between 1971 and 1980 to meet regional power needs.

Coal underlying approximately 18,000 acres in the Nine Mile Draw area northeast of Rock Springs occurs in seams up to 30 feet thick and is extremely low in sulfur content. It will be recovered by surface mining methods.

Start of plant construction was scheduled for 1971. This meant that in a five-year period Pacific Power would have participated in ground-breaking for 3,530,000 kilowatts of new steam power installations — equivalent to the total generating capacity of the entire Northwest Power Pool area in 1944!

Paul McKee, sadly, did not live to see another dream fulfilled in the form of a Pacific-Idaho joint venture for development of 1,500,000 kilowatts from Wyoming coal, with an accompanying expansion of transmission capacity between the Rocky Mountain and Pacific Northwest areas. McKee died on February 26, 1968, at the age of 76.

If any one man deserved a lion's share of credit for the establishment of PP&L's highly favorable position with respect to coal reserves it was Paul McKee. This he would disclaim, insisting it was a team effort, which it was indeed. But leading the team with enthusiasm and vision was an individual whose years of experience nourished rather than diminished a youthful, questing spirit.

The Company's Board in its memorial resolution, characterized McKee "a rare friend, a gallant leader and a noble citizen.

"Few know better than we the breadth and depth of his personal contribution to the preservation and extraordinary development of Pacific Power & Light as an investor-owned public service enterprise. Few had the opportunity to see more clearly how vital a part his imaginative and courageous leadership played in guiding the Company safely through most critical periods in its existence, or to observe how widely the force of his dynamic personality was radiated through and beyond the organization.

"Mr. McKee was president of the Company from February 25, 1933, to September 15, 1958, chairman of the board from 1958 to June 9, 1965, and a member of the Board of Directors throughout the 35 years of his life that were devoted unstintedly to this

296

At the end of 1970 construction was well advanced on first big thermal plant in program of the Joint Power Planning Council comprised of 109 Pacific Northwest electric systems and Bonneville Power Administration. The 1,400,000-kw project near Centralia, Washington, is based on coal reserves proved up and owned by PP&L and Washington Water Power.

enterprise, which today, in a very real sense, constitutes a living memorial and tribute to his remarkable capacity for constructive accomplishment."

The important power development plan worked out by the Pacific and Idaho companies in 1969 was one which McKee's spirit would applaud enthusiastically. It was a logical step forward in the further coordination of regional power resources.

Pacific's system in Wyoming already had a 230,000-volt tie with Utah Power & Light at Kemmerer, where the Utah company had developed 380,000-kilowatts of coal-fired steam capacity and was adding a 330,000-kilowatt unit. Utah, in turn, was interconnected with Idaho to the west and was supplying steam power to the latter under an interim contract to supplement hydro resources.

Idaho Power had approximately 1,500,000 kilowatts of hydro capacity on its system, mostly on the Snake River in the western part of the state. More than 1,000,000 kilowatts of this peak capability was in the Brownlee, Oxbow and Hells Canyon projects spanning the Snake River along the Idaho-Oregon border.

On the other hand, some of Idaho's largest power loads were to the east in the Pocatello area, including the energy needs of important phosphate plants. To serve these loads Idaho maintained large-capacity transmission circuits across the state.

From its Snake River generating complex Idaho also had three 230,000-volt lines to the west in addition to its ties with the eastern Oregon properties of California-Pacific Utilities Company. One line from Brownlee dam connected with the Bonneville grid at La Grande, Oregon. Another, built in part by Washington Water Power, tied in with that company's system at Lewiston, Idaho. A third 230,000-volt line connected with the 78-mile circuit completed by PP&L in 1968 between Walla Walla and Enterprise.

From eastern Idaho there were also north-south transmission connections. An existing 161,000-volt line tied in with the Montana Power system at Anaconda and a paralleling 230,000-volt circuit was being readied for construction. To the south, Utah Power & Light had a 230,000-volt tie with Arizona and the Pacific Southwest and was adding a 365,000-volt line into the area.

Breadth of such system interconnections was commented upon in PP&L's 1967 annual report. It said:

"Since the energizing of the first Pacific Northwest-Pacific Southwest intertie circuit at 500,000 volts, the 40 major power systems of 13 western states and western Canada have formed a Western Systems Coordinating Council. The voluntary organization is pooling the technical personnel of the utilities and government agencies in planning for the highest possible operational reliability of the interconnected systems.

"Personnel of Pacific Power also shared in the planning and testing of the first East-West tie operation linking together 209 major public and privately owned systems across the nation on February 7, 1967, as part of a continuing program to evaluate the limitations and capabilities of large-scale power operations. During the tests, 94% of the nation's generating capacity and 265,000 miles of high-voltage transmission circuits were operated as a single system. A vital section of the tie was the Company's 230,000-volt transmission network in Wyoming."

Chapter 51

The Company Came Far in 60 Years

PACIFIC POWER & LIGHT entered 1970 — its 60th year — with total assets of more than $836,000,000 and annual revenues on the way to reach the $150,000,000 mark before the June 16 anniversary date of the Company's incorporation.

The number of customers served was 492,572. Peak load on the system had reached 2,400,000 kilowatts. The Company had in its own power stations an installed generating capacity of 1,367,000 kilowatts, a figure scheduled to be doubled before 1975.

Annual use of electricity by the Company's residential customers was near the 11,500-kilowatt-hour mark. This was 35 times the 1920 average. Average price received per kilowatt-hour for residential service had come down to 15% of the 1920 figure.

The Company in 1969 had an operating payroll of $20,-000,000 and a construction payroll of $13,650,000. Its taxes for the year were $22,916,000.

By any standard of measurement, Pacific Power had become a large enterprise, ranking 32nd in annual revenues among all the operating electric companies of the nation.

Yet there was something about it which *Electrical West,* in its April, 1964, "Portrait of a Power Company" described as follows:

"How to grow big and prosperous, yet retain the flavor of a small company, is the story of Pacific Power & Light Company. This company has been able to achieve a highly favorable public acceptance, develop and keep dedicated employees and grow at a remarkable rate. This is its story."

The editor further said: "PP&L executives cut their teeth on a work schedule that demands total dedication to the goals of the company. But for all the lore that has grown up about Paul McKee's indefatigable working habits, the actual hours on the job are but a symptom—an outgrowth of attitudes of the top echelon. Says McKee: 'Hard work and long hours are a real chore for the person who doesn't love what he is doing. If you like and believe in what you are doing, you only regret the shortage of time.' "

The article also quoted Don Frisbee, then vice president and assistant to the president. "Our society," he said, "has undergone a substantial change in the makeup of its income producers in the last century. In the past, the production of goods and services was predominantly the effort of many individual entrepreneurs, whereas today the vast majority of our income producers work for someone else in an employee status.

"The challenge in business today is to develop an environment where the spirit of entrepreneurship which motivated our fore-fathers is a real force. To do this, the organization has to be alive to new ideas, have objectives and goals which are worth-while and understood by its employees, and it must create and maintain natural avenues of advancement for its people."

A brief submitted by the Company in 1966 to the Edison Award Review Committee, when PP&L was one of four utilities nominated for consideration due to its work in research and area development, spoke of the activities as "reflecting a basic philosophy that helped make it possible for the enterprise to survive. . . .

"The fact that the people of the Pacific Northwest region are eager for and welcome development of their region's vast resources . . . made it all the more essential that an electric company seeking to live and prosper in the region not only should share in such hopes but give leadership in their attainment.

"If there is any one thing more than another that has brought the Company to its present position, it has been the inspired willingness of its people to work unstintedly to carry out such a philosophy and earn for the Company the opportunity to enjoy both the material and intangible rewards of good citizenship."

These would be fitting words with which to end the story of Pacific Power & Light Company's first 60 years. Board Chairman Glenn L. Jackson, however, instinctively would suggest the addition of one more quotation, this from a report made for the Company in 1967 by Battelle Memorial Institute:

"The challenge which faces the leadership of the region in such an era of growth and expansion is to have sufficient foresight and understanding to achieve progress and at the same time maintain a desirable environment."

Tomorrow, we are sure, will be another busy day!

300

Officers and Directors, 1910-70

The following have served as principal officers of the Company, as Directors, or both, in the years since 1910. Abbreviations: Copco, The California Oregon Power Company; Mt. States, Mountain States Power Company; NWE, Northwestern Electric Company; PP&L, Pacific Power & Light Company.

AINSWORTH, J. C........................Portland, Oregon
  Director 1910-35
ARNETT, HOWARD........................Casper, Wyoming
  Vice Pres. 1966-
BABSON, WALTER S........................Portland, Oregon
  Director NWE 1935-47; PP&L 1947-59; Emeritus 1959-68
BARTHOLOMEW, ALLAN C..................Portland, Oregon
  Vice Pres. 1969-
BASH, F. C............................Medford, Oregon
  Vice Pres. & Treas. Copco 1953-61;
  Vice Pres. PP&L 1961-68
BAUER, ALBERT........................Portland, Oregon
  Vice Pres. & Gen. Mgr. 1961-66
BAXTER, H. R..................Philadelphia, Pennsylvania
  Director Mt. States 1952-54; PP&L 1954-64
BEARD, GEORGE L........................Portland, Oregon
  Vice Pres. & Gen. Mgr. 1966-69; Senior Vice Pres. 1969-
BISHOP, C. M..........................Portland, Oregon
  Director 1970-
BOSWORTH, H. P. JR....................Medford, Oregon
  Vice Pres. Copco 1953-61; Vice Pres. PP&L 1961-66
BOYLE, JOHN C........................Medford, Oregon
  Vice Pres. Operations Copco 1938-41; Vice Pres. & Gen.
  Mgr. 1941-61; Vice Pres. PP&L 1961-63; Director Copco
  1938-61; PP&L 1961-63; Emeritus 1963-
BRAGG, GEORGE T......................Portland, Oregon
  Vice Pres. & Gen. Mgr. 1936-60;
  Director 1937-47; 1949-50; 1955-64
BROWN, F. C..........................Portland, Oregon
  Treas. 1964-69
BUEHNER, PHILIP......................Portland, Oregon
  Director 1910-14
BUNTING, LYMAN J....................Yakima, Washington
  Director 1935-68
CAMPBELL, HARRY H..................Kalispell, Montana
  Director Mt. States 1949-54; PP&L 1954-63
CARPENTER, ALFRED S. V.................Medford, Oregon
  Director Copco 1948-61; PP&L 1961-
CHAPMAN, RALPH A....................Corvallis, Oregon
  Director 1963-68
COOKINGHAM, EDWARD ....Portland, Oregon
  Vice Pres. 1911-36; Director 1910-48
COTTON, W. W........................Portland, Oregon
  Counsel 1912-18; Director 1910-18
CUMMINS, A. S........................Medford, Oregon
  Pres. & Ch. Copco 1941-61; Director 1941-61; Vice Ch.
  PP&L 1961-63; Director 1961-63; Emeritus 1963-
DAHL, G. M............................New York, N.Y.
  Director 1913-17

302

DAME, F. L. . . . . New York, N.Y.
Director 1910-13
DAVENPORT, C. P. . . . . Portland, Oregon
Vice Pres. 1968-
DAVIDSON, J. E. . . . . Portland, Oregon
Vice Pres. & Gen. Mgr. 1912-17
DE LUCCIA, E. ROBERT. . . . . Portland, Oregon
Vice Pres. & Chief Engr. 1951-66; Senior Vice Pres. 1966-
69; Director 1966-69
DIERDORFF, JOHN. . . . . Portland, Oregon
Vice Pres. 1947-66; Director 1952-54; 1964-70;
Emeritus 1970-
EGGLESON, A. W. . . . . Enterprise, Oregon
Director 1936-50
FERGUSON, JOHN. . . . . Coos Bay, Oregon
Director Mt. States 1947-54; PP&L 1954-60
FIELDS, ARTHUR L. . . . . Portland, Oregon
Director NWE 1938-47; PP&L 1947-69
FOGG, FRED S. . . . . Tacoma, Washington
Director 1910-33
FRISBEE, DON C. . . . . Portland, Oregon
Treas. 1958-64; Vice Pres. 1960-65; Exec. Vice Pres.
1965-66; Pres. 1966-; Director 1966-
GEIGER, JOHN H. . . . . Portland, Oregon
Treas. 1969-
GLEASON, ALFRED M. Portland, Oregon
Vice Pres. 1968-
GORDON, S. S. . . . . Astoria, Oregon
Director 1910-33
GRAY, H. S. . . . . Portland, Oregon
Director 1933-36
GRENIER, A. S. . . . . New York, N. Y.
Vice Pres. & Gen. Mgr. 1911-12; Director 1917-33
HALL, E. B. . . . . Klamath Falls, Oregon
Director Copco 1946-61; Emeritus PP&L 1961-65
HARRISON, GREGORY A. . . . . San Francisco, California
Director Copco 1953-61; PP&L 1961-
HAWKINS, J. G. . . . . Portland, Oregon
Treas. 1938-50; Sec. 1941-51
HOOVER, VERYL. . . . . Portland, Oregon
Vice Pres. 1961-68
HUMPHREYS, PHILIP G. . . . . Portland, Oregon
Vice Pres. 1970-
IRVINE, J. H. . . . . Lebanon, Oregon
Director Mt. States 1946-54; PP&L 1954-65
JACKSON, GLENN L. . . . . Medford, Oregon
Vice Pres. Mt. States 1929-38; Vice Pres. Copco 1935-61;
Vice Ch. PP&L 1961-65; Ch. 1965-; Director Copco 1933-
61; PP&L 1961-
JOHNSTON, W. D. . . . . Casper, Wyoming
Vice Pres. Mt. States 1949-54; PP&L 1954-56; Director
Mt. States 1937-54; PP&L 1954-61; Emeritus 1961-
JONES, F. LOWDEN. . . . . Walla Walla, Washington
Director 1934-61
JONES, WILLIAM. . . . . Tacoma, Washington
Director 1910-23
KELLY, RAY F. . . . . The Dalles, Oregon
Director 1936-48

303

LAING, JOHN A..........................Portland, Oregon
    Vice Pres. & Gen. Counsel 1918-36;
    Gen. Counsel 1936-53; Director 1911-36
LAMBERT, HENRY G......................New York, N.Y.
    Director 1950-
LANE, C. HOWARD.......................Portland, Oregon
    Director 1967-
LANSING, JOHN Y.......................Portland, Oregon
    Vice Pres. 1965-
LEWIS, C. HUNT........................Portland, Oregon
    Director 1910-33
LISBAKKEN, R. B.......................Portland, Oregon
    Vice Pres. 1968-
LOVELL, SHERMAN W......................Astoria, Oregon
    Director 1940-61; Emeritus 1961-64
LUCAS, H. C..............Yakima & Olympia, Washington
    Director 1910-35
LUNDGREN, CONRAD F..................Kalispell, Montana
    Director 1964-
MACKENZIE, GEORGE F...................Portland, Oregon
    Treas. 1950-58; Vice Pres. & Controller 1958-60;
    Director 1960-61; 1965-66; Emeritus 1966-
MAJOR, PAUL C.........................Portland, Oregon
    Vice Pres. & Controller 1969-
MCARTHUR, LEWIS A.....................Portland, Oregon
    Gen. Mgr. 1917-22; Vice Pres. & Gen. Mgr. 1922-37;
    Director 1922-47
MCCLUNG, D. R.........................Portland, Oregon
    Vice Pres. & Gen. Supt. 1948-50; Vice Pres. & Asst. to
    Pres. 1950-52; Exec. Vice Pres. 1952-58; Pres. 1958-66;
    Director 1954-66
MCIVER, MILO K........................Portland, Oregon
    Director 1962
MCKEE, PAUL B.........................Portland, Oregon
    Pres. 1933-58; Ch. 1958-65; Director 1933-68
MARSHALL, WILLIAM M...............Spokane, Washington
    Director 1950-65
MERRILL, Z. E...........................Albany, Oregon
    Pres. Mt. States 1937-50; Ch. 1950-54; Ch. PP&L 1954-56;
    Director Mt. States 1936-54; PP&L 1954-56
MERWIN, L. T..........................Portland, Oregon
    Vice Pres. & Gen. Mgr. NWE 1920-1936; Pres. 1936-47;
    Vice Pres. PP&L 1947-49
MILLAY, H. W..........................Portland, Oregon
    Sec. 1951-
MITCHELL, S. Z........................New York, N.Y.
    Ch. 1910-33; Director 1910-33
MOORE, MILES C.................Walla Walla, Washington
    Director 1910-19
MURPHY, PAUL F........................Portland, Oregon
    Director 1959-
MYERS, GEORGE L.......................Portland, Oregon
    Director 1923-35
NEILL, WILL T.........................Portland, Oregon
    Vice Pres. 1936-55; Director 1933-47; 1949-54
NEVINS, GEORGE F......................Portland, Oregon
    Sec. 1910-24; Treas. 1916-24;
    Director 1910; 1912; 1918-24

PENLAND, CLARENCE H................Pendleton, Oregon
Director 1936-62
PERRY, LOUIS B........................Portland, Oregon
Director 1969-
PETERS, A. W.......................Hood River, Oregon
Director 1936-61; 1965-66; Emeritus 1966-67
PLATT, C. W...........................Portland, Oregon
Sec. & Treas. 1924-36; Director 1924-36
PRINGLE, HENRY H.....................Medford, Oregon
Director Copco 1953-61; PP&L 1961-66; Emeritus 1966-
RICHARDS, JOSIAH...................Spokane, Washington
Director 1910-51
RIVES, GEORGE D......................Portland, Oregon
Director 1964-
ROBERTS, GEORGE M...................Medford, Oregon
Director Copco 1947-61; PP&L 1961-65
ROBERTS, J. R........................Redmond, Oregon
Director 1938-61; Emeritus 1961-70
SAMMONS, E. C........................Portland, Oregon
Director NWE 1943-47; PP&L 1947-55
SANDOZ, THOMAS F......................Astoria, Oregon
Director 1963-
SANFORD, CHARLES M...................Portland, Oregon
Sec. 1936-41; Director 1933-39
SHERWOOD, DONALD...............Walla Walla, Washington
Director 1961-
SKELLEY, S. E........................Portland, Oregon
Director 1933-36
SILLIMAN, FRANK JR....................New York, N.Y.
Director 1924-33
SMITH, ALLAN A.......................Portland, Oregon
Director 1949-50; 1957-64; Emeritus 1964-
SOLIDAY, DAVID S...............Philadelphia, Pennsylvania
*Director Mt. States 1940-54; PP&L 1954-66;
Emeritus 1966-69*
STILES, JACK T.......................Portland, Oregon
Vice Pres. 1968-
SYKES, F. G...........................New York, N.Y.
Vice Pres. 1910-24; Director 1910-24
TALBOT, GUY W........................Portland, Oregon
Pres. 1910-33; Director 1910-49
THORNDIKE, EUGENE....................Medford, Oregon
*Director Copco 1953-61; PP&L 1961-66;
Emeritus 1966-69*
TRIMBLE, A. W........................Portland, Oregon
*Vice Pres. & Treas. Mt. States 1942-49; Exec. Vice Pres.
1949-50; Pres. 1950-54; Vice Pres. PP&L 1954-70;
Director Mt. States 1945-54; PP&L 1954-70*
TURNER, H. H...................Walla Walla, Washington
Director 1920-22
VOLLUM, HOWARD......................Portland, Oregon
Director 1964-
WEATHERS, NIEL A.....................New York, N.Y.
Director 1910-11
WILKINSON, M. J......................Portland, Oregon
Treas. 1936-38
WISTING, GEORGE H....................Portland, Oregon
Director 1933-34

305

Index

306

309